SUNDAY SERMONS TREASURY OF ILLUSTRATIONS

VOLUME I

Compiled, Edited and
Composed
By James F. Colaianni

VOICINGS PUBLICATIONS,
PLEASANTVILLE, NEW JERSEY

Library of Congress Catalog Card Number 82-91068

Valued editorial and technical assistance provided by Nancy Fox-Hoover, Rev. William Bray and James F. Colaianni, Jr. is acknowledged with deepest appreciation.

—James F. Colaianni
Editor

We preach not because we have to say something,
but because we have something to say.

"When I came to you, brethren, I did not come proclaiming to you the testimony of God in lofty words or wisdom. For I decided to know nothing among you except Jesus Christ and Him crucified. And I was with you in weakness and in much fear and trembling; and my speech and my message were not plausible in words of wisdom, but in demonstration of the Spirit and power, that your faith might not rest in the wisdom of men but in the power of God" (I Corinthians 2:1-5).

A brilliant clergyman, scholar and preacher who once appeared on Life magazine's list of "Ten Best Preachers in America," had an uncommon sympathy for people who slept during the sermon. He said that when he was still a young preacher, he would notice a certain woman who slept through his sermon every Sunday, without exception. This distracted him severely, until the day he made a pastoral call on the woman at her home. He arrived in midafternoon and was greeted by the sounds of several small children running in and out of the kitchen, slamming doors and making demands on the mother. The telephone was ringing, the washing machine was on the spin-dry cycle, the dog was barking and the woman was trying to quickly get dinner started in the oven. He saw the kind of turmoil she lived in and realized that at this particular stage in her life, probably the best thing the Church could give her was a quiet, comfortable place to sleep on Sunday morning. "Thereafter," he said, "every Sunday morning as she closed her eyes, I just blessed her and let her go off to sleep."

ACCEPTANCE

1 (Blindness; Healing; Sharing)

There is a true story about a little boy who lived in the Midwest. He was blind. His family heard about an eye surgeon at Massachusetts General Hospital who had developed a new surgical technique which was related to the boy's condition. There was a possibility that if he could be sent to Boston for this surgery the boy might have the gift of sight. It was very expensive. The people in the Church contributed to the cause. So did some others in the surrounding community. Finally, all preparations had been made and the boy and his mother were all packed and ready to go. As they were saying their "Goodbyes" to the rest of the family, the mother noticed that the little boy had tucked his old teddy bear under his arm. The teddy bear had seen better days: some of the stuffing was popping out through a broken seam, one ear had been chewed, and an eye was missing. The mother said, "Why take this old teddy bear all the way to Boston. When we get there, we can buy a brand new one." Some of you may be young enough still—if not in age, in spirit—to know why that wouldn't do: it had to be this teddy bear and no other. So the little boy took his much used, much battered, much loved, teddy bear with him to Boston.

In the hospital, the little boy had his teddy bear tucked under his arm through every experience—even into the operating room. Through the long period of postoperative convalescence, the teddy bear stayed with him. Then came the day when the doctor was able to remove the bandages from the boy's eyes. Wonderful! He could see! Imagine what it must have been like for him to see his mother's face for the first time. He had thought of it, imagined it, and now he could actually see it! Imagine what it was like to look out a window and see clouds for the

1

Acceptance

first time. Imagine what it was like for that little boy to see his teddy bear for the first time! When the time came for the boy to be discharged from the hospital, he was dressed in new clothes purchased especially for the occasion. His little bag was packed. Surrounding him were nurses and doctors and other hospital personnel who wanted to say "goodbye" to this lovable little boy whom they had come to know so well during his long confinement. The boy was sitting on the edge of his bed, clutching his teddy bear, when the eye surgeon who had restored his sight came into the room for a last visit. The doctor appeared busy as doctors often do when they are trying to cover up their emotions. Before the doctor could say anything, the little boy spoke: "Here doctor, I want to pay you for helping me," and he handed him the battered old teddy bear. The doctor took the teddy bear into his hands, accepting it without reservation. And for some months after that, if you had gone to the tenth floor of the "White Building" in the Massachusetts General Hospital complex you could have seen the teddy bear. The doctor had put it in a glass case in the corridor. There it sat— one ear chewed, stuffing coming out, one eye missing. Under the teddy bear the doctor had placed his professional calling card and below his name had written this sentence: "This is the highest fee I ever received for professional services rendered."

The doctor had given a great gift to that little boy: the gift of sight. And the boy was so thankful that he offered to the doctor his most treasured possession: the old teddy bear. But that is not the real point of the story. The real moment of excitement in the story occurs when the wise and sensitive doctor accepts his little patient's gift offering. We all know what we would have said if we had been the doctor: "Oh that teddy bear means so much to you, I really couldn't take it from you. Thanks anyway, but you keep it." But the doctor did not say that. By graciously receiving the gift, by showing the little boy that the gift was accepted with gratitude, the doctor allowed him to experience the joy of giving.

ADOLESCENCE

2 (Hopes and Dreams)

The editor of a religious "Youth" magazine once asked her readers to write a short essay entitled, "My Fondest Hopes and Dreams." One 13-year-old reader wrote: "If I could have my fondest dream come true, I would wish for a life using all my natural talents for God's glory until they are exhausted. And if I couldn't have this, I would wish for a color television set."

3 (Parent and Child)

The wife of a Junior High principal was talking about the struggle she had one year with the modern dress-code or, more accurately, the lack of a dress-code for the students. Something cringed inside of her when she saw the youngsters going to school in sloppy clothes. Her daughter, Nancy, was tired of "setting an example for the rest of the students," as her parents had been insisting. She wanted to "dress like the other kids," she said, and she kept nagging her mother about it. Finally, the mother gave in and Nancy was allowed to go to school in rumpled khaki pants and an old Army jacket. When Nancy came home from school, she was bubbling over with joy. She said, "Oh Mom, a girl I didn't even know came up to me and said, 'You must have a wonderful mother to let you come to school looking like that.' "

ADVERTISING

4 (Aging; Humor)

"What is the secret of your long life?" a news reporter asked a man who was celebrating his one hundredth birthday. "I can't be sure just yet," the old man replied. "You see, I'm still negotiating with three breakfast food companies and a mattress manufacturer."

3

AFTERLIFE

5 (Death)

The best-selling book, "Life After Life," by Dr. Raymond A. Moody, Jr., is a collection of actual case histories of persons who appeared to have died clinically and were resuscitated; persons who came very close to death as the result of a severe injury or illness; and persons who were in the act of actually dying. In each instance, these persons claimed to have entered the afterlife world and Dr. Moody's book tells us what they experienced. In one case, a dying man reaches the point where he hears himself pronounced dead by his doctor. Then he hears a loud buzzing, and he feels himself passing through a long, dark tunnel. He sees himself outside of his physical body. Then he sees other persons coming to help him. He begins to recognize the spirits of loved ones and friends who had died before him. Finally, a loving spirit of a whole new kind—"A being of light"—becomes present to him. After publication of the book, Dr. Moody's life changed radically. The response was so heavy, so demanding, that he had little time left for his family, his personal life, or his medical practice. Consequently, he decided to forego any further research into this phenomenon so that he could attend to the needs of his family and practice. He acknowledged that before his research on "Life After Life," he was a nominal Christian only. "But now," he says, "I love the Lord Jesus Christ with my whole being."

6 (Churchgoing; Loneliness)

A prominent medical doctor who has written several books in his field and a well-known "radio preacher" were exchanging ideas about worship. The doctor confessed that he had received no formal religious training. He had always assumed, he said, that people who attend Church on Sunday do so because they want to receive some assurance about afterlife, some hope about life-after-death. The clergyman immediately and strongly challenged that assumption. "Most people go to Church on Sunday not because they fear death, but because they are lonely and want to be with other people," he said.

7 (Death; Reconciliation)

We know from history that Thomas Jefferson and John Adams had hated each other with a passion when they were at the peak of their power. They were real political enemies. But each was blessed with a long, creative retirement. During this period, a reconciling correspondence developed between them and they became great friends. They wrote to each other on a wide variety of subjects, from "How to grow almonds" to "Whether there is a God." When John Adams' wife, Abigail, died (after 54 years of beautiful, creative marriage), Jefferson wrote a letter of consolation to his friend. In it he spoke of "ascending to an ecstatic meeting with the friends we have loved and lost and whom we shall still love and never lose again." Then, he added, "God bless you and support you under your heavy affliction." Adams wrote back, "I do not know how to prove physically that we shall meet and know each other in the future state. My reasons for believing it, as I do most undoubtedly, are that I cannot conceive such a Being could make such a species as the human merely to live and die on this earth. If I did not believe in a future state, I should believe in no God. This universe, this all would appear as a mere boyish firework. But if there be a future state, why should the Almighty dissolve forever all the tender ties which unite so delightfully in this world, and forbid us to see each other in the next?"

AGAPE LOVE

8 (Empathy)

In the U.S. Civil War, the poet Walt Whitman ministered to wounded soldiers. He said he never asked the wounded soldier how he was. He simply became the wounded soldier. That is empathy. That is agape love. That is New Testament love. That is the spirit of the Early Christians—the reason for their boundless enthusiasm and their incredible joy.

AGING

9 (Humor)

A woman of advanced age began to have hearing problems. Reluctantly she gave in to suggestions from family members that she consult an ear specialist. After the doctor had made a thorough examination of the woman's ears, he said to her, "You have a condition which can be corrected by minor surgery. I suggest we do it as soon as possible." To which she replied, "There will be no operation, thank you. I'm eighty-nine years old and I've heard enough!"

10 (Marriage; Humor)

A retired couple, living in Florida, were sitting on their front porch one evening. The wife was just watching the people go by. The husband was reading a book on physiology. The wife turned to her husband and said, "George, let's go inside and watch the Late Show." To which George replied, "I'm too tired. Do you realize that today my heart beat 103,389 times? My blood travelled 168,000 miles. I breathed 23,000 times. I inhaled 483 cubic feet of air. I moved 750 major muscles. And I exercised 7 million brain cells. I'm exhausted. I'm going to bed."

11 (Birthday; Humor)

It was Aunt Sadie's birthday. Aunt Sadie was ninety-nine years old—the oldest resident in a small town in Pennsylvania. Among the guests at her birthday party was her pastor, thirty-nine years old. As the pastor was preparing to leave, he said, "Now, Aunt Sadie, I hope that one year from this very day, I will be able to come and celebrate your one hundredth birthday with you." Aunt Sadie looked at him for a moment, then said, "I don't see why not. You look fairly healthy to me!"

12 (Marriage; Togetherness)

One of the special problems of some newly-retired married couples is too much "togetherness." After years of being apart for half their waking hours, at least five days a week, while one (or both) was at work, they are now together full-time—and that can be a heavy burden. The "Me and My Shadow Syndrome," as someone has called it, means that the husband and wife have run out of space. They find themselves being "accountable" to each other for each minute of each hour, and why wouldn't they get on each other's nerves?

13 (Courting; Humor)

The women residents of a home for the elderly were buzzing with excitement. Two residents of the home had just returned from their first "date": Martha, aged eighty-three and Robert, who was almost ninety. Robert quickly retired and the women began to bombard Martha with questions: Did you have a good time? Where did you go? What did you do? "I had a terrible time," Martha said. "I had to slap him three times in public." The excitement mounted: "Do you mean he got fresh with you?"

one of the women asked. "No, he kept going to sleep on me,"
Martha replied.

14 (Art)

A gigantic retrospective of the late Pablo Picasso's works was
held at the Museum of Modern Art in New York City. More
than 900 of Picasso's works were displayed chronologically,
beginning with when he was a very young boy. Most of the
earlier works were traditional landscapes and still lifes. Then,
as the artist advanced in age, new colors began to emerge, and
the still lifes were no longer very still. Finally, of course, the
works turned into the kind of bold, zesty experiments for which
Picasso is best-known today. One art critic who saw the show
recalled that once, when Picasso was eighty-five, he was asked
to explain why his earlier works were so solemn and his later
works so exuberant and exciting. "How do you explain it?"
asked the interviewer. "Easily," Picasso answered, his eyes
sparkling. "It takes a long time to become young."

15 (Eternal Life)

When John Quincy Adams was 80-years-old, someone met him
in the street and asked, "How is John Quincy Adams today?"
He replied, "John Quincy Adams himself is very well, thank
you. But the house he lives in is sadly dilapidated. It is tottering
on its foundations. The walls are badly shattered, the roof is
worn, the building trembles with every wind and I think John
Quincy Adams will have to move out of it before very long. But
John Quincy Adams himself is very well thank you." The old
man was really in touch with the Christian vision of the Resurrection power of God making us whole for all eternity.

16 (God, presence of; God, relationship with)

A little boy named "Billy" loved to spend time with his grandparents. The grandfather was retired and had available the

thing that children value above all else: time. He had time to be with Billy. On Billy's visits, they would go to a ball game, or they would go fishing, or they would go to the zoo, or they would just sit around and be with each other. One day when they were sitting in the sun, fishing, Billy said, "Grandfather, can you see God?" Now, grandfather had a way about him of not always answering a question immediately. He would think before he answered. This time, however, he paused for such a long time and there was such a faraway look in his eyes that Billy thought that grandfather hadn't heard. So he repeated the question: "Grandfather, can you see God?" Grandfather, with a strange look in his eyes, replied: "Billy, it's getting so lately that I don't see anything else."

17 (Birthday; China)

Chinese author, Lin Yutang, in his book entitled, "The Importance of Living," says he finds no differences that are absolute between Eastern and Western life except in the attitude toward age. In China, one of the first questions a person asks another on an official call is: "What is your glorious age?" If the respondent says, apologetically, "23" or "28," the other offers comfort by saying that he or she still has a glorious future, and may one day become old. Enthusiasm grows in proportion as the individual is able to report a higher and higher age, and if that is anywhere over 50, the inquirer drops his voice in humility and respect. People actually look forward to the celebration of their fifty-first birthday.

18 (God, wisdom of)

In God's Wisdom, the process of aging brings with it the opportunity to achieve a new and enriched perspective on the world, a more total view and a "deeper insight into the true meaning of everything: of life and love, of world and God, of time and eternity. Such wisdom of mature age is different from sharp intelligence or mere information storage. It cannot be learned in books, nor can it be acquired in schools and universities. Only by a life-long process of gradual growth and maturing can this special wisdom of the heart be acquired."— Alfons Deekens, "Growing Old and How to Cope With It."

19 (Communication; Humor; Marriage)

An elderly man and wife who had been together for forty years were sitting in front of the fireplace late one evening. The husband reached out to his wife, patted her on the knee and said, "I'm proud of you." Because a hearing problem had overtaken her in her advanced years, she responded as usual. "What did you say?" she asked. "I'm proud of you," he repeated. She snapped back, "I'm tired of you too."

20 (Family; Motherhood)

The daughter of an eighty-year-old woman was trying to persuade her mother to come and live with her. "Mother, now that Dad is gone, it isn't good for you to live alone," she said. But the mother was not convinced. "No! a thousand times no," she said. "I have always resisted the idea of living with any of my children. It brings on too many problems; too many tense situations." The daughter kept trying. "That's true mother," she said, "but you're different." To which the mother replied, "Yes, I am... but you're not."

21 (Lifestyle)

The American Geriatrics Society has announced that, soon, a normal life-span may cover 100 years. Some scientists are predicting a normal life-span of up to 120 years. Commenting on these findings, in a book called "How to Improve Your Life," Eric Butterworth says...

Now all this is thrilling to contemplate, and I appreciate the dedicated people who give so much of themselves in seeking ways to prolong life. But I am disturbed when I think of the many discouraged, defeated and discarded people I have seen living out their years in loneliness and unproductiveness. It is almost cruel to prolong life without developing the ability to live abundantly... I am convinced that along with the scientists' research in "How to add years to our life," we need to conduct some research in a spiritual laboratory on "How to add life to our years." Everyone of us would do well to echo the prayer, "O Lord, keep me alive while I am living."

22   (Loneliness)

An elderly woman who lived alone had a friend stay with her one night. The friend became curious because although there was a clock in each room of the little apartment, nevertheless the woman called on the telephone to hear the time, just before she went to bed. When her friend asked her why she did this, she answered, "Oh I do that every night. I just like to hear someone's voice before I go to sleep."

23   (Humor)

The following notice appeared in the "Bargain Hunters' Guide" of a Massachusetts newspaper:

> Retired schoolteacher tired of reading and 'rithmetic! Is there a gentleman in late 60's or older who can help me find my way to the playground before the bell rings?

Aging

24 (Humor)

From the front page of a Midwestern newspaper:

> Police were called today to help restore order at
> the Presbyterian Home For The Aged—scene of
> a week-long revolt. Three militant octogenarians
> were arrested after a scuffle in the north parlor.
> They were identified as leaders in an activist group
> that seized control of the parlor three days ago
> and locked the matron in the closet. The eighty-
> year-old spokesman for the activists told report-
> ers the demonstration was staged to enforce de-
> mands that the old folks be given more of a role
> in management. "We have a bunch of young
> whipper-snappers running things around here,"
> he said, "and we don't trust anybody under sixty-
> five." Another one of the activists commented,
> "What is the sense of living a long time if some
> fifty-year-old kid is going to tell you what to do?"

25 (Humor; Speechmaking)

At a reunion of retired executives, each of the guests was invited
to give a two-minute after-dinner talk on his experiences since
retirement. Since some of the former executives were inclined
to be rather long-winded, the toastmaster was instructed to rap
his gavel when the two minutes had expired. The first speaker
was called and, true to his old form, was still on his feet talking
well beyond the time limit. The toastmaster, a kindly old man,
couldn't bring himself to rap his gavel. On and on the speaker
continued, boringly, until the other guests began to murmur
and to signal the old man to rap the gavel. Responding to the
pressure, he wound up and brought the gavel down full force,
accidently on the head of the man sitting next to him. And as

the victim was sinking under the table he was heard to say, "Hit me again, I can still hear him."

26 (Death; Humor)

A certain man in his eighties passes through an extremely tense moment each morning when he gets out of bed. He says, "I put on my robe and rush to the front door for the newspaper. Quickly I turn to the obituary notices, and if my name isn't there, then I have breakfast."

27 (Celebration)

The editor of a Senior Citizens' Newsletter asked readers to send in their ideas for a Bonus Day based on this proposition: "Suppose God gave you an extra day of the year. What would you do with it?" One response read as follows:

> Suppose everyone in the world should celebrate that day as God's day! Suppose everyone would give the wages earned or the services rendered to some helpless person or to some definite Cause they feel is God's work! For twenty-four hours we would not think any negative thoughts, or have any hatred, resentment, fear, anger, jealousy or envy. Instead, for twenty-four hours only thoughts of good will, courage, peace, faith and trust would be vibrating through the air. What wonderful TV and radio programs would be broadcast that day! What wonderful front-page news stories would appear! What wonderful human encounters would take place! What wonderful exchanges between the leaders of nations would occur! What wonderful family gatherings would result! How much love would be poured into every task! My bonus day would be God's Day—Molly Pickens, age 94.

ALCOHOLISM

28 (God, and creation; God, love of)

It is the love of God, ultimately, that gives you the OK feeling about yourself. An ex-alcoholic has written about discovering God's love through Jesus and how this made it possible for her to conquer the alcoholism. "I am a person now," she wrote. "I feel good and clean 'cause now I know that God don't make no junk." That's terrible grammar, but beautiful theology: "God don't make no junk."

29 (Alcoholics Anonymous; Caring; Healing)

"Alcoholics Anonymous" is a fellowship of women and men who help each other to solve their problem of alcoholism by sharing personal experiences with the disease. They also help persons to recover from the crippling effects of intoxication. The Alcoholics Anonymous program centers around a series of "Twelve Steps" embodying faith in God and service to fellowman. The "Twelfth Step" involves the direct care of persons desperately in need of immediate help. They may be vomiting, or shaking and hallucinating. They may be in a jail or a mental institution or a half-way house or a gutter. Alcoholics Anonymous members who do "Twelfth Step" work remember times when someone cared enough to help them in their great need. The Alcoholics Anonymous fellowship is richly imbued with reverence for the healing power of God. Members are invited to find new meaning for their lives by trusting in God's goodness. AA members, through this caring interaction, are constant reminders to one another that "God is not the God of the dead but of the living," and that "All are alive for Him."

30 (Empathy; Despair)

In William Inge's "Come Back Little Sheba," there is a character named "Doc" who is an alcoholic. It is very hard on the members of his family who cannot understand why he is an alcoholic. It is even harder for Doc because even he doesn't understand why he turns to this unhealthy way of solving his problems. Then there is "Lola," his wife—overweight, unattractive, sloppy around the house in many ways, involved in a difficult love/hate relationship with her husband. Lola is really hurt when, after a period of not drinking, Doc takes the bottle and disappears overnight. She is hurt, she is afraid and she calls her parents. She wants to come home for a little while— just to be there. Maybe she can pull herself together. But her father refuses to let her come. She is rejected and you can just feel the heartbreak and the pain and the despair in the drama. How can we help people in situations like that? Doc and Lola need more than words; they need more than facts and formulas. What they desperately need to know is that there is a way out of the deepest pit of degradation and despair. They need to be able to place their trust in someone who can show them the way because he himself or she herself has travelled it.

ANGER

31 (Resentment; Forgiveness; Jesus, mercy of; Reconciliation)

A priest, on pilgrimage to the Holy Land, saw a rusty iron nail on the ground, next to one of the sacred monuments. He picked it up and decided to keep it because it would remind him of the nails that pinned Jesus to the Cross. Because he had a weakness for losing his temper while driving, whenever he took

Anger

the wheel he placed the rusty iron nail on the seat beside him where he could see it and be reminded of Jesus on the Cross, forgiving His enemies. One day, as he was driving through the busiest intersection in town during the peak traffic hour, his car suddenly went dead. Instant traffic jam was the result. As he tried desperately, but unsuccessfully, to get started again, the driver of the car immediately behind him began leaning on his horn. The priest tried to signal that he was doing the best he could, but the impatient driver kept sounding his horn relentlessly. The priest looked in the rear-view mirror and could see that the man was getting angrier and angrier, and was beginning to curse him. Finally, the priest having taken all he could endure, pushed open the door of his car, ready to get out and give the horn-blower a real tongue-lashing. Then he saw the rusty nail and he remembered what it represented. He waited for a few seconds while he calmed down. Then, slowly, he walked to the car behind and said to the driver, ever so gently, "I'll be glad to honk your horn if you will start my engine for me." Many years later, the priest had occasion to recall the incident. This is what he said:

> I was sitting at my desk working on a sermon for next Sunday, trying to think of a good "Love your enemies" illustration. Then I thought of that traffic incident with the horn-blower, and I realized that I was still carrying it with me, after all these years, as a kind of grudge. I realized that I had never relinquished my resentment toward the horn-blower. I realized that, in a sense, I hadn't become reconciled to that enemy. I can remember that he was still angry and still cursing as he drove around me. The truth is that I had been regarding the experience as a clever put-down of that man, a triumph over the enemy. In my heart of hearts, he was still the enemy—and I was ashamed.

16

32

"Anybody can become angry, that is easy," said Aristotle, "But to be angry with the right person, and to the right degree, and at the right time, and for the right purpose, and in the right way—that is not within everybody's power and is not easy."

33 (Parent and child)

A man is driving home from his office somewhat earlier than usual. He stops in a line of cars at a red traffic signal. A sign with large lettering designates the car in front as a "Driver Education" vehicle. The traffic light changes to green but the "Driver Education" vehicle is slow in responding. It lurches forward a few feet, then stops. Again it lurches, then stalls. The young woman driver appears confused. The instructor, sitting next to her, remains calm. But the man in the car behind becomes furious. His horn blasts. His head shakes from side-to-side disapprovingly. His face reveals an attitude of scorn. His car window rolls down and he vocally registers his anger. He doesn't realize that the beleaguered driver in front is his own daughter, a high school senior. She, however, does recognize him clearly in her rear view mirror. Later, when she arrives home from school, she asks, "Where's Dad? Is anything wrong? He seemed to be in a terrible rush earlier today." To which her mother replies, "Dad's fine. He came home early, turned on the TV and fell asleep watching one of those silly 'Game Shows'."

34 (Humor; Travel)

From time to time most of us are bitten by the "travel bug," and usually the bite is not without its sting. One important function of a good "travel book" or travel agent is to anticipate the hazards and the hassles travellers are likely to encounter

17

and to suggest ways and means of avoiding them. Even so, it is a rare trip on which nothing goes wrong. The story is told of a traveller who boarded a train in New York City. Immediately he went to the porter and said, "Look, I want to get off in Washington, D.C., but once I'm asleep it's very difficult for me to wake up. Sometimes I say nasty things I don't really mean. Here is five dollars. Please, no matter what I say, don't be offended; just wake me up and put me off the train in Washington." Hours later, he awakened as the train pulled into the station at Richmond, Virginia, 100 miles past Washington, his destination. The man was furious. He found the porter and angrily denounced him for his incompetence. "What happened?" the conductor asked the porter. "I've never seen anyone that mad!" To which the porter replied, "That's nothing. You should have seen the fellow I put off in Washington."

ANTICIPATION

35 (Friendship; Joy)

"The Little Prince" is one of those rare literary gems, simple enough for children, yet profound enough to keep adults thinking all their lives. The Little Prince comes to earth from another planet, and he needs a lot of help adjusting to our ways. One of the earthly beings who befriends him is the fox. As the fox begins to tell him things and show him things, a deep friendship develops. At one point in the story they are trying to agree on a time for their next meeting. It becomes very important to the fox to know the exact time of the proposed meeting. They finally agree to meet at four o'clock. But the Little Prince cannot understand why the fox must know the exact time. "Oh," says the fox, "if you will come at four o'clock, then I will begin to be happy at three."

ANXIETY

36 (Wisdom)

A wise old woman had listened carefully to a group of malcontents tell her their problems. "I have some advice for you," the woman said to them. "Write down the trouble that worries you most." When they had done this, the woman placed all of the papers in a large jar. Then she said, "Now I want each of you to draw out one of the papers and by all the laws of probability, each will have a brand new trouble to worry about." The malcontents proceeded to do as the wise old woman directed. The result: all of them, without exception, demanded to have their own trouble back.

37

The well-known contemporary poet, W. H. Auden, was one of the first to call our period in history "The Age of Anxiety." Since that time, others have picked up on it because it does seem to characterize our time in history—this feeling of apprehension, of worry, of doubt, of uneasiness about the future. It is a mood that has affected our culture. We find it in our art and literature and music. The Museum of Modern Art in New York City has a painting by Andre Rousseau of a Gypsy woman sleeping out in the open with her guitar by her side. It's all very peaceful, except in the background there is a menacing lion. There is no explanation, no clue as to why the lion is there. That's why the artist does it that way. There is often no rational explanation for our anxieties, but they are there. And, as you look at the painting, you get the feeling of threat, of dread, of tension. You sense that something is very wrong, even though you don't know why.

Anxiety

38

"No matter where we are, we're not there." These words were spoken by a clergyman who had led a group of travellers on an overseas pilgrimage: "When we arrived in London, members of the group immediately became anxious about the next stop. They began reading brochures about Paris. They weren't in London at all! They already were getting ready for Paris. When we got to Paris they immediately began reading about Rome, which was our next stop." This is a real problem in our society. No matter where we are, we're not there.

39

There are many superficial and, therefore, unsuccessful ways in which modern men and women try to handle anxiety:

> Some use alcohol or other drugs. They try to tranquilize away their anxieties. Some use the method of repression. They try to pretend away their anxieties, refusing to confront them. Some use the expedient of work. The "workaholics" try to work away their anxieties. They fear their anxieties will take over should they ever dare to cut down on their work. Some use the gift of speech. They try to talk their way out of anxiety. They never stop talking. They fear that once their mouths stop going the anxieties will catch up to them. Some use the quest for money and power. They try to buy relief from anxiety. Some use the sexual experience. They try to fantasize their way out of anxiety.

40   (Humor; Insomnia)

Edwin Teale, the naturalist writer, tells about a period of anxiety in his life during which he could not sleep. One night he

20

decided to try the old remedy for insomnia: counting sheep. He says he went to bed and closed his eyes, but when the first sheep came along it stumbled and fell. His state of mind was such that he became totally involved with the situation. Would someone come along to help the sheep? How many more sheep would stumble over the fallen one? How much money would the shepherd lose as a result of the accident?

APPEARANCES

41

Lemon trees are pretty, the smell of the lemon flower is sweet, but the fruit of the poor lemon is impossible to eat. Many things in this life look pretty, smell sweet, but taste bitter.

ATHEISM

42 (Cynicism; Revelation)

A young philosophy student at a large university consistently brought home the latest word from her professor as to why belief in God was an utterly preposterous idea. One evening, in a mild state of shock, she said that her professor had had a religious experience and had now changed his tune. While driving alone one morning, a voice clearly said to him: "Why are you fighting me? I want to make you one of my spokesmen, someone who will save people, not destroy them." The professor almost cracked his car up against a telephone pole. There was no one else in the car, no trick was possible. His class met that evening. With passion and conviction, he told his students that he had been wrong, that he had misled them, that God was indeed real and that he had clearly had a revelation from

Atheism

Him. What happened next is almost as remarkable as his story. With razor-sharp reasoning, using his own impeccable arguments, his students pointed out to him the improbabilities of his interpretation of what had happened. They explained away the whole incident on psychological grounds. After all, he had been under considerable tension about this issue because of the class. Obviously, he had temporarily hallucinated the voice. He thought about their arguments for a while and then agreed with the students: he had been silly; he had overreacted to an experience that could be more than adequately explained on a scientific basis. The class could go back to normal.

43 (Communism; Deceit; Humor)

A Communist party leader visited a textile mill in Hungary. The manager of the mill was showing him around and the Commissar asked, "How is the production of textiles here?" The manager answered, "Commissar, production is tremendous. If we took all of our textiles and piled them one on top of another the stack would reach to the feet of God." The Commissar glared at the manager and said angrily, "Comrade, you know there is no God." Whereupon the manager shrugged his shoulders and said, "There are no textiles either."

44 (Faith)

Some of you may remember A. J. Cronin's best-selling novel, "The Keys of the Kingdom." Part of the book is about a young doctor's struggle to believe. He simply cannot believe in God. But he is a sensitive, compassionate person. He goes to China to do what he can to help the victims of famine and plague. Eventually, the doctor himself is stricken. On his deathbed he speaks to his best friend—a missionary priest. But, even now, he remains a non-believer. "Funny," he says to the priest, "I still can't believe in God." And the grief-stricken priest answers simply, "Does that matter now? He believes in you."

45 (Faith; God, presence of)

According to an old rabbinical story, in a small East European country there lived a pious Jewish lad who wanted to become a Rabbi. He walked several miles each day, to and from the synagogue, for his Scripture lessons. Between the boy's home and the synagogue there stood a fruit stand, owned by an atheist. Whenever the boy walked past the fruit stand, the owner would taunt him about his faith. "Where are you going, young man, to see God again?" he would ask. Or, "Did you find God in good health today?" The boy always continued on his way, never answering. One day, in an effort to evoke a response, the non-believer selected the biggest, shiniest apple from his stand and said to the young man as he passed by, "You are wasting your time studying about God. I will give you this apple if you tell me where God is." The boy stopped, reflected for a moment, then replied, "I will give you two apples if you will tell me where He is not."

46

The famous atheist lawyer, Clarence Darrow, once said in a debate, "They tell me there is a God, but I have never seen Him. I have no personal acquaintance with Him." To which his opponent replied, "It is credibly reported that Mr. Darrow has a mind, but I have never seen it. I have never touched it. I have no personal acquaintance with it at all."

47 (Religion; Russia)

A bright, young Russian woman applied for a government position in Leningrad. She was given a long questionnaire to fill out which she handled with ease—except for one question: "What is the inscription on the Sarmian Wall?" After some deliberation, she wrote down her best guess: "The inscription on the Sarmian Wall is, 'RELIGION IS THE OPIATE OF THE

PEOPLE.' " Later, she decided to check her answer. She walked seven miles from Leningrad to the Sarmian Wall. Anxiously, she looked at the inscription. It read exactly as she had guessed: RELIGION IS THE OPIATE OF THE PEOPLE. With a sigh of relief, the young woman dropped to her knees, joined her hands together and exclaimed, "Thank God."

48   (Christmas; Despair; Emmanuel)

One modern atheist has compared man to a "contemptible atom lost in the inert and unbounded cosmos." He says that man's feverish activity is without meaning and without purpose; that his values are valid only for him; and "the fall of an empire or even the collapse of an ideal counts for no more than the destruction of an ant-hill by a heedless traveller's foot." And so the only thing man can do, he says, "is to try and forget the inhuman vastness which crushes him and which is indifferent to his existence." Simply stated, these are the anguished words of a man who knows Christmas isn't coming—ever. There is no Christmas, no "Emmanuel"; because Emmanuel means "God-is-with-us"—and there is no God.

AUTHORITY

49   (Humor)

A company employing several thousand people was attempting to institute a pension plan. But the plan could not be implemented without one hundred percent participation. Every employee signed up except one man. Many efforts were made to win him over, but the man kept on resisting. Finally, the President of the company called the man into his office. "Here is a copy of the proposed pension plan and here is a pen," he said. "Sign up or you're fired." Whereupon the man immediately picked up the pen and signed his name. The President of the company said, "I don't understand why you refused to sign until now. What was your problem?" To which the man replied, "You're the first person who explained it to me clearly."

BACKSLIDERS

50 (Humor; Parish Life)

A pastor compiled a list of parishioners whose Christian powers he felt were withering with disuse. To them he mailed the following message concerning a forthcoming "No-excuse-to-stay-home Sunday":

> There will be ...cots available for those who say Sunday is their only day to sleep; ...eye-drops for those who have red eyes from watching late Saturday night TV; ...steel helments for those who say the roof would cave in if they ever went to Church; ...blankets for persons who think the Church is too cold, fans for those who say it is too hot; ...score-cards for those wishing to list all hypocrites present; ...TV dinners for those who can't cook Sunday dinner and take time to go to Church, both; ...a sanctuary decorated with Christmas poinsettias and Easter lilies for those who have never seen Church without them.

BAPTISM

51 (Children; Holy Spirit; Parish Life)

In a large downtown Church, a communal baptism had been arranged for several children and adults. On the day of the baptism, the Church was filled to capacity. Because he had

Baptism

expected a large attendance, the pastor was careful to remind the younger baptismal candidates to answer the ritual questions "loud and clear." When the first boy was asked, "Do you believe in God the Father?" he answered in a voice all could hear, "I do believe." As each child answered the questions in turn, the urge to upstage took over, resulting in a steady increase in volume, each child answering louder than the one before. Finally the pastor came to the last child and began to ask her the questions of faith. "Do you believe in God the Father?" "I do believe," she fairly shouted. "Do you believe in God the Son?" Still louder came her answer, "I do believe." "And do you believe in the Holy Spirit?" This time there was a pause. Then, in a quieter tone, she replied, "I believe I do."

52 (Children; Humor)

Some children were watching a river baptism from a distance. They were close enough to see the Baptist Minister immerse people and say certain words, but they couldn't hear exactly what he was saying. However, they decided to imitate him. That afternoon they conducted their own baptism ceremony in the back yard. They had a rain barrel full of water. The little girls in the neighborhood all brought their dolls. A little boy was in a frock coat acting as minister. Someone who was observing the proceedings saw him pick up one of the dolls, hold it over the rain barrel and say, "In the name of the Father and of the Son and into the hole you go." Then he dunked it down.

53 (Holy Spirit; Humor)

A woman decided to read the New Testament and investigate the claims of Christianity. Several months later she was baptized. Immediately following the ritual she said enthusiastically, "I could feel the Holy Spirit descend on me. I'm glad I've finally got religion. I can see things differently now. Like that uncle of mine whom I hated passionately. Once I vowed I would never go to his funeral. But now I'll be happy to go to his funeral anytime."

BEAUTY

54 (Pain)

The timeless paintings of the great French Impressionist, Auguste Renoir, literally glow with life and light and color. Renoir seemed to put light inside the people he so beautifully portrayed on canvass. For the last twenty years or so of his life, Renoir was crippled with arthritis. His hands were twisted and gnarled; even his spine was affected, so that he could not stand when he worked, and needed assistance to move from one position to another. The pain he suffered while working caused beads of perspiration to stand out on his face. On one occasion, his prize student, Matisse, asked Renoir, "Why do you torture yourself to go on like this?" Renoir replied, "The pain passes; the beauty remains."

55 (Blindness; Healing; Light)

A man we shall call "Roger" underwent major surgery after several years of blindness. The operation was a success to the extent that he could now see with the help of heavy lenses. When he arrived home from the hospital, he immediately set out to fulfill a longtime ambition: to stroll alone through the neighborhood. But after walking for just a few minutes he rushed back to the house, threw himself on his bed and buried his face in a pillow. His concerned wife asked what had gone wrong. He replied, "I couldn't take anymore. The light hurt my eyes but it wasn't that so much as the beauty. There was so much beauty that I could not take it all in a single dose: human forms; children's faces; faces of old people, wise with the experience

Beauty

of the years; trees and flowers and birds and clouds and the sky. I couldn't stand anymore. I couldn't absorb so much light and so much beauty."

56 (Growth; Pain)

One of the nice things about reading little children's books is the discovery that animals can talk or trees can talk or even teacups can talk. You never raise the question, "Why is this teacup talking?" You just allow yourself to get caught up in the fantasy and get carried along with it. In one such story, a couple in Sussex in England are buying a new teacup. The wife says to her husband, "Look at this one. It is beautiful. I want to buy it." And the teacup says, "Ah, but you know, I wasn't always beautiful." Instead of being surprised at a teacup talking, the couple simply ask the teacup what it meant. The teacup says,"Originally, I was just a soggy, ugly, damp lump of clay. They put me on a wheel and they started turning that wheel until my head became dizzy. Then they started to poke and prod, and it hurt. I cried out, 'Stop!' But they said, 'Not yet.' At long last, they did stop the wheel and put me into a furnace. It became hotter and hotter until I thought I could no longer stand it, and I cried out, 'Stop!' But they said, 'Not yet.' Finally they took me out of the furnace and someone started to put paint on me and the fumes from the paint made me ill. It made my head swim and I cried out, 'Stop!' But they said, 'Not yet.' When at long last they had finished painting, they put me back into the furnace and it was hotter than before. And I cried out, 'Stop!' And they said 'Not yet.' Finally, they took me out of the furnace, and after I had cooled down, they placed me on a table top in front of a mirror. I remembered myself as a soggy, ugly, damp lump of clay. When I looked at my image in the mirror, I lost my breath and I said, in amazement, 'I am beautiful.' And then I knew that it was only the pain that I went through that had made it possible for me to be beautiful."

57 (Humor)

A middle-aged bookstore customer was expressing her obvious annoyance to one of the store clerks. "Everytime I come in here to buy a best-seller, you are 'sold out'," she scolded. "Why can't you people learn to stock your shelves more efficiently?" "And what is the title of the book you wish to purchase?" asked the clerk. "How to Remain Young and Beautiful," the woman answered. "Very well," replied the clerk, "I will place your order for 'How to Remain Young and Beautiful' at once. And I'll mark that order 'urgent'."

58 (Terminal Illness)

An old gentleman is seated on a train, quietly looking out the window, noticing everything that passes by: the lines of houses, the wire-connected poles, the rolling clouds, the children at play. A woman he does not know is seated next to him. Smilingly, he waves to a passing hay wagon. "See," he chuckles, "hay going to the barn. Isn't that wonderful?" The woman is curious. "What is so wonderful about a hay wagon?" she asks. To which the old gentleman gently replies: "You think it strange that a hay wagon means so much. But, you see, last week the doctor told me that I have only three months to live. Ever since, everything has looked so beautiful, so important to me. I feel as if I had been asleep and had only just waked up."

BIBLE

59 (God, glory of)

Spiritual writer Thomas Merton once said, "By the reading of the Scripture I am so renewed that all of nature is renewed around me. The sky seems to be a deeper blue, the trees a deeper green, the whole world is suddenly charged with the glory of God."

60   (Children; Humor)

The parents of a little boy had given him a new Bible to present to his grandmother on her birthday. The boy knew that when a book was to be presented as a gift, it was customary to write something on the front page. Not knowing what to write, he copied an inscription from a book in his father's bookcase. Imagine grandmother's surprise when she opened her brand new Bible and read the inscription: "To Grandmother, with the compliments of the author."

61   (Bible Translations; Lifestyle; Service)

Three persons were talking about some of the recent translations of the Bible. One said, "I like the New English version of the Gospels. It's easier reading than all the older versions." Said the second person, "I prefer the new Jerusalem Bible. The translators have modernized the language without sacrificing reverence." To which the third person replied, "I know an even better translation. I like my mother's translation best. She translated the Bible into life, and it is the most convincing translation I have ever seen. She was a loving person who always took the needs of others seriously. That's what Jesus did, when He was on earth."

62   (God, and the lost; Prison; Luke)

A prison chaplain tells the story of a young man who was locked up in the penitentiary's death row:

> The young man had not been a part of the Church
> at all. Consequently, when I first saw him it was
> difficult to know exactly how to make genuine

contact with him, how to start the relationship. I told him I had come to see him because I cared. I asked him if there was anything specific he would like to talk about. When that first visit ended, I gave him a Bible. I could not help wondering what that young man, who had never looked at a Bible before, would find in it. On my next visit, I found his face pressed up against the cell bars. And before I could say anything, he said to me, "That man Luke wrote a great story." That young man on death row could hardly wait to begin talking about what he had found in Luke's Gospel. Later, as I reflected on that scene, I could hear myself saying, "Of course! Wouldn't it be Luke's Gospel that would motivate a young man in that position! Wouldn't it be the Gospel that emphasizes God's love for the lost: the lost coin, the lost sheep, the lost son who finally came home! Wouldn't it be the Gospel that speaks of a Heavenly Father who neglects not even a sparrow and who knows us so intimately that even the hairs on our head are counted! Wouldn't it be that Word for that young man in that time and place!"

BIGOTRY

63 (Insensitivity; Preaching)

A certain Army Chaplain once preached an entire series of sermons on a very brief conversation he had overheard while serving on a military base. The camp had been suddenly struck by a severe storm, with very high winds, and heavy rains coming down in sheets. Two officers' wives were watching the storm through a big picture window in the Officers' Club. The chaplain was sitting at a desk nearby. Suddenly, through a flash of lightening, one of the women saw a soldier outside doing guard duty—totally at the mercy of the raging elements. "Oh dear," she said, "look at that poor soldier out there in the storm." To which the other woman replied, "My dear, it's perfectly all right. He's only a private."

BIRTH

64 (Children; Family; Humor)

A mother of three was trying to acquaint two of her children with the wondrous mystery of their new baby sister. Her son, Billy, was noticeably self-conscious about the whole process of discovery. The mother encouraged Billy to talk to the tiny babe. "Just let her hear your voice," she said. "Say anything." Billy hesitated, then with a shy, but loving glance at his baby sister, he blurted out, "The Los Angeles Rams won again."

65 (Children; Humor)

"I hear you have a new little sister in your family," said a kindergarten teacher to one of her pupils. "Yes," answered little Johnny, glumly. "Why aren't you happy about it?" the teacher asked. Johnny replied, "I wanted a brother so that I could play boys' games with him when he got bigger. And we can't exchange the baby now. We've used her for four days."

66 (Children; Humor)

An elementary school teacher was telling her class about statistics which indicate that more twins are being born these days than in the past. "Why?" asked a little boy. "Because," answered a little girl, "Little children are afraid to come into the world alone."

67 (Children; Humor)

A little girl was given her birth certificate to take to her new school. "Be sure not to lose it," her mother said. So she lost it, and when someone saw her crying and asked her what was wrong, she answered, "I've just lost my excuse for being born."

BIRTHDAY

68 (Joy; Lifestyle)

A pastor received a birthday card from a young woman parishioner whose marriage ceremony he had recently performed. The card bore the following message:

> Dear Pastor, It dawned on me this morning that today is your birthday. I hope you are having a good day. I wanted to be sure to send you our warmest wishes for a happy day. What a far-out thing it is to be born, and to know life. Each day is so new and exciting. How quickly it passes. How essential it is to live each day in fullness and love. I will be celebrating my birthday on Sunday and I hope my parents realize how happy I am to be given this miracle of life. May this beautiful day be a memorable one for you. May the celebration of life continue into each new day. What a far-out thing it is to be born, and to know life. This is the day which the Lord has made. Let us rejoice and be glad in it.

BOREDOM

69 (Humor; Loneliness)

It was a rainy Sunday afternoon and Margaret White was bored silly. She didn't know what to do with herself. Then the telephone rang. "This is State Police Sergeant Hill speaking and I would like to speak with Miss Margaret White," said the voice on the other end. "This is Margaret White speaking," the woman replied. "I'm sorry to tell you this," said the police sergeant, "but I have a warrant for your arrest charging you with failure to answer a traffic summons." "Wonderful!" she answered. "How soon can you come and get me?"

BORN AGAIN

70 (Boxing; Salvation)

George Foreman, the former world heavyweight boxing champion, had been attending some Bible classes and prayer groups, but not getting too serious about it. One night, after a boxing match, he was in his dressing room, shadow-boxing and dancing around, trying to cool down, when suddenly he said he began to feel Christ wanting to come inside of him. He didn't understand what was happening and so he sat and put his head in his hands, and his hands felt wet. He saw blood on his hands and realized he had been injured in the fight. Some of the blood dripped on his feet. Then he suddenly realized these were the wounds of Christ: the head, the hands, the feet. He said, "I felt for the first time that Jesus is the Son of God and that Christ, the Living God, wanted to come inside of me." Imagine that!

After a boxing match, in a locker room! But George Foreman said "Yes!" When he tried to tell his handlers what had happened, they thought it was because he had been hit in the head during the fight. They thought he was hallucinating...crazy. And they sent him to the hospital to have x-rays taken. Of course it sounds crazy ... to the world. Later, George Foreman said, "Christ has come inside of me and has never left my heart or my life since then."

71 (New Life; Salvation)

Twenty years ago, a Washington, D.C. clergyman agreed to do a series of thirty-two weekly TV programs on "The Life and Teaching of Jesus." "Immediately after I made the commitment, I panicked," he said...

> There I was, an ordained minister with a Doctor's Degree in Theology, but I didn't really know enough about Jesus Christ to talk about Him on television for thirty-two weeks. So I started trying to get myself ready. I read the Gospels over and over again. I waded through all the translations I could find; I drew on all the resources of my earlier training, including what I could remember of my seminary Greek; I read "Lives of Jesus" written by many different scholars. I was trying desperately to "find" the real Jesus. "Where is Jesus?" I was asking myself, quite literally. After several months of preparing myself in this way, I finally found myself saying, "Yes! Yes! Yes! Whatever may come, whatever happens, Yes to Christ." If you ask me what day, I can't tell you. If you ask me what week, I can't tell you. I didn't see a bolt of lightening, but I know that in that period in my life I was born again. And, come what may, I am Christ's man.

Bureaucrats

72 (Humor; Parish Life)

In appreciation of his fifteen years of loyal service, the members of a Baptist congregation gave their pastor an all-expense-paid trip to Europe. When he returned, they asked him about the trip. He replied, "The only thing I can say is that I wish I had gone to Paris before I was 'born again'."

BUREAUCRATS

73 (Humor; Responsibility)

Several years ago, a clever U.S. Government bureaucrat organized the "National Association For Professional Bureaucrats." The motto of the organization is: "When in charge, ponder; when in trouble, delegate; when in doubt, mumble."

BLINDNESS

74

Helen Keller, as you know, early in her life lost the ability to see, to hear or to speak. She was less than two-years-old when the fever came and left her in this disabled condition. And yet, through the help of Anne Sullivan, her teacher, and the Perkins Institute for the Blind [where she lived and studied for a time], she became one of the most sensitive, most alert, most aware persons in contemporary life. She was a very sensitive and a very beautiful Christian. This little girl who was blind and deaf—babbling like a wild animal sometimes, often having violent temper tantrums in her frustration at not being able to express herself—this little girl developed into one of the most gracious, most cultured persons of our time. As the years went by, she became especially concerned about the insensitivity and the blindness of her friends who had eyes to see. Because of her handicap, she learned to read with her fingers. She learned to sense the reality of life around her. On one occasion, she was walking in the woods with a friend. It was Springtime and Helen Keller was using her fingers constantly to read the signs of new life bursting out in that forest. She felt a slender birch tree and the vibrations of a bird singing in its limbs. She felt flowers and leaves beginning to sprout. She felt stones in a cool brook. And when she returned home, she had the memory of many things that she had seen on the walk, even though she was blind. She asked her friend [who had perfectly good eyes] what she had seen. The friend said, "Nothing in particular." Helen Keller was astounded: to walk through a woods in the Springtime and see "nothing in particular." She began to ask other people, and she discovered that there were persons all around her who had eyes to see but were more blind than she was with her sightless eyes. She was amazed to discover that few persons could really describe the face of a close friend. She discovered many husbands and wives who couldn't tell the color of one another's eyes, from memory. She said once, it would really be a blessing if everyone, early in adulthood, could be blind for a short period of time—because then they would learn to appreciate the gift of sight.

CALAMITY

75   (Football; Humor)

Great calamities on earth already are part of our life experience. And we have no guarantee that things will not get worse before they get better. Our human situation sometimes can make us feel like the skinny lad, weighing in at 145 pounds, who turned out for the first practice of a major college football team. His enthusiasm quickly diminished, however, as he explains: "The coach handed me the football and said, 'Let's see what you can do, son.' I tucked the ball under my arm and began to run down the field. One big bruiser grabbed my left leg. A second big bruiser grabbed my right leg. Then I heard the first big bruiser say to the second big bruiser, 'Make a wish!' "

CARING

76 (Repentance)

During the Vietman War, journalist Arthur Hoppe, famous for his political satire columns in the San Francisco Chronicle, joined an organization called the Foster Parents' Plan and became the foster parent of a Vietnamese orphan boy numbered 8944. When Hoppe was sent a photograph of the boy, he became alarmed. It upset him to realize that he had gone out of his way to become burdened with another human being. He began to resent carrying out the committment he had made to correspond with the boy. Six months passed. Then Hoppe received a letter regretfully informing him that his foster-child's village had been overrun and, therefore, contact with him had been lost. Mr. Hoppe then conveniently forgot about the boy. "I should have felt grief and worry, but I felt relieved," he said. "After all, I had never known the boy." Two years later there was another letter, written by the boy in Vietnamese with a translation attached:

> Dear Father, I thank you for your last month's
> gift, which were $950 Vietnam [$8.11 U.S.], two
> bars of soap and a towel...

The lad went on to say that he had been ill but was all better now, that his sisters were in good health, and that he would like to have a picture of his foster-father "so that whenever I think of you, I'll take it out and look at it." Hoppe reacted angrily at first. "I felt trapped," he said. He said that he knew that for years to come he would have to write regularly to the boy, send him presents and be concerned about his welfare— "not so much out of generosity as out of guilt." So he resented the child's intrusion into his comfortable life. However, Hoppe slowly came to see what a fitting penance this was. How easy it had been over the years to be expressing intellectual concern in his columns for the fate of millions of war victims and how terribly hard it was to be honestly concerned with the fate of just one of them. "God give me the grace to do it well!" he said.

77 (Service)

In a documentary film on Mother Teresa, winner of the Nobel Peace Prize, there is an interview with a young man who had gone to India to help her in her mission to the poor and the sick. He was given the task of working with a small group of eight or ten boys who were homeless, parentless. He became parent, teacher and friend to them—living with them, bringing them up. When a reporter asks the young man if there were not times of discouragement when he realized how many thousands of children there were whom he could not help, a look comes over the young man's face which seems to say, "That is the most stupid question I have ever heard." What he finally does say is, "Here are some boys who need me. I am able to help them. That is all that really matters."

78 (Sensitivity; Teaching)

A school superintendent and an elementary school principal were conducting a review of an eighth grade teacher's work. As they entered the classroom through the back door, they heard the teacher say to the tallest boy in the class, "Otto, would you please raise the window?" When Otto had raised

Caring

the window, the teacher said in a voice all could hear, "I don't know what I would do without Otto. He is the only one who can raise that window for me." After they had left the classroom, the principal said to the superintendent, "I hope you noticed what a beautiful and sensitive thing that teacher did for the boy named Otto. Otto is large for his age—and very awkward. He is slow to learn and desperately needs encouragement. You see, the window really didn't need raising. But Otto needed to raise the window. He needed recognition. And the teacher, bless her, was responding to this need." A very simple act, a small act of kindness, yet very important to all of us, because before this week is over we will have dozens of similar opportunities to be sensitive to another's need; opportunities to care!

79 (Sacrifice)

On February 2, 1925, in the hills of Kentucky, an event took place that attracted the attention of the entire U.S.A. Within hours of its occurrence, dozens of nurses and Red Cross workers arrived at the scene. They were quickly joined by two surgeons, piloted there by a Chicago woman. Special telephone and telegraph lines were hastily installed. All this and much more because one man—an underground explorer names Floyd Collins—was trapped in a cave, sixty feet below the earth's surface. Floyd Collins' left foot had become wedged in a crevice, and a large boulder had fallen on his leg. He was powerless to move back up the long, narrow tunnel through which he had descended. His family and friends were topside, but inaccessible to him. For seven days, hundreds of men and women worked furiously to try to rescue Floyd Collins. His brother repeatedly risked his life squirming on his stomach down the dark, wet, winding passage in order to bring him food and drink. At one point in the rescue operation, a human chain, sixty feet long, stretched down through the shaft of mud and slime. But despite these and many other heroic efforts, Floyd remained cut off from the outside world. Then a frightening thing happened: the walls of the narrow shaft caved in. Trying to dig through the debris might have endangered the trapped man's life. Consequently a new shaft had to be dug. Heavy digging equipment was moved in, but huge rocks were encountered and the work of sinking a new shaft went slowly. More and more hundreds of people arrived, offering assistance. National Guard troops were ordered to keep the well-meaning crowds from hindering the rescue operation. All of this massive, frenzied activity had suddenly erupted because one man—one solitary person—was lost, and the community would not rest until he was found. One man was suffering and the community could not rest until he was comforted. One member had been denied access to the other members, and the community could not rest until access was restored.

CATEGORIES

80 (Family)

A woman we shall call "Kathy" had worked as a pharmacist until her marriage to a physician, the widowed father of two lively children. Then, Kathy who had spent years measuring liquids and pills with precision, began spending her days coping with dirty socks and noisy youngsters. Soon there was trouble on the home front. Kathy wanted the house to be immaculate and the children to be orderly and well-behaved, but things did not always turn out that way. One day the doctor offered the pharmacist his diagnosis of her difficulty. Bluntly he told her that anything she couldn't stick a label on or put in a file was not important to her. He told her she needed to learn that people cannot be neatly categorized, treated like prescriptions!

Celebration

81 (Humor)

Psychologists categorize us as "mature" or "immature." Psychiatrists count us as "normal" or "neurotic." To the sociologists we are "inner-directed" or "outer-directed." Educators classify us as "achievers" or "non-achievers." And waitresses see us as "big spenders" or "cheapskates." Wherever we turn, it seems, we are being pigeonholed and slotted, classified and characterized, categorized and dehumanized. It is impossible, of course, to imagine a world without categories. We need them to help us to organize and to communicate. But in recognizing their value and necessity, we see also that they can be easily misused. We can misuse them to oversimplify, to serve as a substitute for a closer look, or to shield ourselves from our own ignorance. As an old folk-proverb goes, "It ain't what you don't know that hurts you; rather, it's what you know that ain't so." And so much of what we know that "ain't so" is found in our hastily arrived at, easy categories. A woman driving around a hairpin turn on a narrow country road swung a bit wide and forced a man coming in the opposite direction to swerve sharply to avoid collision. To add insult to injury—or so it seemed— as the woman passed by the man she cried out, "Pig!" Hastily categorizing her as a crass ignoramus, he shouted back, "Jackass!"—and as he rounded the curve he crashed into the biggest pig he had ever seen.

CELEBRATION

82 (Beauty)

Picture the making of a large and beautiful "Persian" rug. A large loom is set up in a vertical position. Standing in front of the loom is the artist. Behind the loom are several young men standing on a scaffold. Their job is to run back and forth on the scaffold weaving the threads in and out, in accordance with the artist's instructions. From their position, the work of art is very ugly. They can see only knots. They cannot see the pattern taking shape on the other side. But, when the last thread is woven, the artist calls them out front where they can see the finished beautiful work of art. And together, they can celebrate.

CHANGE

83 (Despair)

Shakespeare's Macbeth lamented, "Tomorrow and tomorrow and tomorrow creeps in this petty pace from day-to-day, to the last syllable of recorded time; and all our yesterdays have lighted fools the way to dusty death...life's but a walking shadow, a poor player that struts and frets his hour upon the stage, and then is heard no more; it is a tale told by an idiot, full of sound and fury, signifying nothing" [Act V, Scene 1]. This is the sound of a worldview of cynicism and despair. This is the view of people who fear and resist the future to the point of preferring the evil that is known over the change that is unknown. It is said that some people are so fearful of change that had they been present at creation they would have voted for chaos.

84 (Humor)

A man became disenchanted with the city life he was living. He decided to move to the country and start a chicken farm. He bought a farmhouse with some land around it and, after he had move in, he bought 200 baby chicks. But they all quickly died. He bought 200 more baby chicks but, again, they all died a short time later. Puzzled and distressed, the man wrote to the County Agricultural Agent and described everything that had happened. "I want very much to be a successful chicken

Change

farmer," he concluded. "Therefore, can you tell me: Have I been planting the chicks too close together or too deep?" Whereupon, the County Agent wrote back and said, "I can't answer your question until you send me a soil sample."

85   (Despair; Education)

There is a wonderful story about the college alumnus who went back to his Alma Mater for a twentieth year class reunion. He dropped in to see his old math professor and was amazed to discover that the examination questions that year were the same ones his class had received twenty years before. "Doesn't this present a problem?" he asked the professor. "Doesn't each class pass the questions on to the next class?" "Yes, they do that," the math professor said, "but it's no problem because every year now we change all the answers." That's the way it is these days. The answers are all changing. The thing you build your life on today you suddenly discover tomorrow is all wrong because of some new evidence, some new discovery. These are times of convulsive change. Things are moving so fast that people are confused and, even worse, they are giving up hope.

86   (Humor; Paul)

In a midwestern Church, the crib-room is filled to capacity every Sunday without fail. As you enter the room, you see a large framed sign hanging on the wall over the long line of cribs. It reads, "Not all of us shall fall asleep, but all of us are to be changed." Bible experts know that this line is a direct quote from St. Paul, First Corinthians, Chapter 15, Verse 51: "Not all of us shall fall asleep, but all of us are to be changed."

87   (Grace; Repentance)

John Newton had fallen into a state so sordid that his own devout Christian mother never would have recognized him.

Change

Things began to happen in his life, however. He was at sea and one of his shipmates, for some unknown reason, had brought a copy of Thomas A'Kempis' "Imitation of Christ" on board. With time on his hands, John Newton began to read it. And something began to stir within his soul. The seeds that his mother had planted long years before began to sprout. Then the ship ran into a storm of such force that even the most seasoned sailors thought it would surely go down. In this confrontation with death, John Newton realized that he was not ready to die. As a result of these and other events, he turned his life completely around. Talk about amazing Grace! At age thirty-nine, he became an ordained clergyman in the Church of England. He was assigned to a parish, where the people came to love him because of his generous, kindly, pastoral manner, because of his preaching, and because there was one thing he could do better than most other clergymen: sing! He could sing the glory of God, and he began to write hymns about it. His first collection of hymns [named the Olney Hymns after the parish he was serving] included "Amazing Grace."

88 (Politics)

A college student was working in her first political campaign. After two tedious days of door-to-door canvassing she sighed, "There must be some better way to change the world."

89 (Death; Humor; Jesus; New Life; Resurrection)

A mother whose only son was preparing for college, wrote the following letter to the college president:

> Dear Sir: My son has been accepted for admission to your college and soon he will be leaving me. I am writing to ask that you give your personal attention to the selection of his roommate. I want to be sure that his roommate is not the kind of person who uses foul language, or tells off-color

45

Change

> jokes, smokes, drinks, or chases after girls. I hope
> you will understand why I am appealing to you
> directly. You see, this is the first time my son will
> be away from home, except for his three years in
> the Marines.

Nothing, apparently, could make that mother let go. Not even
the United States Marines. But Jesus comes to us telling us
we've got to let go: "Unless a grain of wheat falls into the
earth and dies, it remains alone. But if it dies, it bears much
fruit" [John 20:24]. God works through a process of death/
resurrection.

90 (Children; Daily Deaths)

The bestselling book, "Passages," reminds us that moving
through the various stages of life is a kind of dying. When the
need to let go of certain things signifies that you'll never again
be the same as you were, it is a kind of dying. A child's going
off to school for the first time is a kind of dying. For some
children it can be very painful. After one week in school, a little
boy was asked if he liked it. "Not bad," he said, "but it sure
cuts into my play time."

91 (Freedom; God, presence of; Grace)

A woman had been going through a particularly trying period
in her life. Instead of turning to God, as many of us do when
real problems come, she simply made herself busier and busier,
burying herself in her work and other activities. In the midst
of this, she was seriously injured in an accident and was hospitalized. While there, she had time to reflect on what had been
happening in her life. She had time to pay attention, to close
off everything else and just listen. It became for her a life-
transforming experience, a new awareness of God's Presence.
In her own words:

The one implicit feeling I had in this moment was a sense of freedom, of being in all ways unencumbered. It was as though the windows of my life had been washed. It was as though some part of me had been left behind, a part that was old and hard. In that hospital bed, the world was a very private world and I was quite alone. Then, all at once, I was not alone. There was no increase in light; there was no sound, no motion. Lying utterly still, I was aware of a Presence and I simply waited. Previously unable to accept, I was now accepting. I was allowing myself to be claimed. I was allowing this Grace to wash over me, to cover and to penetrate the self I had been, just as the tide rises to cover what formerly was dry and bare. Now I knew what this Presence was. It was God, the Father. Here was the glory of His patient Presence. Feelings of wonder gripped my soul and, with the wonder, peace. Not the peace the world knows, but at-one-ness with God. And I understood. I understood that I had been forgiven!

92 (Caring; Psychoanalysis; Service)

Dr. Richard D'Ambrosio tells in his book, "No Language But A Cry," about an experience early in his practice as a psychoanalyst. In response to a friend's request, he visited a dreary-looking institution for homeless girls. He tried to be realistic: "I have already enough patients to take care of." But something caused him to read some of the case histories—a collection of human misery that some doctors might not encounter in a whole lifetime of practice. One case evoked his particular attention. It was the case of a girl he calls "Laura," the worst case of all.

Change

Laura was twelve-years-old. At the age of one she had been snatched from the stove where her drunken parents were literally trying to cook her. Since that day she had not been able to speak. In addition, her body was bent from a severe curvature of the spine; she had crossed eyes and burn scars on her face. Because of her lack of response to therapy, she was classified as a mental defective. "Too big a job," was the doctor's first reaction. But, again, an inexplicable something caused him to become very unrealistic: he would try to help the child.

The young doctor worked with the girl, week after week, in a small office he had set up in the institution and decorated with toys. He visited with her for hours on end. He talked with her. He took her for walks. He built a dollhouse for her and stocked it with a family of dolls and doll furniture. But she showed no sign of interest. As the years passed, he could count only little gains. Gradually, very gradually, her walk improved. One day, as a group of roller-skaters careened toward her on the sidewalk, she grabbed the doctor and clung to him in fright. After three years, Doctor D'Ambrosio felt the time had come to give Laura a shock that might break through the protective shell she had built around her, after her terrifying babyhood experience. As Laura watched, the doctor played the role of a puppet master. He caused the mother doll and father doll to change from loving parents to angry ones. They began to yell at the crying infant dolls, and to beat them. It was then that Laura's breakthrough came. She trembled and shook as the doll battle continued, and then the doctor heard a scream: "No! No! No!" She had uttered the first words anyone had ever heard from her. She continued to scream as she hit the mother and father dolls and sent the dollhouse crashing to the floor. Thereafter Laura made a rapid entry into the real world. She began to talk. She studied. She grew. She underwent surgery to straighten her back and her eyes, and to remove the burn scars. Ten years after Doctor D'Ambrosio began to work with her, Laura left the institution—trained as a teacher of other children who need special attention.

48

93 (Humor)

The story is told of a farmer who had lived on the same farm all his life. It was a good farm, but with the passing years, the farmer began to tire of it. He longed for a change—for something "better." Every day he found a new reason for criticizing some feature of the old place. Finally, he decided to sell, and listed the farm with a real estate broker who promptly prepared a sales advertisement. As one might expect, it emphasized all the farm's advantages: ideal location, modern equipment, healthy stock, acres of fertile ground, etc. Before placing the ad in the newspaper, the realtor called the farmer and read the copy to him for his approval. When he had finished, the farmer cried out, "Hold everything! I've changed my mind. I am not going to sell. I've been looking for a place like that all my life."

94 (Paul)

So complete was the Apostle Paul's response to Jesus' call to new life that not only did he change from a power-hungry pharisee into a humble servant of the Lord, he changed his name too.

CHILDREN

95 (Humor)

A little boy came in from play to ask his mother, "Who am I?" Assuming that he was playing a game, she answered, "Why, you're Superman." But the little boy remained very serious. "Oh, mom," he said, "The lady up the street is right." The mother asked him what he meant and he replied, "She said I was so dirty my own mother wouldn't recognize me."

Children

96 (Humor)

A little boy answered a salesman's ring at the front door. As he opened the door, the caller asked him, "What is your name, little boy?" "My name is 'Eddie Don't'," the boy replied.

97 (Declaration of Independence; Education; Humor)

The students in a fifth-grade class in American History were given an examination. Among the questions to be answered was the following: The Declaration of Independence was written chiefly by... [fill in the blank]. On one of the papers, a student had neatly penciled in, "Candlelight."

98 (Grandmothers)

A third-grader was asked to write a theme for school on "What is a Grandma?" She said, "A grandma is a lady who has no children of her own, so she likes other people's little girls. A grandpa is a man grandma. He goes for walks with boys and talks about fishing and stuff. Grandmas don't have anything to do except be there. Grandmas drive you to the supermarket where the pretend-horse is and they have lots of dimes ready. Or if they take you for walks, they slow down past pretty leaves and caterpillars. Grandmas never say, 'Hurry up.' Sometimes grandmas are fat, but not too fat to tie kids' shoes. Grandmas wear glasses and funny underwear. They can take their teeth and gums off. They answer questions like, 'Why do dogs hate cats?' and 'How come God isn't married?' When they read to us, they don't skip words or mind if it's the same story again. Everybody should try to have a grandma, especially if you don't have a TV, because grandmas are the only grown-ups who have got time."

99 (Humor)

A boy was visiting his grandmother for the first time in several years. She lived in a small Wyoming town—cowboy country. On arrival, the boy's initial reaction was to cry out, "Grandma, look at those bowlegged cowboys." The grandmother was shocked and embarrassed, fearful that someone might have heard the outburst. Consequently, she immediately took her grandson to her home and there devoted much of the day trying to refine his vocabulary. The next morning, as they were walking through town, the lad again commented on the local gentry, this time trying his best not to embarrass his grandmother. He said, "Grandma,

> Hark! What manner of men are these who wear
> their legs in parentheses!"

100 (Humor)

A little boy asked his dad for permission to go outside and "have a game of 'Catch' with God." Dad was puzzled. "How do you play 'Catch' with God?" he asked. "Easy," answered the little boy, "I just throw my ball up in the air and God throws it back!"

101 (Humor)

There once was a little girl who dreamed of becoming a great writer. Whenever she visited her grandmother she brought along her latest composition, and the grandmother was always happy to read it and make suggestions for improvement. On one occasion, the grandmother's advice was, "Never use the same word twice in the same sentence, if you can possibly avoid it." The grandmother soon discovered how well that lesson had been learned when the child presented her with a sampler she had made in sewing class. It read: "Home Sweet House."

Children

102 (Humor)

A mother of eight had been next door visiting. When she returned home, she went into the living room and there, on the new carpet, she saw her five smallest children gathered around something in which they seemed very interested. On closer examination, and to her total dismay, she discovered that the children were gathered 'round a family of skunks. In her horror she screamed, "Run, children, run!" Whereupon, each child grabbed a skunk and ran.

103 (Humor)

A mother was engaged in a heated discussion with her twelve-year-old son because he had refused to take his little sister fishing with him. "I've already told you," the mother said, "it will be all right. I've talked to her and she has promised not to make any noise. She won't frighten the fish away this time." The boy replied, "Mom, it's not the noise that's the problem. Last time she ate all the bait."

104 (Humor)

A little girl named Jenifer decided to write a letter to God. "Dear God," she began, "are boys better than girls? I know you are one but please try to be fair!"

105 (Humor; Teaching)

A big-city school teacher brought a rabbit into class to show her small pupils, many of whom had never seen one. The children were delighted and asked many questions about the animal. Finally, one little boy asked, "Is it a boy rabbit or a girl rabbit?" The teacher was a bit flustered but finally confessed that she did not know. "We could vote on it," said one little girl.

Children

106 (Birth; Good News; Motherhood)

"I've got good news for you," a father said to his little girl. "God has just sent you a baby brother." "Great!" she exclaimed. "Where's Mom? I can't wait to tell her."

107 (Parent and Child)

"From the day your babies are born you must teach them to do without things. Children today love luxury too much. They have abominable manners, flaunt authority, have no respect for their elders. They no longer rise when parents or teachers enter the room. What kind of awful creatures will they be when they grow up? They must be taught to know and do the right thing." These words of counsel and advice were written by an internationally famous scholar just before his death: Socrates, in the year 399 B.C.

108 (Jesus, faith in)

A University student went around asking little children about Jesus. Susan, age six, said, "I don't know if there was a Jesus but I believe in Him anyway." John, age nine, said, "There had to be a Jesus or it wouldn't make sense to have B.C. and A.D." Rory, age eight, offered this marvelous insight: "If I asked Jesus if He loved me, He probably wouldn't answer me. He probably would just send me another kid to play with. He does things like that."

109 (Aging; Awe)

Several years ago, singer Tony Bennett popularized a song entitled, "This Is All I Ask." The lyrics are the poignant response of an elderly person to a group of children happily at play. Perhaps you are familiar with this line, "Children everywhere... Take me to that strange, enchanted land grown-ups seldom

53

Children

understand..." These lyrics reflect the unique sense of awe and wonder in the presence of little children that seems specially reserved for older people.

110   (Humor; Obedience; Rebellion)

A little girl had done something to displease her mother and was banished to a corner of the kitchen. "You will sit there until your father comes home," the mother said. "I'll stand in the corner, but I won't sit," the child said defiantly. Whereupon, the mother put her hands on the child's shoulders and literally forced her into the sitting position. When the father came home he asked his daughter what she was doing over in the corner of the kitchen. She said, "My head tells me I'm sitting here, but my heart tells me I'm still standing."

111   (God, wisdom of; Prayer; Retreat)

A pastor delights in telling the true story of a wonderful experience he once had at a clergymen's "retreat." He was assigned to a room which had just been vacated by a little girl at the conclusion of a family retreat. And, as he was settling into the room, he found a prayer which had been composed by the child during one of the retreat exercises. Here it is, in the little girl's own grammar:

> Dear God, I have had a B-E-E-U-T-T-Y-F-U-L-L time here. The hills are so beeuttyfull and the lakes were ice. I was getting boring because there was no one to play with hardly. But you know best, Amen.

112   (Humor; Parent and Child)

There is the story of two little boys talking about their respective family situations. One of them said, "My father is a doctor.

54

I can get sick for nothing." The other boy said, "Big deal! My daddy is a minister and I can be good for nothing!"

113 (Humor; Teaching)

A pre-kindergarten teacher found an exciting new thing to do with her class. She wrote a song about popcorn, taught it to the children, then had them crouch down on the floor to sing it. At the appropriate point in the song, all the children would "pop up." The teacher had them "popping" all over the classroom. One day, the popcorn song was in full sway, when the teacher noticed one little boy who remained crouching on the floor while the other children "popped" all over the room. "What's wrong?" the teacher asked, "Why can't you 'pop' like the other children?" The little boy replied, "I'm burning on the bottom of the pan."

114 (Humor)

A little boy was looking through a book on "Child Psychology, Ages Five Through Ten," that his mother had been reading. Turning to one of his friends, the boy said, "Wow, you should read what a stinker I'm gonna be next year!"

115 (Christmas; Humor)

The owner of a big, shaggy dog called the local veterinarian on Christmas morning. "It's my dog, Prince," he said. "There is a large swelling at the corner of his mouth." But it's Christmas morning," the veterinarian replied, "can't it wait until tomorrow?" "Please", said the dog owner anxiously, "please let me bring him to you now." "All right. Bring him right now," said the vet. When the dog arrived with his master, the vet made a brief examination, then said to the man, "Do you have any children?" "Good heavens," the man replied, "is it contagious?" "No," said the vet, "it's bubble gum."

CHOICE

116 (Humor)

While on a motor trip, a husband and wife stopped at a little roadside restaurant. The counter was dirty, so they sat at the only table in the place. But the tablecloth was unclean and the chairs were dusty. They were trying to decide whether or not to leave when the waitress came to take their order. "I'll have a cup of coffee," said the husband. "I'll have coffee too, and be sure to bring it in a clean cup," said the wife. A few moments later the waitress returned with the two coffees on a tray. "Which one of you wanted the clean cup?" she asked.

117 (Decision; Principalities and Powers; Paul)

The relentless call to decision is necessary because of the kind of world in which we live. Clearly things are not as they ought to be. The creature is in rebellion against the Creator. Look around you at the wars, the barbarity, the injustice, the hatred, the stupidity that fill every day's News. The Christian, writes St. Paul, must resist what he calls "The Principalities and Powers of this present age" [Eph. 6:12]. The Christian must decide. The Christian cannot approach life simply "taking things as they come."

118 (Decision; Neutrality)

Journalist Heywood Broun observed that many persons act like the donkey standing midway between two stacks of hay. The animal starved to death because he spent his time just standing there, evaluating the two stacks. He preferred to die rather than give up his neutral position. He preferred to die rather than make a decision, make a choice.

119 (Preaching)

An elderly woman in a nursing home was faced with a very hard choice. Being a rabid baseball fan, she had been following the World Series then in progress, and on Sunday morning she was happy to learn that the deciding game would be televised at three p.m. However, three p.m. also was the time scheduled for Church Services, to be conducted by an as yet unidentified clergyman from a neighboring community. Consequently, our elderly baseball fan was faced with an extremely hard choice because she was a deeply religious woman too. Finally, the moment of decision arrived. "Are you going to attend Church Services or watch the World Series game on T.V.?" she was asked. "I haven't decided yet," she replied. "It all depends on who is pitching and who is preaching."

120 (Courtship; Humor)

A young man, seeking a friend's advice, confessed the following: "I've got to make a choice. The girl I'm dating wants us to get married. I want to buy a new car. I can't afford to do both. She's a wonderful girl, but every night I dream about the new car."

CHOIR MUSIC

121 (Bible)

Members of the combined choirs of Los Angeles were looking forward with great anticipation to their performance of Bach's "Matthew Passion" because the great Leopold Stokowski was to conduct. After the final rehearsal, Stokowski tapped for silence and said to the several hundred singers and orchestra: "I suppose you know the notes well enough. But the spirit is lacking. I want each of you to sit down tonight with your Bible and read St. Matthew's account of the Life of Christ. Try to grasp it all. Perhaps that message is just what our listeners need in a time of doubt and despair. Then let us come to our performance and try to give to our audience the meaning and inspiration in these sacred words." Said one of the singers later: "We did as we were told, and the next day we sang our hearts out."

CHOSEN PEOPLE

122 (Jesus, ascension of)

In the famous play, "Fiddler on the Roof," Tevye, the leading character, is a pious Russian Jewish peasant who loves to stare up into the sky and argue with God. In one particularly dark moment, when everything seems to be going wrong in his little Jewish community, Tevye looks toward the sky and says to God: "It's true we are the Chosen People. But once in a while can't you choose someone else?" Undoubtedly, this same question was on the apostles' minds as they witnessed Jesus' disappearance from the earth. They had been chosen by Jesus for the great adventure. They had followed Him, listened to His Word, agonized through the painful events of His passion and death. Now, standing on a hill with the Resurrected Christ, they receive His commission: "Go, therefore, make disciples of all the nations." [Mt. 28:19] And with this formidable mandate still ringing in their ears, the apostles find themselves alone. Jesus has disappeared. And there they stand, "looking up at the skies." It is easy to imagine that in that moment of parting they, like Tevye in Fiddler on the Roof, felt constrained to ask, "Why us, Lord? Why couldn't you have chosen someone else?"

CHRIST CHILD

123 (Cross)

Raphael, the great Italian artist, painted the "Alba Madonna" which hangs in the National Gallery in Washington, D.C. In the painting, the Christ Child holds a little stick shaped in the form of a cross. Raphael understood that the shadow of the cross is present to the Christ story from the very beginning.

CHRIST, IMAGE OF

124 (Christ, as King; Compassion)

The Danish sculptor, Thorvaldsen, had a burning ambition to create the greatest statue of Jesus ever made. He began by shaping a clay model of a regal figure with head thrown back and arms upraised in a gesture of triumph. It was his conception of Christ the King: strong, dominant. "This will be my masterpiece," he said when the model was complete. But in the night, fog and sea-spray seeped through a partially opened window of his oceanside studio. The moisture affected the shape of the model so that when the artist returned to the studio in the morning, he was shocked to find that the head had drooped, the facial expression had been transformed from severity to compassion, and the arms had dropped into an attitude of welcome. Thorvaldsen stared at the figure for a long time, agonizing over the time wasted and the need to begin all over again. But something came over him to change his mood. He began to see that this image of Christ was the truer one. Then he wrote at the base of the newly-shaped figure: "Come unto Me."

CHRIST, IMITATION OF

125 (Faith)

The story is told of a zealous priest who was fond of asking perfect strangers if they believed in Christ. One day, he said to a young man passing by, "Do you believe in Christ?" The young man paused, then replied, "No I do not." "Why not?" asked the priest. "Well," said the youth, "you believe that Jesus is God. If Jesus is God, He should be able to do almost anything. God made tigers and the tigers made other tigers; God made oak trees and the oak trees made other oak trees; God made birds and the birds made other birds. If Jesus is God, as you say He is, then He should be able to make other Jesuses. But have you ever seen another Christ? I haven't!"

CHRIST, AS KING

126 (Service)

You have perhaps seen the nineteenth century painting that shows a long row of beggars waiting in a soup line. They are all ragged and sleazy looking. But around the head of one, barely perceptible, is a halo. One of them is the Christ! You may see no halo around the heads of your brothers and sisters in need, yet to serve them is to serve Christ, for the King is hidden in them.

127 (Christian Ministry)

The King of Denmark once went out horseback riding all alone. A visitor to the country was very surprised to see this and asked one of the citizens if the king didn't have a bodyguard. The citizen replied very proudly, "We are all his bodyguard." There is a great day coming in the life of the Church and the world, when we will be able to look at Christ our King and say: "We are all His ministers."

CHRIST, PRESENCE OF

128 (Caring; Prison)

A psychologist has written an account of a man who was serving a long prison term in a U.S. federal penitentiary. We shall call him "George." George had had a tragic childhood. When he was only three, his mother died. When he was seven, his father abandoned him. He grew up to be a loner. He was surly, mean, hostile. In prison he kept himself isolated from the other inmates. Serving time in the same prison was a man much older than he. He tried to befriend George. He consistently went out of his way to let George know that someone cared about him. He refused to let George's hostility turn him off. He just kept trying to let George know that someone cared. Finally, the older man was released from the penitentiary. A short time later, word came back to the prison that he had died. When George heard the news, to the astonishment of the other prisoners, tears ran down his cheeks. He sobbed softly for a time and then he said quietly to the other prisoners, "He was the only Christ I ever knew." It was through the unlikely circumstance of that relationship that the Living Christ became real to him.

CHRIST SPIRIT

129 (Transformation)

A New York City manufacturer produced a batch of T-shirts bearing the slogan, "This is YOUR LIFE, not a dress rehearsal." This is our life and our life's mission is now. It is not a dress rehearsal, not a trial run. The cosmic Christ Spirit dwells among us now, transforming death into life, despair into hope, tears into laughter, sorrow into joy, sickness into health. The Christ consciousness in God is acting that way in our world now.

CHRISTIAN MINISTRY

130 (Discipleship)

Said Zorba the Greek: "In order to really be alive, you have to have a touch of madness." Many of us are so uptight, so folded away inside, so afraid of what people will say, that we have no "touch of madness," even in our love affair with God. One of the modern persons who symbolizes this "touch of madness" most is the late Albert Schweitzer. The word "waste" has often been used by people speaking about his life. Dr. Schweitzer had a doctorate in Philosophy, a Doctorate in Theology, a Doctorate in Music and, of course, a Doctorate in Medicine—all earned. He went to Africa and when people asked him why, he said, "I was obedient to Christ." He didn't go for a short Peace Corps term, he went for his whole life. This brilliant man who could have enjoyed world recognition in any of his fields, simply went out to Africa and made himself available—full-time—to those who were hurting and for whom there was inadequate medical care.

131 (Discipleship; Zest For Life)

The Circles, Squares and Triangles who lived in "Flatland" had a very ordinary existence until, one day, they were visited by a Sphere. Said the Sphere to one of the circles, "What can you do?" The Circle did a few tricks, whirling 'round and 'round. The Sphere asked, "Can you go up?" "What's up?" asked the Circle. The Sphere tried to describe what it is like to go up and to see life from a new dimension. Unable to get his point across, the Sphere then took the Circle by the rim and stood him up on end, saying, "Now, that's up!" It was the most wonderful experience that the Circle had ever had and he wanted to share the new dimension of life he had discovered. But the other Flat People laughed at him, and then persecuted him for his revolutionary ideas. Finally, they sentenced him to death. Before he died, the Circle said, "I see you will never understand until you experience it yourself."

132 (God, love of; Lepers; Service; Sacrifice)

Damien DeVeuster was a Belgian Priest who gave his life to the care of lepers in the colony at Molokai, Hawaii. He died in eighteen hundred and eighty-nine at age forty-nine. Molokai is the island where lepers were sent to rot and die, literally. Partly as a carryover from the myths of those who lived in Biblical times, a leper was considered unclean and a person to be isolated from "clean" society. And for many years these unfortunate people were dispatched to Molokai where they were left to die in the most horrible conditions. Damien, as a young priest, felt that when Jesus said "You shall be witnesses in Judea and Samaria to the ends of the earth," it included the Island of Molokai. Nobody else, it seems, had figured that out yet. But Damien had. He went to his bishop and asked permission to move to the island and be with the people and do what he could. The bishop loved this young priest, a man of great promise, and he tried to argue him out of it. It didn't seem fitting that this young man with so much potential should throw himself away in that forsaken place. It was what some-

Christian Ministry

one later called "Holy Waste"—a beautiful phrase. But Damien persuaded the bishop and soon thereafter he entered the leper colony at Molokai. He said that in the early weeks he was often dreadfully sick at his stomach as he moved among the people and saw the horror of the conditions under which they were living. It was all he could do to force himself to stay in spite of his strong intention. But he went to work. First of all, he found up in the mountain a source of fresh water. And he was able to build a little system that would bring the fresh water down to the village. From this came the colony's first sanitation system. Then he showed the lepers how to build little houses to replace the flimsy shacks and hovels they had been living in. It was the colony's first housing project. He built a clinic and, although he had little medical knowledge, nevertheless he could at least dress their leper sores himself and give them some comfort. Talk about the cup of water, talk about visiting the sick, talk about being there with love—it was all there in his ministry and in his life.

Damien helped them build a small chapel, and he would preach each Sunday. The lepers became accustomed over the years to seeing him go into the pulpit every Sunday, cross himself, and begin the sermon with these same words: "You lepers know that God the Father loves you." And then he would go on to preach a sermon that always was full of hope, full of life, and full of joy. Several years went by in this way, until one Sunday morning he went into the pulpit, crossed himself and said, "We lepers know that God the Father loves us." It was everyone's first indication that Damien had contracted leprosy by living so close to them. He continued to pour himself out in this ministry of love until he died, a leper among the lepers whom he loved.

133   (Parish Life; Preaching)

There is a story of a young clergyman who went to the pulpit and proceeded to thrill the congregation with his very first sermon. The following Sunday the people returned with great anticipation and, to their surprise, he delivered the same sermon he had preached a week earlier. On the third Sunday and then the fourth Sunday he did the same thing, much to the congregation's dismay. Finally, a committee called on the clergyman and demanded an explanation for his strange behavior. "Is that the only sermon you have?" they asked. The young preacher replied, "No. I have several sermons and I'm working on still more. But you haven't done anything about the first one yet."

134 (Service)

Do you remember Leo Tolstoy's beautiful story entitled, "Where Love Is, God Is Too"? It is the story of an old shoe cobbler who hears a voice in his deep sleep one night. The voice tells him that on the very next day the Lord Jesus will visit him. Next morning he begins his work in a spirit of high expectation as he eagerly awaits the coming of the Lord. But the only visitors he has that day are people in distress. First, there is an emaciated old beggar with a racking tubercular cough. The old cobbler takes him in, warms him by the fire and gives him food. Next comes a half-frozen, thinly clad woman carrying her hungry baby in her arms. She needs food and clothing—and the old cobbler obliges. Then, an old apple woman comes. She is terribly upset because a boy has tried to steal her apples. The cobbler knows the boy and he is able to bring the two together and reconcile them. This day has not turned out as expected, but the cobbler has not forgotten the promise of the Lord's visit. Tired now, he falls asleep in his chair and he hears the same voice from the previous night: "I was hungry and you fed Me. I was thirsty and you gave Me drink. I was sick and you ministered to Me."

135 (Compassion; Service)

William Wasson, now middle-aged, was raised in Phoenix, Arizona. He had studied for the priesthood but was denied or-

Christian Ministry

dination by Catholic Church authorities because he was in poor health. After surgery for a thyroid condition, he journeyed south to Mexico in order to convalesce. Following a period of recovery, he decided to remain in that country. In 1953, he finally was ordained and assigned to a parish in Cuernavaca. One day, in his Church, he came upon a 16-year-old lad who was trying to rifle the poor box. He called the police. At the Cuernavaca Police Station he learned that the boy was an orphan. He put down the pen with which he was about to sign his name as complaining witness, and announced that he was going to adopt the boy. He took the orphan home with him and, within days, the Cuernavaca Police Chief had sent him eight more homeless boys who had gotten themselves into trouble. The priest immediately began to beg or borrow the resources he needed to care for his new charges. For housing, someone lent him an old building that had been a brewery. Another donated an old store. A woman appeared with a big bag of oranges. The youths in his charge hammered some doors and wood scraps into crude beds, tables and chairs. Such were the humble beginnings of the orphan community William Wasson was to name "Nuestros Pequenos Hermanos" [Our Little Brothers and Sisters]. A year later, William Wasson rushed to the city of Tampico which had been devastated by a hurricane. He went into the jails and hospitals and the streets, gathered up 35 abandoned children and brought them into the community of Our Little Brothers and Sisters, thereby doubling its population. The population rose to about 1200. Scattered throughout Mexico today, William Wasson's proteges include over 500 teachers; many accountants, lawyers and doctors; and many others skilled in various trades. Each graduate returns to the community to contribute one year of service to the current members.

136 (Values)

Oscar Wilde once wrote that, in modern society, "People know the price of everything but the value of nothing." Someone else has characterized our time as the "Age of the Sellout," in which

"Everything is for sale. Every person has his or her price. Honesty and integrity are traded off, like chattels, for money and power." Although this assessment may be an overstatement, nevertheless it contains more than a grain of truth—enough truth, in fact, that it should be a matter for our deep concern. Whether it is the "Age of the Sellout" or the "Age of the Fallout" or the "Age of the Blowout," it is our Age. This is the Time into which we, as a Christian People, have been called to give light. This is our one and only opportunity to be the "salt of the earth."

137 (Holy Spirit; Service)

Mother Teresa, winner of the Nobel Peace Prize, is a frail little woman who for years has been laboring unceasingly from morning 'til night ministering to people dying in the gutters of India, and to abandoned children, and to the poorest of the poor. And, in between the cracks, she runs around the world raising money for her hospitals and refuges. Reading about her exploits, one can only say, "I don't know how she does it!" People have asked her how she does it and her answer is always the same: "Without the Holy Spirit of God I receive from Christ, I could not get through one single day or one single hour of the life I have chosen." Mother Teresa is comforted as she reaches out to comfort others.

138 (Compassion; Leprosy)

Leprosy was the "cancer" of the twelfth century and it caused great fear among the people. Not only did the lepers suffer the terrible pain caused by the rotting away of the limbs of their bodies, but also they suffered because of isolation. They were forced to live in the tombs, outside of town. They had to ring a little bell and call out "Unclean, unclean," wherever they walked. Francis of Assisi felt great compassion for the lepers because they were the poorest of the poor. Nevertheless, he had a great personal fear of leprosy. One day, as he was riding on

Christian Ministry

his horse, he came upon a leper in the road. Francis instinctively went around the leper. But something within him drew him back. He realized that, for him, this was a critical confrontation. He dismounted, walked over to the leper, gave him some money, got back on his horse, and began to ride away. But when he looked back, he saw no one on the road. The leper had vanished. Francis was convinced that he had actually encountered the Living Christ, in the form of a leper. For the rest of his life Francis ministered to the lepers, always convinced that when he did so he was ministering to Christ.

139 (Preaching)

There is a scene in Herman Melville's "Moby Dick" in which the minister is preaching in a seaside chapel to the men who are going out to search for the great white whale. He stands in the pulpit which is shaped like the prow of a ship and he preaches a powerful message. During his sermon, perhaps to emphasize his own authority he says, "Shipmates, God has laid but one hand upon you. Both His hands press upon me." Unfortunately, that statement is unbiblical, unchristian, unhealthy and untrue. If you are a disciple of Jesus Christ, if you have given yourself to Him, then both His hands press upon you just as surely as they do on me. The words, "Fulfill your ministry," apply just as surely to you as they do to me.

140 (Work)

A certain skylark came from a nobel skylark family. He loved to fly high above the earth and sing beautiful melodies. One thing he did not like was the daily work of having to dig worms in order to receive nourishment and stay alive. You can imagine how excited he was when one day, soaring high above the earth, he saw a little man dressed in a scarlet coat walking down the road and hollering "Earth worms for sale. Earth worms traded for skylark feathers." The skylark zoomed down and said to the man, "What's the deal?" "Two worms for one feather," the man answered. "Try it, you'll like it! It's a good deal!" So the skylark tried it and he liked it. He had so many feathers, after all. Who's going to miss one feather? He plucked a feather out, got his worms, and had a lot more time to just coast around that day. Day-after-day the skylark plucked another feather and traded it for worms. Then the awful day came when he tried to fly but was barely able to get himself off the ground and came crashing down again. He realized what had happened. He was a bedraggled skylark, unable to fly. A contradiction in terms: a skylark that can't fly. And so he spent the whole day digging feverishly for worms. When evening came, the little man in the scarlet coat came by. The skylark said to him anxiously, "I've got to trade back." The little man just kept on walking, laughing as he went and shouting over his shoulder, "No deal, friend. Worms for feathers is my business, not feathers for worms."

And so we go on, day-after-day, trading off the bright-colored feathers of the spirit, avoiding the daily work of our Christian mission, until we reach a point of no return. We become a contradiction in terms: a Christian without a mission.

141 (Service)

The American Quaker, Thomas Kelly, has written of his life-transforming experience in the great Cathedral at Cologne, Germany. He said that during a time of intense prayer in that Cathedral, God gave him a vision, a great experience. He became aware, as he said, "of the whole congealed suffering and need of all humanity," and God laid it right on his shoulders. It was a burden too great to bear except that, at the same time, God gave him Grace and strength to rise up and to give the rest of his life to doing what he could to relieve that suffering and to meet that need.

Christian Ministry

142 (Sacrifice; Service)

Shortly before his death, the famous American missionary doctor, Thomas Dooley, returned to the U.S. to raise additional funds for his hospital in Southeast Asia. As a doctor, he knew he had terminal cancer and would soon be dead. However, the big question on his mind was whether, under the circumstances, he should spend his last days in the country of his birth or return to his hospital in Southeast Asia where the people needed him. While he was debating this in his mind, a telegram arrived from some of the medical corpsmen he had trained to be his helpers at the hospital. "We need you here," the message read, and then went on to say: "While you are gone, we are the fingers of your flesh to heal the sick. We are your ears to hear their cries of pain. We are your heart to love them." And that is precisely the response Jesus asks of us, as He sends us from our places of worship out into a world and a community where people need us. Consequently, we pray to the Lord Jesus: "We are the fingers of your flesh to heal them, we are your ears to hear their cries of pain, we are your heart to love them."

143 (Epitaph; Service)

In a tiny Churchyard in England there is an inscription on the gravestone of a woman who had spent all of her adult life in sacrificial service, ministering to others in the community. The inscription reads: "SHE HATH DONE WHAT SHE COULDN'T."

144 (Healing; Light; Sacrifice)

In her modest but lovely little home in Japan, the widow of Toyohiko Kagawa, one of the great Christians of modern times, often receives visitors from foreign lands who want to learn more about her late husband. She talks about his early life when he had been orphaned, left with relatives who mistreated him. He contracted tuberculosis and believed that he was dying

70

[which he was]. She talks about the dramatic religious experience that came to him: he saw a blinding light in his room and immediately sensed that he was surrounded by God's healing presence. And he was healed by this experience: transformed, physically and spiritually, both. After all the hardship and suffering Kagawa had been through, one might readily sympathize with him had he said, "This is God acting in my life. I'm going to savor the experience, treasure it within myself. Just God and me!" Instead, he opened himself up totally by moving into an incredibly horrible slum where, for many years, he ministered unselfishly to the people there: counseling them; feeding them; clothing them; finding shelter for them; listening to them; identifying with their pain. These slum-dwellers lived by the thousands in little dog kennel-like places. One out of two babies died either at birth or within the next few days. Kagawa himself contracted an eye infection which partially blinded him for the rest of his life. He gave of himself in every possible way, not only in a direct, personal way but in organizing the distribution of medical supplies and food and clothing. His ministry in that slum, giving light where he could give it, is a most beautiful example of what Jesus is talking about in the Gospels; Kagawa had received the Grace, he had received the Faith, he had experienced healing, but always with the understanding that he would go forth to share it with others. Among other things, Kagawa was a poet. And, early in his slum ministry, he wrote these lines:

> I came to bring God to the slums
> but I am dumb, dismayed, betrayed
> by those I would aid—
> pressed down so sad
> I fear that I am going mad.

> IS THERE NO WAY THAT HELP CAN COME?

But even as Kagawa asked the question, he became part of the answer by going into that slum and giving his life – giving the light – wherever he could.

Christian Ministry

145 (Boy Scouts; Humor; Procrastination)

Members of a Boy Scout troop were out on a first-aid training exercise. Two young scouts were sent into the woods to play the role of victim. "Lay out there and wait for us to come and give you first-aid" was the instruction. The troop found the first little boy but they took so long to minister to him the second little boy became discouraged. When the troop finally got to the place where he was supposed to be, they found a note that said, "I have bled to death and gone home."

The trouble with our Christian Ministry of loving other people is that we allow ourselves to be diverted. We find good excuses for delay. We procrastinate. We put it off and we put it off, and there are many people who will bleed to death and go home. And the opportunity for us to be there will be lost forever.

146 (Jesus, savior; Redemption)

In Alan Paton's beautiful novel, "Cry the Beloved Country," there is a young man who was born late in his parents' lives. He leaves his home in the hill country and goes down to the city. He never writes or sends back news. Finally, his elderly father decides to go to the city to find his boy. Because he hasn't spent much time in the city, he has a hard time of it there. He is bewildered and confused and he doesn't know which way to begin. Then he is befriended by a city minister who hears his story and resolves to help him. The old man moves in with the minister who goes out of his way trying to help the father pick up clues, get on the trail of this boy. And when they seem to be making progress, the old man, with tears in his eyes, is trying to thank the minister for all he has done. He can't quite find the words and says simply, "You're a good man." The minister replies, "I'm not a good man. I am a sinful and a selfish man. But Jesus Christ has laid His hands on me, that's all."

CHRISTMAS

147 (Devil)

A letter has been preserved, from the year 1827, in which an American bishop made the following observation: "The devil has stolen Christmas from us. The devil has stolen Christmas, the day of our spiritual redemption, and converted it into a day of wordly festivity, shooting and swearing." To which, quite recently, someone added these words: "If the bishop thought the situation bad in 1827, he should see us now! December is an absolutely chaotic month! Frantic shopping, double and triple parking, office partying, and all the rest. The devil has stolen Christmas from us too!"

148 (God, love of; Incarnation)

Once upon a Christmas Eve, a man sat in reflective silence before the fireplace, pondering the meaning of Christmas. "There is no point to a God who became man," he mused. "Why would an all-powerful God want to share even one of His precious moments with the likes of man? And even if He did, why would He choose to be born in an animal stall? No way! The whole thing is absurd! I'm sure that if God really wanted to come down to earth, He would have chosen some other way." Suddenly, the man was roused from his reverie by a strange sound outside. He went to the window and saw a small gaggle of blue geese frantically honking and aimlessly flopping about in the snow. They seemed dazed and confused. Apparently they had dropped out, in exhaustion, from the flight formations of a larger flock on its way from the Arctic Islands to the warmer climes of the Gulf of Mexico. Moved to compassion, the man tried to "shoo" the poor geese into his warm garage, but the more he "shooed" the more they panicked. "If they only realized I'm only trying to do what's best for them," he thought to himself. "How can I make them understand my concern for their well-being?" Then, this thought came to him: "If for just a minute, I could become one of them, if I could become an ordinary goose and communicate with them in their own language, they would know what I am trying to do." And suddenly... suddenly, he remembered Christmas and a smile came over his face. Suddenly, the Christmas Story no longer seemed absurd. Suddenly, he pictured that ordinary-looking Infant, lying in the creche in that stable in Bethlehem, and he knew the answer to his Christmas problem: God had become one of us to tell us, in human terms we can all understand, that He loves us.

149 (Christmas Shopping)

The time is early December. A family of four drives to a suburban mall to do some Christmas shopping. They decide to shop separately so that the presents they purchase for each other might be kept secret. Before they split up, the father says, "Let's synchronize our watches and agree to meet in the parking lot at five o'clock sharp." The four adjust their respective watches. Then the mother turns to the father, and with hand outstretched says, "O.K. Now let's all synchronize our wallets!"

150 (Christmas Tree; Humor)

On January 1st, one man's New Year's resolution was to become a non-conformist. For instance, he resolved never again to take part in the over-commercialization of Christmas. He would become a shopping mall dropout. "To think," he said angrily, "That I paid fifteen dollars for a Christmas tree, and on Christmas Day, my wife wore it as a corsage!"

151 (Children; Expectation; Jesus)

One Christmas season, members of a New England Church were preparing for their annual Christmas Pageant. A little boy who had been crippled by polio and who walked with crutches, wanted to play a part in the pageant. All of the major roles had been given out—Joseph, Wise Men, Shepherds—and the boy understandably was dissapointed. Finally, it was decided that he would play the role of the innkeeper. The boy was heart-broken because he was the only person in the play who would have to reject Jesus. All during rehearsals this very sensitive young lad was deeply troubled by the role he had been given to play. The night came for the pageant to be presented, the auditorium was packed with parents and others from the Church, and the play began with Joseph's knock on the door of the inn. The little boy's big moment had arrived! He couldn't restrain himself any longer. He threw open the door of the inn and shouted at the top of his voice, "Come in! I've been expecting you." The audience roared, thunderous applause broke out, and they all agreed later that this was the greatest Christmas play they had ever seen. In his own special way, the little boy had expressed the spirit of the Gospel, crying out to God, "Come in! I've been expecting you."

152 (Christmas Shopping; Children; Credit Cards; Santa Claus)

In a shopping mall, a five-year-old walked up to a department store Santa Claus and said, "You don't have to worry about me this year. We have 'Master Charge' and 'American Express'."

153 (Church Choir; Parish Life)

It was Christmas Eve in Washington, D.C., and a group of young tourists from all parts of the country were being guided through one of the city's historic Churches. The Church choir director happened to be there, preparing the Christmas music program and, in the Christmas spirit, he volunteered to lead the young tourists in some carolling. The first two songs went well. But as the improvised choir began the third, the choir director looked troubled. Something had gone wrong. "It didn't sound quite right," he said, "but I finally located the source of the problem. One of the carollers, a young woman from the deep South, had been singing, "O lil' ol' town of Bethlehem."

154 (Fellowship; Soldiers; War)

The Royal Argyle Sutherland Highlanders, a Scottish Regiment famous for its kilts and bagpipes, has a proud tradition of loyal military service to the British Crown. Surviving veterans of the regiment's World War I campaigns still tell the story of a strange encounter with the enemy on Christmas Eve, 1916. In deference to the Christmas Feast, there was a brief, if unofficial, "cease-fire." Floodlights pierced the eerie darkness of the "no-man's land" lying between the opposing armies. Soldiers from both sides climbed out of their trenches and slowly walked toward the other side. In the words of one of the Argyle Sutherland Highlanders, "The first German soldier I came into contact with offered me a drink of cognac. I, in turn, gave him a bit of candy. Then we stood there, silently, each looking into the other's face. Suddenly, spontaneously, we embraced and we both broke down and cried in each other's arms. After a while, the signal came, we returned to our trenches, the lights went out, and it was time again to point my rifle in the direction of the man I had just embraced as a fellow human being."

CHRISTMAS CUSTOMS

155 (Santa Claus; "St Nicholas Day"; Christ, and Christmas; Christmas Tree; Puritans)

There was no Santa Claus back in Eighteenth Century America, but some of the Dutch Colonists in New Amsterdam did celebrate "St. Nicholas Day." A man dressed in red bishop's robes would visit the children and put candy or a birch rod in their wooden shoes, depending on whether they had been "good" or "bad" that year. It is that little tradition among a few of the Colonists which has been blown up into the incredible Santa Claus "thing" we have with us now. Today Santa Claus is at the center of the American National Christmas. And it was Clement Moore, clergyman and professor of theology, who wrote the poem that did this to us. "The Night Before Christmas" was written by this Christian theologian and not one line, not one word about Christ. It is purely secular, from beginning to end.

The Christmas tree came to us largely from the German tradition. We know that during the Revolution, Hessian soldiers decorated their trees. Washington chose to cross the Delaware on Christmas night partly because he knew that the Hessian and British guard would be down. They would be busy celebrating around the Christmas trees they had decorated. It wasn't until the middle of the Nineteenth Century, however, that the Christmas tree custom began to take hold around America.

The custom of feasting came from the English and to some extent from the Dutch. But again, in Colonial times, whether or not one partook of the "bountiful table" depended upon where one lived. Many of the Colonists feasted on Christmas Day, but the Puritans worked, as if to make the point that everything else being done that day was sinful.

CHURCH

156 (Parish Life)

I think I shall never see
  a Church that's all it ought to be:
A Church whose members never stray
  beyond the straight and narrow way.
A Church that has no empty pews,
  whose Pastor never has the blues.

Church and State

> A Church whose Deacons always "Deak,"
> and none is proud and all are meek.
> Such perfect Churches there may be,
> but none of them are known to me.
> But still, we'll work and pray and plan
> to make our own the best we can.

CHURCH AND STATE

157 (Christ, lordship of; God, judgment of; Patriotism)

"Kurios Christos" [Christ is Lord], was the creed of a group in the Roman Empire of the first century, A.D. The members of this group, called "Christians," were far more politically concerned than their simple faith-formula might suggest. They lived in a time and place when all "loyal, patriotic" citizens were required to assert, once every year, "Kurios Caesar," which means "Caesar—the State—is Lord!" Thus when these Christians pronounced their creed, "Kurios Christos," they were not only saying "Christ is Lord," but also "The State—Caesar—is not Lord." They were affirming what their Jewish forebearers had said at Mt. Sinai: "We will have no other gods before the one true God." They were affirming a higher loyalty than their loyalty to the State. They were performing a supreme act of loyalty for which many of them were thrown to the lions. Saying "Yes" to the hard demands of one's country can be the manifestation of a noble patriotism, but there are times when precisely the opposite is true. There are times when a noble patriotism comes in the form of an emphatic "No!" There are times when the true patriot must say, "This nation under God," not to provide comfort but to disturb. There are times when "This nation under God" must mean "This nation under the judgment of God", as well as under His protection.

158   (Bible; Patriotism)

In the United States Capitol there is a prayer-room. In the prayer room there is an open Bible. This is good. But when you go in, the Bible is not at the center of your attention. The real worship center to which your eye is drawn is the stained-glass window. That is what you are looking at as you pray and meditate. The stained glass window depicts George Washington [kneeling], and the Great Seal of the United States, and the American Eagle. One can see how it is easy to mingle and to mix all of these things until they become very confused. We find so many sincere well-meaning people tending to confuse the "American Way of Life" with genuine religion, getting it all twisted into a kind of "civil religion."

CHURCH DENOMINATIONS

159   (Courtship; Jesus, command of; Marriage; Somnambulists)

"Be constantly on the watch! Stay awake," Jesus commands. The signs-of-the-times are such that, clearly, this is no time for somnambulists. A somnambulist, as you know, is a person who walks in his sleep. On the eve of his wedding, a young man decided to confess all to his fiancee. He went to her and said, "My love, there is something I feel I must tell you before we are married; something you must know. It may make a difference in your feeling toward me: You see, I am a somnambulist." The young lady thought for a moment, then replied, "Oh that's all right. There's no problem. I was raised a Methodist. So, we can go to your Church one Sunday and to mine the next."

CHURCH–GOING

160 (God, presence of; God, word of)

Sunday after Sunday there are persons in the congregation who feel like the football team that takes the kickoff and runs all the way back to the opponent's twenty-yard-line. It's wonderful, but they never go on to score from that vantage point. And the reason they don't score is because they have settled into what has become a Twentieth Century idea that all you have to do is be here. That is not enough. Being a passive "hearer" is not enough. If we leave Church Sunday after Sunday merely having heard, it's like pouring water into sand. We must experience the Word of God, the very Presence of God.

CITY LIFE

161 (Humor)

A woman lived in a big city neighborhood that was going downhill very fast. The area was becoming increasingly over-crowded, noisy and dirty. It was a bad situation. The woman decided something would have to be done about it. She knew that money would be required to change the situation. Consequently, she started a fund-raising drive. She called people. She sent letters. She got some financial support from private foundations. She finally raised $85,000 and then she used the money to move to another neighborhood.

CLERGY

162 (Humor)

Early one Saturday morning, the pastor of a large Church was on the golf course preparing to tee off when a stranger asked if he might join him for the round. The pastor agreed, and the two men played the eighteen-hole course together. As they were leaving the final green to return to the clubhouse, the stranger said, "I enjoyed playing with you. Would you like to join me again tomorrow morning?" The pastor replied, "I can't. I work on Sunday mornings." Puzzled, the stranger asked, "What in the world do you do on Sunday mornings?" To which the pastor replied, "You know, I've been asking myself that question for many years."

163 (Humor; Resurrection Power)

There's a wonderful story about a clergyman who woke up one morning, looked out the window and saw a dead donkey in his front yard. He hadn't the slightest idea how it got there, but he knew he had to get rid of it. He called the Sanitation Department. He called the Health Department. He called several other agencies, but no one in the bureaucracy seemed able to help him. In desperation, he called the mayor and asked what could be done. The mayor must have been having a bad day. "Why bother me with your problem," he answered. "You're a clergyman. It's your job to bury the dead." Whereupon the clergyman lost his cool and snapped back, "Well, I just thought I'd better notify the next of kin." If you have a dead donkey on the front yard of your life and you don't know what to do with it, the Resurrection Power of God is present to you at that point of need.

164 (Children; Humor)

An ordained minister was having some personal problems and decided to leave the ministry. He ran into trouble, however, when he couldn't find other work. Finally, in desperation, he took a job at the local zoo. It seems that the gorilla had died and since it had been the favorite animal of the children, the zoo officials decided to put someone in a gorilla costume until

Comfort

a real replacement could be found. It was the minister's job to don the costume, hop around the cage and entertain the kids. To his amazement, he found it to be the best job he'd ever had. He found that people were paying more attention to him now than they ever did when he was in the pulpit. He had all he wanted to eat. He could take a nap in the sun anytime he wanted to. It was all part of the act. One day, as he hopped up and down, he felt so frisky that he decided to try the trapeze. He began flying around and then suddenly lost his grip, flew over the bars and into the next cage. In his semi-dazed condition, he looked up and saw a lion charging right at him. Naturally, he forgot he was supposed to be a gorilla and started to holler, "Help! Help!" Whereupon the lion said, "Be quiet you fool. I'm a minister too!"

COMFORT

165 (Compassion; Death)

In order to become the person God intends us to become, we need regularly to acknowledge our dependence upon Him and to reaffirm our trust in Him. It seems, however, that the majority of us have to be knocked down before it actually happens. A woman who had recently lost her husband, has written of such an experience. She says:

> A sudden loss...a loved one, so dear to me... my body rejects the news with violent motions. Family and neighbors begin to arrive. Arrangements have to be made. Then, the lesson from God: As I stand beside my loved one, I look up to see faces that I know. But I see with new eyes. I see their pain. I see their lives, etched in their faces. I feel compassion for their grief and their heartache. It's as if God has opened my spiritual eyes and I see familiar faces for the first time—as they really

are. God has allowed me a momentary understanding that I have never known before. They came to give me comfort. But God used them to give me so much more.

COMMENCEMENT EXERCISE

166 (Change; Prayer)

At a high school commencement exercise, one of the senior girls delivered a closing prayer which she herself had written. The young woman began to read her prayer at that time when the confusion and the shifting at the edges of the crowd begins, as people's thoughts turn to the parking lot. But, as the prayer unfolded, the noise quickly subsided and a miraculous silence settled over the crowd. It lasted until the last word of the prayer was uttered. Here is a portion of that prayer:

> Dear God, grant us one thing before we leave the sheltered reassurance of our childhood. Show us life. Not an empty, shallow world of shallow people and shallow dreams, but real life...For we have known the bliss of childhood as well as the passion of adolescence now. We've heard the cry of babies, and we've seen the fear of death on a soldier's face. We want to change the world but we don't know how. We want to throw our arms around our brothers but our hands cannot reach. We want to break the bonds of conformity that tie us to the ground, but we're not strong. Smile on us when we drink from the waters of truth. And, when we are old, reassure us that our struggle helped to make the world a world of peace, compassion and wisdom. And please don't let us die without ever having lived!

COMMITMENT

167 (Discipleship; Jesus, and disciples)

Twenty centuries ago, Jesus summoned twelve committed disciples and sent them out two by two to communicate God's Love, to bind up wounds, to be peacemakers in a troubled world. And to this day, He is calling the committed to go and do likewise. Christian commitment:

> I can skip one day and I know it.
> I can skip two days and my friends know it.
> I can skip three days and the world knows it.

168 (Courting; Humor)

"My dearest Susan," wrote a lovesick Romeo, "I would swim the mighty ocean for one glance from your lovely eyes. I would walk through a wall of fire for one touch of your delicate hand. I would traverse the widest river, climb the highest mountain for a single word from your warm lips. As ever, your faithful Arnold.—P.S.: I'll come to see you next Saturday if it doesn't rain."

169 (Jesus, death of)

A young man put his arm around his girl friend, saying, "I adore you, I need you, I can't live without you, I love you." The girl pushed him aside and said, "Billy, I don't want to get serious." Billy replied, "Who's serious?" In our personal relationships and in our religion we often use language carelessly. We need to understand that what is happening in the death of Jesus is that God is saying to you, "I love you, I want you for My own. I'm serious about this and I want you to be serious about this too. I want you to respond to this. I want you to be moved by this Event."

170 (Resolutions)

Late one December, an elementary school principal said to his teachers: "Let's all write out New Year's Resolutions about how we can be better teachers and I'll put them on the staff bulletin board. In that way, we can be mutually supportive in our efforts to keep those resolutions." The teachers agreed, and when the resolutions were posted they all crowded around the bulletin board to read them. One of the young teachers in the group suddenly went into a fit of anger. She said, "He didn't put up my resolution. It was one of the first ones in. He doesn't care about me. That just shows what it's like around here." On-and-on she ranted and raved. The principal, who overheard this from his office, was mortified. He hadn't meant to exclude her resolution. Quickly rummaging through the papers on his desk, he found it and immediately went to the bulletin board and tacked it up. The resolution read: "I resolve not to let little things upset me anymore." Resolution, but no commitment!

COMMUNICATION

171 (Bureaucrat; Humor)

There once was a plumber who wrote a letter to the government agency in charge of plumbing regulations. In it he said he had discovered hydrochloric acid to be a marvelous substance for cleaning out clogged drains. A government bureaucrat wrote back saying, "The efficiency of hydrochloric acid is indisputable but the corrosive residue is incompatible with metal permanence." The plumber obviously misunderstood this letter because he wrote back and said he was glad the government agreed with him. The agency official, somewhat alarmed at this response, sent a second letter which said, "We wish to emphasize that we must refrain from assuming responsibility for the production of toxic and noxious residue with hydrochloric acid and consequently, we most emphatically recom-

Communication

mend some alternative procedure." Again the plumber misunderstood and, again, he wrote back saying he was glad the government agreed with him. Finally, in desperation, the government official wrote the plumber the following: "Don't use hydrochloric acid. It eats the heck out of pipes!"

172

There is a true story about a number of literary critics who had gathered together to discuss the poetry of the celebrated American poet, Robert Frost. They zeroed in on a particular poem of Frost's and spent hours discussing the deep metaphysical symbolism of these lines:

> The woods are lonely, dark and deep,
> but I have promises to keep
> and miles to go before I sleep.

Finally, after many hours of speculation about what the poet really had in mind when he wrote those lines, they went to see Robert Frost and asked him about it. Frost said to them, "Shucks, all I meant was I was tired and I wanted to get on home and go to bed."

173 (Outer Space; Science)

Since the dawn of human curiosity, man has climbed mountains and gazed into the night sky wondering whether there is life somewhere out there. Hoping, or perhaps fearing that we are not alone in the universe, today's scientists enlist the latest technology in an effort to communicate with man-beyond-the-moon. Did you know that right now powerful transmitters are sending a message into the vast unknown? It is a simple message: one click, then two clicks, then three clicks, then four clicks, then a pause, then the whole sequence is repeated. What is the message? Order! Scientists are hoping some curious beings will hear the message, know it comes from earth and respond. Inter-stellar communication is not likely to be the liveliest conversation in town. But we are already listening. Giant radio telescopes are examining tiny bits of static from deep space hoping to discern a "message" from out there.

174 (Family; Humor)

There was a family in which the brother, who lived in another city and worked for a zoo, often stopped by to visit when he was travelling. Usually, he was transporting an animal of some kind. The family became so accustomed to this that they were not very shocked when he appeared one day with an alligator in tow. With the alligator safely reposing in the family bathtub, they all went out to breakfast. What they should have remembered, but didn't, was that the twice-a-week cleaning lady who had been with them for years would be coming that day. When the family returned a few hours later, they found a note from the cleaning lady: "I am very sorry that the house is not clean, but I quit! I will not work for a family that keeps an alligator in the bathtub. I'm sorry I didn't mention this before, but the subject never came up."

175 (Prison)

Soon after Al Smith was elected to his first term as Governor of New York, he made an inspection tour of the state prison, Sing Sing. After Smith had toured the plant, the warden explained that prison morale was low and he asked the governor to speak some encouraging word to the inmates. Smith agreed and, characteristically, began by saying, "My fellow citizens." Then he remembered that when one goes to State's Prison he loses his citizenship. Nervously, he tried again. "My fellow convicts," he said. But that didn't sound quite right. Embarrassed almost beyond words, Smith then said, "Well, anyhow, I'm glad to see so many of you here." Despite his good intention, the Governor did little to uplift prison morale that day.

176 (Ephesians; Family; Love; Marriage; Parent and Child; Paul)

In the novel, "Dearly Beloved," by Ann Morrow Lindbergh, there is a moving passage in which Deborah, the mother, is

Communication

adjusting the wedding veil for Sally, her daughter. They have lived in the same house for twenty some years but never really enjoyed deep sharing or real communication. And the mother is feeling this very deeply now on the wedding day. With great feeling, Ann Morrow Lindbergh describes the scene: "Deborah went to her daughter, kissed her lightly on the forehead and hesitated for a moment, looking urgently, almost pleadingly into her wide eyes. Wasn't there something she could say at this moment, mother to daughter, something real? Sally, too, seemed to be pleading, asking for confirmation. 'Your father will be up in a moment,' Deborah blurted in a rush." That was all she could say. The words for something deeper never came. The real thing never got said. That's the commentary on life for so many of us in marriage, in the family, and with friends and others. We go places and do things together, but the real thing never gets said, the real communication never takes place. But that's what St. Paul was so excited about, you see. You can't read the Letter to the Ephesians without feeling the throb of high enthusiasm in his life. Paul discovered that because God loves us so much it is possible for us to move down to deep levels of loving, where the real thing can be said and where the real sharing of life can take place. When you know how much God loves you, you have a new sense of your own worth, of your own integrity as a person.

177 (God, love of; Humor; Parent and Child)

The Germans have two words for the verb "to know." One word is "kennen" which means to know with your mind. The other word is "wissen" [pronounce vissen] which means to know at the deepest level of your being. The problem is that many of you know the Good News of the Gospel in a "kennen" kind of way. You know it intellectually. You accept it! "I accept; I believe," you say. And you wonder [sometimes out loud] why preachers keep going on this way about God's love for us. The answer is—and the problem is—that so few of us know this in a "wissen" kind of way, down at the deepest level of our being. The proof of this is in the way we live. We don't translate this into our daily lives because we haven't allowed it to take hold of our full beings. We know, but we don't "understand." Like the teenage girl whose mother picked her up at high school to take her to the dentist. All the way to the dentist's office the girl chattered about an English Placement Test that she had taken. She said, "Oh mommy, I'm in the top eight per cent in the nation in the ability to understand sentences, and to give meanings to words." She was also in the top three per cent in her ability "to understand direct statements" and "to perceive the motive and ideas behind them." And she just rambled on about this. The mother said that when they arrived at the dentist's office there was a big sign on the door that read "Pull"— and her daughter pushed, and the dental work had to be postponed on account of a swollen lip.

178   (Family; Parent and Child)

Psychiatrist Paul Tournier has written of a case in which a father had a problem with one of his daughters, a little girl who was very quiet, very shy, unable to express herself outwardly. The father was an outgoing person and most of the other children were too. And he was just puzzled and bewildered and confused about this, but he tried to understand. On one occasion he gave his quiet little daughter a present. It was an elegant little glass elephant on a gold chain, to put around her neck. He put it down on the table in front of her and said, "I've brought you this present." Well, she was just overwhelmed! Her mouth dropped open and she stared at this beautiful, beautiful thing. She sat there for several minutes, staring at this thing, unable to speak. Then she got up and went into the other room to try to tell her mother what had happened. When she came back she was thunderstruck because she saw her beautiful little elephant dangling from her sister's neck. The father said, in a kind of offhanded way, "Well, you didn't want it so I gave it to your sister." Didn't want it? He wasn't

Communication

listening! He wasn't listening to the joy of her silence. He hadn't listened enough to this child to know who she was and how she expressed herself. And years later she was in therapy, trying with her analyst to trace back the tragic feeling she had that no one was listening down through the years. Even in the family we don't know one another because we're not listening! One of the great joys of parenthood is discovering that every child is different and unique and unlike any other child—even in the same family. You can get to know the uniqueness of each child and identify with it, and call it forth and rejoice in it. But only if you listen enough to hear who the child is, to hear the life that is developing and trying to come through.

179 (Missionaries)

There is the story of an old missionary out in the field who needed an assistant. They sent him a young scholar with a Ph.D. in Theology. When he arrived, the young man had to speak to the natives through the old man because he didn't know the language yet. In his first talk to these simple but wonderful people, the young man delved deep into his learning and said: "Truth is absolute and relative. The Gospel is absolute truth but its application is relative to immediate needs." When the old missionary heard this, a frown came over his face for a moment. Then he arose to translate and said: "He says he's glad to be here."

180 (Honesty; Prayer)

The question of how to tell the truth becomes very important, obviously. A supervisor in an engineering plant found himself in a deteriorating relationship with one of his employees. The employee obviously disliked him and he had stopped trying to do a good job under his supervision. This situation prevailed for months, during which time the supervisor wrestled with the problem of how to handle it. Finally, he talked to his pastor about the problem and it was decided that he would begin to pray for guidance. "While I was praying," he said later, "it came to me that I could no longer put off having a frank, honest, open discussion with that man. Then I carefully wrote down everything I needed to say. I told it the way it was: he was not doing a good job, he was upsetting the other workers and he was upsetting my life because of his prejudicial attitude toward me. I showed the paper to my wife and she suggested that I simply give it to the man. In that way, she said, he could have time to digest it and reflect on it before responding. I followed her suggestion and, a short time later, I received a note from the employee in which he thanked me for what I had written, admitted that much of it was true,and expressed a desire to talk to me more about it." In the days that ensued they not only arrived at a solution to their work problem but also they began what subsequently developed into a lasting friendship. Enmity and bitterness were transformed into a deep friendship because a caring person was able to "tell it the way it was" in a way that enhanced the life of the other.

COMMUNISM

181 (Humor)

A man named Walenska, a long-time Communist in Poland, went to the Polish Emigration Office and applied for a visa to Canada. The emigration official was shocked. "You have been a loyal party worker for many years," he said. "Why do you wish to change your way of life so drastically?" Walenska replied, "I have two reasons, sir. A friend recently told me when this present regime collapses, all of us Communists—even you, sir—who joined the Party in order to get along, will be executed. I want to leave before that happens." The official said, with a knowing smile, "Comrade, there is no danger of this regime collapsing. You can be sure of that." To which Walenska replied, "That is my second reason."

COMPASSION

182 (Christian Ministry; Service)

The late Toyohiko Kagawa was a Japanese Christian who made important contributions to religious education and to the Japanese Labor Movement during his lifetime. Long an advocate of international good will, Kagawa was twice imprisoned during World War II for his refusal to approve his country's war policies. What made him really great, however, was his commitment to a ministry of service. Kagawa had moved into an incredibly horrible slum, ministering unselfishly to the people there for many years: just a simple matter of feeding and clothing and ministering to the needy in a hundred different ways. He was small in stature, but very strong. On one occasion, in the slum, he found a baby who had been thrown away. [It was customary then to throw babies away when parents couldn't take care of them.] When he saw this little girl baby in the filth of the gutter, he picked her up and took her to his home. He called her Ishi [little stone] because she was so cold and so pale and so white. This strong man took this little baby to his room and nursed her back to life. And if you can just get this picture, you're getting the very end-point of the Christian life. Kagawa knew the little child was dying and he wept. And as his tears hit the child's face, they shocked her back to life. His poem, which is called, "When Tears are Mingled," describes the incident. It ends with these lines:

> Will she not cry?
> Here in my close embrace, I kiss her wan lips—
> growing grayer. My drawn face touches her face.
> Fast are my frightened tears falling,
> falling on Ishi's eyes.
> With her cold, still tears, they are mingled.
> Oh, God. At last: She cries!

183

Several years ago, a fascinating book entitled "Mister God, This Is Anna" was published. It is a heart-rending, true story of a little girl, a young man, and the world they shared. The author is identified only by the pseudonym, "Fynn." The story begins when four-year-old Anna is discovered alone and hungry on London's fog-shrouded docks by Fynn, then nineteen years of age. Fynn takes the little girl into his home where he lives with his mother and younger brother. He soon discovers that Anna has an astonishing ability to ask—and answer—life's largest questions. Rarely does conversation with Anna exclude mention by her of the Creator, whom she always calls "Mister God." Anna loved to talk with old people, to tell them stories. One night she told a story to a group of old hoboes which included a rough, wild character they called "Convict Bill". Anna said that there once was a king who was going to execute one of his subjects. But the king suddenly had a change of heart when he saw a little child smile. Convict Bill, hearing these words, nodded in agreement. "A smile," he said, "is pretty powerful stuff."

Compassion

Be as little children! Let God see on your face the trusting smile of a little "Anna", and—Wham! There He will be, smiling at you!

184 (Bible; Protest; Slavery)

Abraham Lincoln was a man of deep, brooding compassion. He carried the burden of the widow and the orphan, as he said in his Second Inaugural Address. There were many times when his compassionate nature got him into real difficulty with his generals. A boy was caught sleeping on guard-duty and was sentenced to death. Lincoln talked with him, excused him, saved him from execution. And the generals complained: how can you run an army and have discipline, with a commander-in-chief who caves in like that. It is hard to believe because Lincoln was such a thin man, but between the Battle of Gettysburg and the end of the war, he lost sixty pounds, brooding over the fact that young men were dying needlessly. He felt the war was already settled and yet it ground on and men were still killing each other. He was a man of deep, quiet compassion and yet he was a man of prophetic protest. He loved the Bible and the Old Testament prophets especially. When Lincoln was a young man, he took a riverboat down the Mississippi to New Orleans. He saw, for the first time, a slave market. He saw families being separated forever–mothers, fathers, children, being sold separately. And Lincoln turned to a companion and said, "If I ever get a chance, I'll hit this hard." And he did. These two Lincoln anecdotes illustrate the balance of compassion and protest. And it is important for us to understand that it is often more loving to raise a voice of protest than it is to wait around to pick up the pieces.

185 (Caring; Peacemaking)

Four law enforcement officers were escorting a violence-prone insane man to a mental institution. The man resisted. He fought them all the way. The full strength of all four officers was needed to keep him under restraint. When they reached the hospital, the officers forced the man through the door, dragged him down a long corridor and pushed him into a chair. A cleaning woman watched intently as the man continued to struggle, Then the woman calmly walked toward the man and gently touched him. The man looked up and saw in the cleaning woman's face a look of deep concern and compassion. She put her hand on his shoulder. He relaxed. He stopped struggling. Someone brought the woman a chair. She sat down and began to speak in a caring way—as though she were speaking to a sick child. The officers released the man from their grip. The cleaning woman continued talking and, thirty minutes later, the man was led away by a nurse. He went calmly.

186 (Change)

In an ancient tale, Francis of Assissi is riding on horseback through the countryside. He sees a poor leper by the side of the road holding out his wooden bowl—begging. The leper's grotesque features jar St. Francis' sensibilities and he recoils in horror. Then, recovering from the shock, he tosses some coins at the man and gallops away. Soon, however, Francis slackens the pace. He seems unsure of his direction now. Then, he wheels the horse around and gallops back to the leper's station where he jumps to the ground and lovingly embraces him.

187 (Healing; Hope; Judgment; Reconciliation)

A 16-year-old boy was arrested for stealing a car. He was a previous offender. He was very rebellious, outwardly very hard. All attempts to get through to him and to counsel him had failed. In the trial, the prosecuting attorney was harsh and judgmental, attempting to break the boy down, pointing out

Compassion

to the jury and others that he was incorrigible, that he had caused trouble before, that he should be put behind bars to protect society. The judge, also in a harsh spirit, continued trying to break this boy down. When he had finished, the boy startled everyone in the courtroom by saying to the judge, "I'm not afraid of you." There was a man in the courtroom named Mr. Weston who runs a farm for delinquent boys. The judge turned to him and said, "Mr. Weston, I feel that this boy is hopeless and that there's no need sending him to your farm. We'll have to send him to jail." Mr. Weston got up and said, "Your Honor, I don't feel the boy is hopeless at all. I feel that beneath that rough, bluff exterior he is very frightened and confused. I happen to know that he has never had a father's love and has never had a chance to make anything of himself. I would like to give him that chance." The only sound in the courtroom was the sound of this boy breaking down and crying. As it turned out, this moment, this statement at this particular time in his life, was the turning point toward that boy's rehabilitation. A full half-hour of harsh, judgmental condemnation had only driven him deeper into himself and into his rebellion. One statement—non-judgmental, compassionate—had released within him the powers of reconciliation and healing and hope.

188 (Parish Life; Preaching)

Dr. Howard Thurman, clergyman and scholar, who once appeared on Life magazine's list of "Ten Best Preachers in America," had an uncommon sympathy for people who slept during the sermon. He said that when he was still a young preacher, he would notice a certain woman who slept through his sermon every Sunday, without exception. This distracted him severely, until the day he made a pastoral call on the woman at her home. He arrived in midafternoon and was greeted by the sounds of several small children running in and out of the kitchen, slamming doors and making demands on the mother. The telephone was ringing, the washing machine was on the spin-dry cycle, the dog was barking and the woman was trying to quickly get dinner started in the oven. He saw the kind of turmoil she lived in and realized that at this particular stage in her life, probably the best thing the Church could give her was a quiet, comfortable place to sleep on Sunday morning. "Thereafter," he said, "every Sunday morning as she closed her eyes, I just blessed her and let her go off to sleep."

COMPETITION

189 (Humor)

Two businessmen became involved with each other in a highly competitive kind of game. Whatever one did, the other immediately outdid. When one bought a $250 suit, the other bought a $300 suit. When one bought a Cadillac, the other bought a Rolls Royce. Finally, when one man installed a plain black phone in his car, the other installed a pastel blue princess phone in his. Then he dialed the other man's number. "Hello Jack," he said, "this is Bill. I'm calling you on your black, plain car phone from my pastel blue, princess car phone." To which Jack replied, "Can you hold on a minute, Bill? I've got a call on the other line."

COMPLACENCY

190 (Indifference; Pride)

Theodore Roethke, the American poet who won the Pulitzer Prize in 1953, wrote a poem called "The Sloth." It portrays one

Conscience

of those shaggy, slow-moving, primitive mammals which seems
to spend most of its life hanging upside down from the branches
of a tree:

> In moving-slow he has no Peer
> You ask him something in his Ear.
> He thinks about it for a Year.

The poem emphasizes the sloth's standoffishness. He inhabits
his own little world, nestled there in his tree as though he were
alone on a remote island. Call him "smug," and he just sighs
and settles back against his branch. He couldn't care less about
anything you might have to say to him. Nothing can disturb
his complacency. He knows everything worth knowing. Moreover, "he knows he knows," as the poet says. Nothing can
convince him that he might be too narrow-minded; that he is
not the wisest of all creatures; that he might be even a little
provincial; that a source outside himself could enrich his life.

CONSCIENCE

191 (Humor; Willpower)

A man consulted with his doctor. "I've got this terrible problem," he said. "Lately, I've been misbehaving and it's getting
worse. My conscience is troubling me very deeply, and I was
wondering if you could prescribe something that would help."
The doctor said, "Oh, I see, you want something to strengthen
your willpower!" The patient protested. "No," he said, "you
don't understand. I want something that will weaken my conscience."

CONSEQUENCES

192 (Sharing)

Aesops' Fables includes the story of a man who owned a proud and handsome horse and an ugly, broken-down old donkey. One day, as they set out on a long journey, the man placed the full burden of carrying the supplies on the donkey. This weakened the donkey so that the poor animal asked the horse to bear part of the load. "If you would take a fair portion, I shall soon get strong again; but if you refuse to help me this weight will kill me," the donkey said. The horse told the donkey to get on with his work and refused to carry part of the burden. Because the horse would not "lift a finger," so to speak, the donkey dropped dead, overcome by his burden. The master then unloosed the pack and placed it upon the horse's back. To this he added the burden of the donkey's carcass. Then the horse cried out: "Alas for my ill nature! By refusing to bear my just portion of the load I have now to carry the whole of it, with a dead weight into the bargain."

CONVERSION

193 (Born Again; New Life; Religion)

Pollster George Gallup Jr. once called a Press Conference to announce the results of a new poll strongly indicating that the United States was on the threshold of a profound religious revival. A reporter asked Mr. Gallup about his own personal

Conversion

religion. "I am a practicing Episcopalean and I strongly believe in spreading the Faith," he answered proudly. But when a reporter asked, "Are you a 'born-again' Christian?" he became apologetic. "I do not remember ever seeing a bolt of lightening," he said. It is important for us to understand that God in His goodness gives us all kinds of experiences when we make our once-and-for-all decision. We needn't feel uneasy because we haven't seen a bolt of lightening. It can be a very gentle, a very tender, a very healing, a very peaceful experience. Have you made that conscious once-and-for-all decision to follow Christ in all things? For some of us who call ourselves "Christians," the unfinished business of our lives is to make this decision down at the deepest level of our being. Some of us have not yet understood that the fullness of life we long for will never come until we make that life-transforming decision to say "Yes!" to Christ.

194 (God, relationship with)

A young woman who had converted to Christianity was asked to explain the difference it had made in her life. She answered, "The old gods that I believed in demanded so much of me. The Christian God gives so much."

195 (Change; Paul)

Dr. Thomas Harris, author of "I'm O.K., You're O.K.," tells the story of two men who met on the street. One of them was the kind of person who dominates every conversation. "Hey Max," he said, "you've grown taller." He then went right on talking without giving the other person a chance to say anything. They parted, only to meet again the very next day. "Hey Max, you've put on a lot of weight," the man said and then went right on talking as he had the day before. Next day they met for the third time. "Hey Max, you've grown more hair." This, at last, was more than the other fellow could take. He immediately broke in and said, "But I'm not Max." But the other man went right on talking. "Oh, you've changed your name, too," he said. All of which reminds one of St. Paul. When Paul changed from being a power-hungry Pharisee to a servant of Christ [as he called himself], he changed his name, too!

COURTSHIP

196 (Humor; Sinners)

A young man was on his first date with the girl of his dreams. He was madly in love with her and, as they were walking home, he wanted desperately to give her a kiss. Having been raised in a strict, religious family atmosphere, however, he hesitated. Then, in a loud voice beamed toward the heavens, he posed this question:

> Father, Father, up above,
> should I kiss
> the girl I love?

And, from out of the sky came a big, booming voice with the answer:

> Sinner, sinner, down below,
> pucker up
> and let her go!

At this very moment in your life there are persons who need you, need your help, need your support, need your love. Do not be afraid to touch them, to talk with them, to listen with understanding, to give them hope! Do not be afraid to give them love!

> Sinner, sinner, down below,
> pucker up
> and let her go!

197 (Commitment; Humor)

"You stopped smoking because she asked you to?" "Yes!" "And you stopped drinking because she asked you?" "Yes!" "And you stopped cursing because she asked you?" "Yes!" "And you stopped gambling because she asked you?" "Yes!" "Then why didn't you marry her?" "Because after all that changing I found I could do better!"

198 (Humor)

A man consulted with his pastor about a certain problem he was having. "How can I help you? What seems to be the trouble?" the pastor asked. "I feel all hollow inside, my life is empty," the man replied. "Can you tell me why?" the pastor asked. The man bowed his head and said, dejectedly, "The woman I love turned down my marriage proposal." The pastor tried to lift up the man's spirits. "You musn't feel that way," he said, "surely you know that a woman's 'No?' often means 'Yes!'" "But she didn't say 'No!' the man replied, she said 'Phooey!'"

CREATION

199 (God, and creation; Mystery)

There is a mighty tug on the human spirit to cancel out and pervert the mystery in God's creation into something we can manage on our own:

Twinkle, twinkle, little star,
I know exactly what you are:
An incandescent ball of gas
Compressed into a solid mass.

200 (God, and creation)

The story is told of four angels watching God create the world. "Why did He make it?" asked the first. "How did He make it?" asked the second. "Give it to me!" demanded the third. "It's so marvelous! Let me go and take care of it!" said the fourth. The question, "Why did He make it?" is the philosophical approach. "How did He make it?" is the scientific approach. "Give it to me!" is the selfish approach. "Let me take care of it!" is the religious approach which acknowledges that all is God's. All the lands are God's. All the skies, all the waters are God's. All the animals are God's. And all the people are God's: the proud and the humble; the rich and the poor; the Caesars and the subjects, without distinction.

201 (Mystery; Science; Universe)

Consider the mystery of the universe. Many centuries ago, Ptolemy could count no more than one thousand and twenty-two stars; centuries later, Galileo could see five thousand through his telescope. Seventy years ago, scientists' best estimate was three hundred billion. The figure soon doubled, then trebled. Now they talk of galaxies and meta-galaxies until the mind boggles. Our own galaxy is about one hundred thousand times six trillion miles wide, yet we know it is but a tiny part of the larger, unknown star-system. We know there are atom particles travelling in outer space at incredible speed [we call them "cosmic rays"] but we don't know where they come from. Getting down to earth, we know there is a vast quantity of salt in the ocean, but we still don't know how it got there. The more we learn about creation, the more we realize how little we know about it—how immense the mystery of it.

CRIME

202 (Planning)

There was a man who decided to rob a bank. "It would all go according to plan," he reasoned—the perfect crime. For many months he plotted out the details of his proposed "caper." He knew the exact time that he would enter the bank. He knew precisely where each of the bank employees would be positioned at that time. He carefully diagramed his escape route. Finally, on the appointed day, he carried out his plan—to a point. Sometime later, as he stood before the Criminal Courts Judge, he was asked if he had anything to say before sentence was pronounced. "Yes I do your honor," he said, "my plan was all so perfect. The only thing I didn't figure on was getting that speeding ticket. I guess you can't know everything!"

CROSS

203 (Crucifixion; Christ, blood of)

It is the closing scene in the motion picture, "Ben Hur." The sky is disappearing behind ominous looking cloud formations. The movie camera takes a long shot of three crosses rising out of a distant hill. Then the camera moves in close, ever-closer, on the figure stretched out on the center cross. Lightening reveals a man squirming in silent agony to the rhythm of the flashes. It is raining—hard. With each flash of light, the pool of rain water at the foot of the cross grows larger. Suddenly, a single drop of blood drips into the pool and scatters. Then another drop falls. And then another. The pool is now tinted light red. The blood now begins to flow into the pool, coloring it an even deeper red. The rain comes harder and the pool overflows into another pool immediately below it. The second pool reddens and enlarges, overflowing into still another pool which, in turn, overflows into a small stream. The blood-stained stream flows into a larger stream which meets a river which flows into an ocean.

204

Down through the centuries artists have struggled mightily to portray the sheer beauty of the mother/child image on canvass. "Madonna and Child" masterpieces hang in museums all over the world. Giorgione (who dominated the art of Venice), Albrecht Durer (the German-born master), Hans Memling (Flemish), El Greco (Spanish), Boticelli (Florentine), are but a few of the world's greatest artists who have contributed richly to our "Madonna and Child" painting legacy. Each of these paintings makes its own unique, reverential statement on the elegance, the serenity, the grace and the mystery of this beautiful image. But, perhaps, the most poignant of them all was created by the great Italian artist, Raphael. In his work entitled "The Alba Madonna," the faces of the Madonna, the Infant, and the child John the Baptist are serene and quiet as they gaze at the thin Cross Jesus holds in His baby hand.

205   (Death; Glory; New Life)

There is the story of three trees which were talking among themselves about their future. The first tree said, "I'd really like to be made into a cradle so that a baby could be laid in me and I could support that new life." The second tree said, "I'd like to be made into an ocean-going ship and be able to carry useful cargoes all over the world." The third tree said, "I don't want to be made into anything else. I just want to stand here as a tree and point upward as a way of reminding men and women that there is a God in Heaven who loves them."

Cross

At harvest time, the woodcutters came to the forest. As they cut down the first tree, one of them said, "We'll make this one into a manger." The tree protested: it did not want to become a feed-box for animals. But the woodchoppers made it into a manger and sold it to an innkeeper in Bethlehem. And when the Lord of all the earth was born, He was placed in that manger, and it became a cradle that all the world would always remember. As the woodcutters cut down the second tree, they said, "We'll make it into a little fishing boat." The tree protested: "I want to be part of an ocean-going ship." But they made him into a little fishing boat, and a man named Simon Peter bought the boat. And when the Lord of all the earth needed a place to stand and address the crowds that were pressing in upon Him, He got into the little fishing boat and it became a place from which the Good News of the Kingdom of Love was spread across all the oceans of the world. The woodcutters came to the third tree and said, "The Romans are paying good money for crosses these days. We'll make this tree into a cross." The tree protested, but was cut down and made into a cross. The Lord of all the earth was crucified on that cross and the cross to this day is pointing toward heaven to remind us that there is a God who loves us. And did you notice, in this simple story, how in every case, being cut down was the price they paid for entering into their glory?

206

On the heavy wooden door of an old Scandanavian Church, there is a strange, very large handle, shaped in a circle and made of wrought iron. Inside the circle is a large Cross. The Cross is cradled in a wrought iron hand. To open and close the door, you grab hold of the Cross and when you do that the hand points directly at you. And you get the impression that the artist who designed the handle is saying to you as you take hold of the Cross, "What does that Cross mean to you and what are you going to do about it?"

207 (Crucifixion; Chief Priests; Scribes)

On Calvary's hill, "People going by kept insulting Him, tossing their heads and saying, 'Ha, Ha!...Save Yourself by coming down from that Cross!' The Chief Priests and the Scribes also joined in and jeered: 'Let the Messiah, the King of Israel, come down from the Cross!' " (Mk. 15:32). Thank God He didn't come down! Because He didn't come down we are given the healing power to overcome our hardness of heart. Because He didn't come down we can see God and one another in a whole new way.

208 (Parish Life; Wedding)

"Alec" was one of those wonderful old Church sextons who seemed to have worked in the parish forever. Over the years he had assumed certain pastoral roles that went beyond the ordinary duties of a Church sexton. For example, it was not unusual for him to take over a "Sunday School" class when one of the regular teachers couldn't make it. And it was Alec who conducted all wedding rehearsals. His pastor once said that Alec "kind of held the Church together." Alec was a real pillar in that sense. At every wedding rehearsal, Alec encouraged the people parading down the aisle to keep their heads up, and to smile, and to look happy. Often someone in the wedding party would say, "But if I am looking up like that I'll stumble, I'll fall." And Alec answered always with the same line. He would point to the Cross hanging high in the sanctuary and say, "If you keep your eye on the Cross, you won't stumble." Right on, Alec! If we keep our eye on the Cross, we won't stumble.

209 (God, love of; Truth)

In John Masefield's play, "Good Friday," when the day of the Crucifixion has come to an end, one of the characters speaks these lines:

Cross

> Friend, it is over now,
> The passion, the sweat, the pains,
> Only the truth remains.

The truth is that we are free to love others because God has first loved us. The incredible worthwhileness of each individual human being derives from the reality that each of us has been first loved by God Himself.

210 (Crucifixion; Jesus, as victim; Russian Orthodox Cross)

In most Christian traditions, the symbol of the Cross is fashioned from an upright and one crosspiece. However, in the Russian Orthodox tradition, it is shaped somewhat differently. In addition to the usual upright and one crosspiece, there are two smaller crosspieces. One is positioned slightly above the central one and the other down toward the foot of the upright. The small one above represents the sign hung over the crucified Lord's head, bearing the inscription, "Jesus of Nazareth, King of the Jews." St. John tells us that these words appear in three languages–Latin, Hebrew and Greek—so that everyone would be sure to get the message: "Here hangs the king—some king!" The little crosspiece below depicts the wooden block placed under Jesus' feet for support, in order to prevent Him from dying too quickly. This crosspiece is set on the upright at a slant to indicate how Jesus must have pushed down hard with one foot when the pain became most severe. Therefore, the Russian Cross emphasizes that Jesus suffers still, wherever anyone suffers in this world; that Jesus the Victor is Jesus the Victim still.

211 (Sacrifice)

There is an old oriental saying that goes like this: Consider the worm; his day is two feet long. Meaning, just as a worm can do only so much, travel so far, given his physical limitations, so too men should learn to submit to the human condition's apparent limitations. But Jesus' Passion Story asks us to change all that. We say, "I can't do the impossible"; Jesus says, "Follow me, however impossible it seems." We say, "But I can't go too far"; Jesus says, "If anyone orders you to go one mile, go two miles with him." (Mt. 5:41) We say, "How much can a person do?"; Jesus says, "My soul is sorrowful to the point of death...Take up my cross."

CRUCIFIXION

212 (Death; God, love of)

In Ingmar Bergman's famous film, "Winter Light," one of the characters is the church sexton, a horribly crippled man who lives in constant pain. The man is deeply troubled by his reflections on Jesus' crucifixion. He says, "The pain in my life goes on and on, in my back and in my bones...It's not the physical pain that burdens me about the Crucifixion, but that He had given so much, He had loved so much, He had healed so much—and nobody cared. Nobody understood. When he died, He seems to have died absolutely uselessly; utterly, utterly alone; utterly, utterly abandoned."

When we get close to the Crucifixion Story, we find that it can profoundly affect us in this way. But there is more to it than this. From the very beginning, the Christian Community has attached a special meaning to Jesus' death that goes far beyond the agony of the crucifixion. This death is a death that gives us life. In the Crucifixion of Jesus Christ, Almighty God is saying "I love you." Almighty God is saying to us through the Cross, "I love you so much I will go to this extreme to show you, to make it real to you, to move you to do something about it. I love you so much I will go to this extreme to show you how the Power of Love conquers all–even death."

Crucifixion

213 (Preaching)

In a novel by C. E. Montague called "Rough Justice," a little boy is in Church with his mother listening for the first time to a sermon on Jesus' Crucifixion. The little boy gets so caught up in the preacher's description of the Event that he begins to cry. It can be very difficult to cry silently, so he is sniffling and making little nose-noises. People are beginning to turn around and look at him. Then, the boy's mother leans down and whispers, "Don't take the preacher so seriously. What will people think?"

214 (Grief)

A famous singer, after a severe bereavement, went to India in search of peace. There she visited the famous Indian poet, Rabindranath Tagore, whose works had been a source of inspiration to her. When it came time for her to leave, she asked Tagore if he would like her to sing him a song. The poet was delighted, of course, and waited to hear what song she had chosen for the occasion. As the song began, Tagore and a second guest were startled to hear the words of an old "Spiritual" fill the air:

> "Were you there when they crucified my Lord?
> Were you there?...
> Oh, sometimes my heart begins to tremble.
> Were you there when they crucified my Lord?

The second guest was deeply touched by the experience. When he retired, he lay awake under the stars long past midnight thinking of the song and the scene it referred to—the scene at Calvary that had taken place under those same stars. And he wondered if he would have had the courage to stand by his Master's side, not when the crowds were shouting "Hosanna!" but when the wild mob was crying, "Crucify Him"; and when His pierced hands and feet were dripping deep red lifeblood.

The words haunted him, "Were you there when they crucified my Lord?"

215 (Deafness; Jesus, symbol for; Preaching)

A well-known preacher was invited to deliver a sermon in the chapel of a college for the deaf. He described it as a "Preacher's paradise, because you get two laughs for every joke: when you reach the punch line one laugh comes from those who can hear and a few seconds later when the sign language interpreter catches up, you get a second laugh." He said he noticed that on several occasions during the sermon the sign language interpreter, in a very graceful way, would point to the palms of her hands. Later he learned that pointing to the palms of the hands is the sign for Jesus Christ. How appropriate! Of all the signs that might have been chosen for Jesus they chose the nailprints in the palms of Jesus' hands to symbolize who He was. The New Testament writers take the same approach, saying to us that somehow the Crucifixion sums it all up. If you really want to get close to Jesus, if you really want to know who He was and what He was doing, you do it through the Crucifixion.

CYNICISM

216 (Advertising; Children; Television)

Columbia University Psychology Professor Thomas Bever has said that our daily fare of misleading TV ads is "permanently distorting children's views of morality, society, and business." His statement was based on an in-depth study of TV viewers between the ages of five and twelve. Professor Bever concluded that at age twelve, many children already have been turned into cynics by TV. They find it easier to decide that all TV commercials lie than to try to discover which, if any, are being truthful. In Professor Bever's words, "They become ready to believe that, like advertising, all businesses and all adult institutions are riddled with hypocrisy."

DAILY DEATHS

217

Every day we die a little. A newborn baby gives up the comfort and warmth of the mother's womb in order to have life. A child gives up the security of home life in order to start school. A student gives up the comfort of the structured academic life in order to graduate. A young man or woman gives up the accustomed family life in order to marry. The daily deaths come in countless other ways too: broken relationships, illness, divorce, death of a loved one. One man counts his daily deaths by the number of times he gets up in the morning to go to a job he hates. Another's daily death is not to be able to find work at all.

DANCE

218 (Praise; Thanksgiving)

Antol Dorati, former conductor of the National Symphony Orchestra in Washington, was talking to an interviewer about Dance—the ballet. Mr. Dorati said he was convinced that the work of a great choreographer is an act of praise. He said, "I imagine that the very first dance was a movement of adoration or praise for that which is—the body simply moving to give thanks to the Creator. In earliest times, as a person became

Death

aware of the wonder of creation and the wonder of life, the body began to move in an expression of praise and thanksgiving." Maestro Dorati has given us a very beautiful image of Faith's beginnings.

DEATH

219 (Compassion; Service)

From Doctor Elisabeth Kubler-Ross, the internationally-known psychiatrist and author of several books on death and dying, comes the true story of an old woman who worked for many years in a Chicago hospital, mopping floors. The doctor says that whenever the old scrub woman left the room of a dying patient, that patient–always, without exception–was happier and more at peace than before. Having observed this phenomenon over a period of time, Doctor Kubler-Ross was determined to find out why it was happening. She invited the old woman to her office for a conference. There she learned that this poor, uneducated, wrinkled, old cleaning woman had faced a great deal of poverty and suffering and tragedy in her life. The woman told her of the time when she had waited in a public health clinic for her three-year-old son to be treated for pneumonia. But, before the little boy's turn for treatment came, he died in her arms. "You see, doctor," the old woman said, "dying patients are just like old acquaintances to me, and I'm not afraid to touch them, to talk with them, or to offer them hope." As a result of this talk with Doctor Kubler-Ross, hospital authorities offered the old scrub woman a newly-created position of "Counselor to the Dying."

220 (Happiness; Understanding)

The following beautiful insight was composed by a young man afflicted with terminal cancer. The Christmas after he died, his

113

mother shared it with relatives and friends, instead of the usual Christmas card:

> Reflection . . .
> Why is it that so many people can't see . . . including myself, that life here on Earth can be a beautiful experience almost beyond belief. I believe God has shown me some answers. Take people for instance. God made everybody and He doesn't make mistakes; there is something beautiful in every person and all it takes is a little effort to see and respect it and you've got a friend. It's too easy to be critical: nobody is perfect, nobody, but everybody needs happiness and someone to understand them and to do that gives a very special feeling to those who make the effort. I'm talking about a true happiness. –David Kerr.

221 (Salvation Army; Service)

When William E. Booth, founder of the Salvation Army, was dying, he called the children around his bed in order to pass his work on to them. With his dying breath he said to them, "Remember the homeless men!" He stopped for a few moments to regain his strength and then he said, "Remember the homeless women!" Then finally, almost inaudibly because he was so weak, he said, "Remember the homeless children!"

222 (Churchgoing; Faith)

There is a very moving story about a major plane crash of several years ago in which a small boy was the sole survivor. All of the other passengers were killed instantly. Almost miraculously, the boy had landed in a thick snow bank that cushioned his fall. Although he was severely injured, he remained conscious throughout the entire, painful ordeal. At the hospital, a team of doctors and nurses worked feverishly, but unsuccessfully to save his life. And, as the boy lay dying, he startled everyone by suddenly looking up into the eyes of one of the nurses and saying, "I go to Church on Sundays." What statement was that little boy trying to make? Was he trying to say, "Because I go to Church I have scored some points, earned some favors with God which I desperately need now?" Or, was he saying, "By going to Church I have learned to trust and have faith in God?"

223

Thomas Hardy was a poet who wrote with considerable cynicism about life and death. One of his poems, called "Are You Digging On My Grave?," tells of a young woman who had died and been buried recently. She hears a stirring up on the surface of her grave and she thinks to herself, "Oh, it must be my lover!" But she realizes, "No he already has married another woman and forgotten me." Then she speculates, "It must be the members of my family!" Again she reconsiders: "No. It cannot be them. I know them too well for that. They're so practical they wouldn't waste time like this on someone who is dead." Then she thought, "Maybe it's my enemy, come to gloat. But, oh no, my enemy wouldn't even bother hating me anymore, now that I'm dead." Who could it be then, digging around on the grave's surface? "Ah, it's my little dog!" she says. Wouldn't you know? Her faithful dog! All you dog-lovers can really understand the fidelity of a dog. But wait! The dog apologizes for having disturbed the woman, saying, in the poem's last stanza,

> Mistress, I dug upon your grave to bury a bone
> In case I should be hungry on this spot
> when passing on my daily trot.
> Sorry, I quite forgot
> it was your resting place.

Death

Sadly, the feeling of rejection and isolation that comes through in the poem often begins long before we are in our grave. We are pronounced "terminally ill" and we begin to feel the vibrations from the very ones we want most to be present to us: "I don't want to touch! I don't want to draw near to death. I don't want to be an intimate part of it!"

224   (God, longing for)

Rudyard Kipling was muttering deliriously on his deathbed, obviously making some last request. Those in attendance could not understand what it was he was struggling so hard to say until one of the nurses leaned over and said, "Mr. Kipling, Mr. Kipling, what is it you want?" Kipling stopped tossing for a moment and replied with the last bit of strength he could muster in his weakened body, "I want God!"

225   (Alcoholism; Resurrection; Temperance)

A New England matron always had been regarded by her relatives and friends as being predictably straight-laced, whatever the occasion. But she was tired of living up to this image. Consequently, when she was offered a cocktail at her grandniece's wedding reception, to everyone's surprise, she accepted. In the middle of the first sip, she suddenly had guilt feelings and blurted out, "Oh, I must refuse. I am a member of the "Women's Temperance Union." Then, after a moment's reflection she reconsidered. "Well, I don't suppose it really matters," she said, "I haven't paid my dues for this year." And she promptly resumed her sipping. The death/resurrection process by which God works is necessary. Our dues must be paid: there are day-to-day deaths that we must die and there is final, physical death. I will die. You will die. Everyone we love will die. But the Good News from Jesus is that God is at work in our daily deaths and our physical death, both, in order that we may have new life.

226 (Education)

A Maryland weekly newspaper ran an article which was critical of the State University's introduction of a Course entitled "Death Education." The author of the article treated it in purely economic terms. "With tight budgets everywhere," he wrote, "why this far-fetched offering in which students will be made aware of all aspects of dying?" As a society, we cannot afford to talk about death is what he seems to be saying. What should be said is that we cannot afford not to talk more about death.

227 (Churchyards; Epitaphs)

Most 18th Century New England cemeteries were put next to the Churches. And it was a regular Sunday afternoon custom to take a walk in the cemetery. Just a leisurely stroll. It was good exercise, a good way to spend a Sunday afternoon. The people who cut the gravestones in those days knew that many people would be seeing them and so it became an Early American art form. They created pictures on the gravestones that could convey real meaning to the Sunday afternoon strollers. Also, there was the epitaph. Imagine you are walking through the cemetery on a Sunday afternoon and suddenly you are confronted with this gravestone epitaph:

"Behold and see as you pass by
As you are now, so once was I
As I am now so you will be
Prepare for death and follow me."

228

Philip of Macedon gave one of his slaves a strange standing order. Every morning this slave was to march into the king's chamber, and no matter what the king was doing, announce in a loud voice, "You must die!" Would many of us appreciate

Death

that kind of daily reminder of the inevitability of our own death, much less order it?

229 (God, and death; Happiness)

Legend has it that when a certain saintly woman was dying she pointed to the wall of her room and cried out: "Oh! Death for me means to see the wall crumble away and to fall into the arms of God." The wall crumbles away and the arms of God stretch out to embrace you, wonderfully to embrace you and loneliness is no more, and you are happy beyond all imagining!

230 (Gambling; Humor)

In Las Vegas, at the funeral of a notorious gambler, a friend was delivering the eulogy. The speaker went on and on with those flowery phrases that try to cover up the fact of death. At one point he said, "Let us not look upon our dear friend as dead, but merely asleep!" To which one of the deceased's gambling pals standing in the rear of the funeral parlor said to those around him, "I'll give you eight-to-five he's dead." There were no takers.

231 (Identity Crisis)

Each in his own way is like the millionaire whose final, bizarre request was to be buried in his gold-plated cadillac, sitting in the driver's seat with his hands on the wheel, a $2.00 cigar in his mouth, and the air-conditioning running. After his request was fulfilled, and as relatives and friends left the graveside, one of the grave diggers looked down at the spectacle and exclaimed, "Man, that's really living!" However misguided his attitude and approach to life (and death), it can at least be said of the deceased man that he was acutely conscious of the nagging question, "Who am I?" Not only had he spent a lifetime trying to prove that he indeed was somebody, but in his own pitiful way he seemed to be expressing the hope that not even death could destroy his unique identity.

232 (Caring; Parent and child)

Author John Rowen has written about how his great grandfather used to sit for hours at a certain window of the house, watching the mountains in the distance. In his last days, the old man began to think that he was back in the "Old Country," in Europe, and that the mountains he saw were the mountains of his childhood. Sometimes, as he did this, night would begin to fall or a storm would be gathering. Then a tear would come in his eye. A look of real fear would come over his face. And he would say to his daughter, "Sophie, may I stay the night with you? The way is very difficult!" And his daughter would always say to him, very gently, "Papa, you may stay the night with me." It was then that the leathery, wrinkled, old face would break into a beautiful smile and the old man would drift off into a peaceful sleep. The time of dying is a time when "the way is difficult." And the greatest gift that we can give to another, in their time of dying, is the gift of caring. The gift of being there.

233 (Communication; Sharing; Sickness)

At the annual meeting of the National Hospice Association, one of the speakers gave an illustration that generated a great deal of discussion among the doctors and the nurses present. The speaker told the story of a young nurse who was ministering to a young man her own age. The patient had terminal cancer. The nurse knew that the young man wanted to talk with her but because she was afraid that she wouldn't have "the right answers," she decided to back off. In her own words, "I know he wanted to talk to me, but I always turned it into something light: a little joke or some evasive reassurance, which had to

119

Death

fail. The patient knew, and I knew, but as he saw my desperate attempt to escape, and as he felt my anxiety, he took pity on me by keeping to himself what he wanted to share with another human being. And so he died, and did not bother me."

234

A man wrote a little piece about what he experienced when his father died. He said that people began to console him, saying: "Isn't it fine that your father lived to be 96? It must be easier for you since he lived such a long life." Although he was grateful for their attempts to console him, he also was very disturbed. He wondered why they didn't realize that to die is to die, at any age. "This was my father's death," he said, "and it was not diminished in importance because he was almost 100. It was his death, the only one he would have." For each of us, our death is our death. Each of us has but one death to die!

235

Dr. Bernard Seltzer, an outstanding surgeon, discovered in midlife that he also had a gift for writing. Among other works, he has written a best-selling book that has been much discussed. It is called, "Mortal Lessons: Notes on the Art of Surgery." One of the "mortal lessons" in the book is Dr. Seltzer's insistence that when death occurs, especially the death of someone we deeply love, it is essential for us to contemplate the dead body as it is—not to turn away from it or to try to disguise it. He says, "He who shrinks from this contemplation is like an Elizabethan 'dandy' who breathes through a handkerchief that has been soaked in vinegar in order to avoid the rank whiff of the poor."

236 (Change; Lifestyle)

When a 50-year-old man was told that he had a terminal illness, he wrote this to a friend:

I suddenly asked myself, "What am I doing? Why
am I working at something I don't enjoy? Why
am I building up a bank account that will do me
no good when I am dead? Why am I pretending
to be one way when I feel another?"

He went on to tell his friend about how he was going to change
all that. He lived 18 months longer and, just before he died, he
said that those 18 months were the best, the fullest, the richest
of his life. And he had lived through that entire period with a
death sentence hanging over him.

237 (Reality)

In the Broadway musical, "A Little Night Music," the grandmother proposes a toast: "To life," she says. Everyone at the
dinner party enthusiastically joins in her toast to life. Then she
spoils the party. She proposes a second toast, saying, "And to
the only other reality, death!" The others cannot join her in
this toast. They are embarrassed. A pall of gloom falls over the
party and you feel it for the rest of the evening. The guests are
unable to face that "other reality."

238

In one of Dylan Thomas' poems, he talks of death in many
moods and ways, but each stanza ends with the beautiful phrase,
"But death shall have no dominion." Death is real. Death is
coming. There is no way we can escape it. But death shall have
no dominion. This is what the New Testament is saying to us.

239 (Afterlife; New Life)

There is a haunting story about a wealthy merchant in Bagdad
who sent his servant to the market place one morning. There
the servant saw the figure of death moving among the people.

Death

Death seemed to look at him very menacingly and the servant became panic stricken. He rushed home and begged his master to give him a horse so that he might leave Baghdad to escape death. He wanted to flee to a city called Samara. The merchant had pity on his servant and gave him his fastest white Arabian horse. And the servant immediately galloped off for Samara. Later that day, the merchant himself went to the marketplace where he too saw the vision of death. He approached the figure and asked him why he had stared so threateningly at his servant that morning. Death said to the merchant, "That was not a threatening look. It was a look of surprise. I was surprised to see that man in the City of Baghdad. You see, I have an appointment with him tonight, in the City of Samara." The story is troubling in one respect. We know that there are some things we can do to delay the appointment with death. We can fasten our seat belts. We can get proper exercise and eat the right foods. We can stop smoking, and so on. There is a dangerous fatalism that comes through in the story when we confront it head-on. But the basic truth it embodies is a truth! We all, ultimately, will have to keep an appointment with death. We die! But... the same God who gave us life in the beginning, gives us new life in the beauty of our spiritual body.

240 (Afterlife; Growth)

Journalist William Allen White, famed editor of the "Emporia Gazette," wrote an editorial the day after his 17-year-old daughter died that has since become a classic. Her name was Mary. She was dearly loved not only by her own family but by the whole community. She was known for her boundless energy. She always had a project of some kind underway. One such project was organizing the delivery of Thanksgiving Day baskets of food to the poor. She did this not in any pious way, but in the manner of a joyous, life-filled, life-loving 17-year-old. She loved to ride horses. One day, her head struck a tree limb as she was riding and she died. In the editorial, Mr. White writes about how the simple funeral service reflected his faith and the faith of the people in the community. Finally, he concludes his description of the burial scene in these words:

> A rift in the grey clouds through a shaft of sunlight upon her coffin, as her energetic little body sank to its rest. But the soul of her, the glowing, fervent soul of her, surely was burning with eager joy upon some other dawn.

This is our dying conviction: that we are safe in the Lord's hands; that we will enter through the true Gate; that we will grow again.

DECEIT

241 (Humor; Politicians)

Famed Louisiana politician, Huey Long, was about to open an election campaign. One of the local leaders reminded Long that he would be campaigning in an area populated largely by Roman Catholics. Consequently, wherever he stopped that day, Huey Long began his speech with the same story. He said:

> When I was a boy I used to get up at six o'clock
> on Sunday, hitch the old horse up to the buggy
> and take my Catholic grandparents to Mass.

With those opening lines, he had every audience with him from the beginning. Later, the local leader congratulated him for a successful campaign. Then, he said, "I didn't know you had

Deceit

Catholic grandparents." Huey replied, "Don't be a darn fool. I didn't even have a horse."

242 (Humor)

There is an amusing story about a man who was driving through the countryside when suddenly his car stalled. He got out to see what was wrong and, as he bent over the motor, he heard a voice say, "That trip to Japan was wonderful last Spring." He looked around but saw no one. All he could see was an old horse standing in the meadow. The horse looked straight at him and said, "Yes, that trip was almost as good as the one to Paris and Rome the year before." Well, the man became almost hysterical with excitement. He ran to the farmhouse at the edge of the meadow, pounded on the door, took out his billfold and said, "I want to buy that horse at any price." Calmly, the farmer replied, "Oh, you mustn't pay too much attention to that horse. He hasn't been to half the places he talks about."

243 (Clergy; Humor)

There is a wonderful story about a horse-trader in the hills of West Virginia. He was a sharp dealer but he always justified his horse-trades by quoting the Bible. He knew just what passage to use in each case. On one occasion, he had a very sick horse on his hands. He tried to sell it but everybody in the area knew the horse was sick and they wouldn't touch it. Then a stranger came along and it wasn't long before he was riding out of town on the sick horse, as the horse-trader counted a thick wad of bills. This upset the horse-trader's wife very much. "Don't tell me you sold that sick horse to someone?" "Yeah," he said. "A preacher passed through and I sold him the horse." "Really, a man of the cloth! You would do this to a clergyman?" she asked. "Oh, it's alright," he replied. "As the Bible says, 'He was a stranger and I took him in.' "

DEPRESSION

244 (Despair; Healing; Suicide)

In the tragic play "Endgame," by Samuel Beckett, the characters rattle on about the miseries of life. They play cruel tricks on each other to get their minds off the agony. It's all very depressing. Following a performance of "Endgame," a psychiatrist told the director he had brought a patient to the performance. She was a sixteen-year-old who had attempted suicide three times. "But why this play?" the director asked. "Why such a hopeless statement as this for a girl already wallowing in fear and depression?" The doctor pointed out that, on the contrary, this play opened up entirely new channels of hope for this girl. "Through it," he said, "she had come to realize that there were other living persons who totally identified with her. It was obvious to her that the author of the play knew how she felt. This was worth months of therapy. She began to see that her problems were truly shared by others and she virtually danced out of the theater that night. Had I taken her to a bouncy musical she would have been completely turned off. I have to work with her where she is."

245 (Meaninglessness; Success)

J. Richard Kennedy wrote a novel called "Short Term." The principal character is a forty-two-year-old businessman named Ken Preston. Ken Preston was "successful" in the business sense of the word. He had all the money he needed. But he was not a joyful man. He was afflicted with a kind of low-level depression that never left him. Because he wasn't really being himself ever, he knew something was very wrong. He said at one point that he felt like a person who was shouting "Rah! Rah! Rah!" for absolutely nothing. He said at another time that he felt "like a quarterback on a timeless Monday morning who kept

125

seeing the scoreboard and the big zero." For Ken Preston there was this continuous depression with only a few strokes of light along the way to keep him going. One thing that he kept remembering was the French girl he had met overseas during World War II. He had thought for a time that he loved her very much, but she had chosen to go her own way and they were separated forever. Yet, he kept remembering something she had once said to him in a moment of brutal honesty:

> You are a very bright man and sometimes you are very kind. But inside, you are nothing.

And that was Ken Preston's trouble to the very end.

DESPAIR

246 (Humor; Suicide)

There is the story of a man who felt such despair about life he climbed up on a bridge to commit suicide. A policeman came along and tried to get him down, arguing with him. Finally, in desperation, the policeman said, "Let's take ten minutes now. You take five minutes and tell me what's wrong with the world and why you want to kill yourself. Then I'll take five minutes and tell you everything that is right with the world and why you should go on living." After each had taken his five minutes, they joined hands...and jumped off the bridge, together.

247 (Cross; Emptiness; Handicapped)

"Elephant Man" is the true story of a man named John Merrick who, in the late eighteen hundreds, was afflicted with a disease that left him terribly deformed. He could hardly walk. He had to sleep in a sitting position. He had a very enlarged head (which is how he acquired the name "Elephant Man"). When the play opens, the "Elephant Man" is in a freak show—his only means of earning a living. A young doctor becomes interested in the "Elephant Man" and from the very beginning of their relationship the contrast between the two men is obvious. The doctor is tall, handsome, physically healthy. He has a charming wife. His medical practice is flourishing. He owns a fine house—with swimming pool. In short, he has it made. In one of the opening scenes of the play, the doctor stands before a class in medical school, delivering a lecture. Seated beside him is the Elephant Man. The doctor is using him as a live model to demonstrate to his students the freakish effects of the Elephant Man's disease.

As the play unfolds, one suddenly becomes aware of an amazing role reversal. One can see that the handsome doctor, who outwardly has everything, really has nothing. He is a hollow man. His inner-universe is empty. As a person, he is nothing. And he becomes more-and-more depressed. But, John Merrick, this "Elephant Man" who outwardly has nothing, who is a loser, a freak in the world's eyes, begins to come to life. He learns how to love and be loved. He becomes aware of beauty all around him, and he is able to appreciate that beauty. His inner-life begins to flourish. At one point he says, "I think my head is so large because it is so full of dreams."

At the end of the play (after the Elephant Man has died) there is a strange Epilogue. In it, the doctor is now seated in the chair and the Elephant Man is standing beside him, lecturing the medical students on the hollow man's disease: the disease of non-belief; the disease of hopelessness; the disease of the spiritless man who despairs of finding any real meaning and purpose for his life; the disease of the empty man who refuses to let God's promise of eternal life fill his soul with the joy of expectancy.

John Merrick, the real "Elephant Man," had spent much of his time building a large model of a Church building—perfect in

Despair

every detail. This symbol appears all through the play as the Elephant Man reconstructs the model Church onstage, adding different parts from scene-to-scene. At the very end, he takes the steeple, puts it in place on the model, and says, "It is finished!"—the exact statement Jesus made from the Cross meaning not merely that the job is ended, but is completed. Then the stage goes completely dark except for one spotlight shining on the beautiful model of the Church.

248

When the famous modern sculptor, Marino Marini, was a young man, he fashioned the nude figure of a man on a horse, in bronze. It was the first of a series of such bronzes that Marini created well into his old age. In the early versions, Marini's rider appears confident, even triumphant, with his arms outstretched and his eyes looking upward. The artist described these early versions as "symbols of hope and gratitude." But, as Marini grew older, the rider's image appeared less-and-less confident, less-and-less hopeful, and more-and-more abstract. Reflecting on these changes, the artist said, "If you look at my equestrian statues of the last twelve years, you will notice that the feeling of panic steadily increases. Even the animal is frozen with terror and stands paralyzed rather than taking flight. That is because I believe that we are approaching the time of a sorry end to the world. In every figure, I tried to express a deepening sense of enslavement by uncontrollable forces."

249   (Hell)

In his play entitled "No Exit," Jean Paul Sartre tells the story of a woman and a man who find themselves in a living room. There they are given to understand that they are in hell. At first they appear to be quite comfortable and not at all upset by their predicament—until they are told that there is no exit from that room. They will be there together forever. Knowing this, they proceed to make a hell out of the situation. "That's the way it is," Jean Paul Sartre is saying in this play. We find ourselves together in this world in an impossible, absurd situation. There is no exit. There is nothing for us to do but to take our frustration out on one another and make the world a living hell. That is one of the dominant moods of our time. Many people are feeling this way as they try to work their way through the complexities of modern living.

DESIRE

250   (Humor; Travel)

A jetliner pilot forgot to turn off the intercom microphone. Consequently, the passengers found themselves eavesdropping on the following conversation:

> Co-Pilot: "I think beautiful thoughts about how wonderful life can be whenever we start climbing up into the sky." Pilot: "Me too. I was just thinking that the most wonderful thing in life for me right now would be to have one hand wrapped around a hot cup of coffee and the other around that beautiful, new stewardess we took on this morning. That would really make it for me."

Hearing this, one of the stewardesses in the back of the aircraft immediately rushed up the aisle to tell the pilot to turn off the microphone. She was halfway down the aisle when a little old lady stopped her and said, "Honey, you forgot the coffee."

DESTINY

251 (American Indian; Names)

In American Indian culture it was considered important to instill a sense of destiny in the young male Indian as he entered teenage. An Indian youth would be dispatched alone into the mountains or the desert, there to meditate on life and to seek inspiration for the direction his own life would take. A majestic waterfall might deliver the message that he was destined to become a strong and powerful leader. As he reflected on this, the youth would choose a name for himself in keeping with the source of his inspiration—like "Mighty Waters." Or, the message might come to him in the distant chant of the "medicine man" ministering to a sick child. If this inspired him to dedicate his life to the alleviation of human suffering, he would choose a name like "Good Medicine." Although in old joke books we find evidence of the sad fact that Indian names were commonly invoked to be laughed at by non-Indians, nevertheless it is true that the Indian youth was taught to take the name he bore as seriously as life itself; to regard it as a profound expression of his life's destiny—something to be lived and lived up to.

DEVELOPMENT

252 (Growth; Struggle)

Alfred Russell Wallace, the famous naturalist, has wrtten of a time when he was observing several cocoons, waiting for the moths to come out. One of the larger moths was beating desperately with its yet undeveloped wings to break out of the cocoon. After several hours, Wallace could not bear to watch anymore, and with a sharp knife he split the cocoon, freeing the moth from its desperate struggle. But, in the ensuing days, as he observed this moth, he discovered that it was not developing naturally. Missing were the beautiful tints and shades of color that should have come into its wings. The wings' growth had been stunted, and they remained underdeveloped. In a few days, the moth died—long before its time. Wallace realized, of course, that the struggle against the cocoon was Nature's way of strengthening and developing the moth's wings.

DEVIL

253 (Betrayal; Humor; Jesus, loyalty to)

There was a "Revival Meeting" in a little Church in which the congregation always worked up to a high emotional pitch in their worship services. Because the Church building was old and in need of repair, a contractor was engaged to do the work, which was extensive. After the job was done, the contractor discovered that he was going to have a hard time collecting on his bill for services. Deciding to force the issue, he bought himself a devil's suit, complete with horns and tail and pitch-fork. The next Sunday, when the congregation had reached its emotional peak, he jumped through the open window of the Church and stood there leering at them in his devil-suit. It was too much: they all got up and left in a hurry. Except one elderly woman who was sitting down in front. She didn't make it. In her haste, she tripped and fell right at the devil's feet. As he stood menacingly over her, she looked up and said, "Now wait just a minute, Mr. Devil. It's true, I've been a member of this Church for twenty-five years. I've sung in the choir, I've taught in the Sunday School, I've baked more pies and cakes than anyone else. But, Mr. Devil, I've been on your side all the time." Surely, there were many times when Jesus wondered what side the disciples were on. Surely Jesus must wonder, all too often,

Discipleship

just what side we are on. Is our goal to minister or to be ministered to; to lose your life to the devil or to find it in the Lord Jesus?

DISCIPLESHIP

254

A corporation president once read a book called "Men of God." He was so impressed with it that he ordered three hundred and seventy-five copies to be distributed to all the high echelon employees of the corporation. He sent his order by telegram to the book distributor in Chicago. The distributor immediately wired back saying, "We do not have three hundred and seventy-five men of god in Chicago. Try Los Angeles." What a fantastic thing it would be if we could say in all sincerity that we have three hundred and seventy-five men and women of God in this Church Community, ready for God to use them.

255 (Christ, cause of)

During the terrible winter at Valley Forge, a government official arrived on the scene to obtain a firsthand report on the actual field situation from General George Washington himself. After Washington had dutifully received him, the government man immediately began complimenting him on his ability to hold the Army together under such terribly trying circumstances. "General Washington, you are a great leader, a great man, an inspiration to us all," the man said. Whereupon, General Washington, standing in the midst of his suffering troops, broke in impatiently, saying, "Never mind all that. Just tell me where you stand in relation to the Cause I represent."

We are like that man. We arrive at church each Sunday praising the Lord and acknowledging His greatness. But each Sunday, if we are really listening, we can hear Him say to us, "Never mind all that. Just tell me where you stand in relation to the Cause I represent."

256 (Preaching)

In his book, "Beside the Briar Bunny Bush," Ian McClaren tells of a young Scotch clergyman, recently ordained, who had come to the little Church of his youth to preach his first sermon. The congregation received him very warmly. Their enthusiasm told him that they were expecting much from his sermon that coming Sunday. Consequently, he labored over the sermon for days until he was confident that it amply reflected his superior scholarship (in which he took great pride) and that it was theologically solid. He was staying with an elderly aunt, an uneducated woman, but a woman wise in the ways of life. She was extremely proud of her young nephew whom she had dearly loved since his birth. It was Saturday night and he had come down from his room to put a few finishing touches on the sermon. After dotting the last "I" and crossing the final "T", he began to discuss the sermon with his aunt. She said to him, "You'll say what is right. No doubt of that. And the Body will be pleased with you. But, oh laddie, when you stand up to preach, be sure and say a good word for Jesus." And he realized that in spite of the theological solidity of the sermon, he hadn't done that. He retired quickly to his room, tore up the sermon and stayed up all night writing a new one. And, as he wrote, he came upon a whole new understanding of this Christian reality: that one of the most fulfilling and one of the most creative things we will ever do is to say a good word—for Jesus.

Discipline

257 (Gospel; Jesus)

"Go, therefore, and make disciples of all nations." Making disciples is more than broadcasting the words of the Gospel. It is confronting people with the Lord's invitation to a new way of life. When Jesus chose His first disciples, He said, "Follow Me": Do as I do. Live as I live. Be like Me. Be different. Jesus was "different" because He was what He taught others to be.

258 (Preaching)

Several years ago, in England, Sir John Barbirolli was conducting a great symphony orchestra before a "standing room only" audience. The concert hall was unusual in that it was used for cultural events on weekdays and for religious services on Sundays. On this particular Saturday evening, one of the patrons of the orchestra noticed that the clergyman who was to preach there the next day was in the audience. He leaned over and said to him, cynically, "When are you going to fill this hall on Sunday the way Sir John Barbirolli has tonight." The clergyman looked his antagonist straight in the eye and said with a steady voice, "I will fill this hall on Sunday morning when you give to me as you gave to Sir John tonight, eighty-five disciplined men and women to be with him and to work with him."

DISCIPLINE

259 (Children; Education)

A little boy attended a school where the students were permitted absolute free expression: they could do whatever they wanted to do. One day he complained to his teacher, "Do I have to do whatever I want to do?"

DOUBT

260   (Annunciation; Faith; Mary)

A young woman named Mary who lived in the Village of Naz-areth was confronted by an angel of the Lord. The angel told her that she was to become the mother of the long-expected Messiah. Mary was "deeply troubled" by the angel's words, Luke tells us, and her first word in response was a word of doubt: "How can this be since I do not know man?" she asked. The angel told her more about the situation and reaffirmed the call that God was issuing to her for this special function to be the mother of the Messiah. Mary replied, "I am the servant of the Lord. Let it be done to me as you say" (Lk. 1:38). In these beautiful words spoken by Mary we can see how an honest, creative doubt can actually strengthen our faith. In our own experience, as we read, as we study and as we discuss, we discover that honest searching and probing and questioning can help us grow in our faith and enrich our faith response. Feodor Dostoevski once was asked about the vitality of his religious faith. His answer was, "My hosanna comes forth from the crucible of doubt."

261   (Faith; God, goodness of; God, presence of; Holy Spirit)

Scientist Edward Stein has written about his passing through a period of severe doubt into a new understanding of God. He says that when he began to experience a real reverence for what he called the "Ultimate," he would ask, "What is it?" (Notice, the "it".) Then it became, "Who is He?" until he began to have difficulty of thinking of God as a "He." Finally, his question became, "Who is the Mysterious Spirit that heals us, that binds us together, that rebuilds broken families, that heals the psy-chotically estranged, that evokes tenderness and forgiveness and hope in us? Who is the Mysterious Spirit that conceived

135

the delicate wonder of childhood, the sensuous warmth of mature beauty, the gnarled gray wisdom of age, the endless mystery of life and death, tears and laughter?" "I don't know," he says, "but I trust this love, I sense this presence, I have felt the power." Here is a modern man who has begun that inward turn toward the "Holy" which is vital and crucial in dealing with the problem of belief. Only a deep sense of awe and wonder and reverence for the Ultimate can open us up to the evidence of God's goodness we receive from Jesus.

DROPOUTS

262   (Football; Humor)

A college football game turned out to be a terrible mismatch. One team outweighed the other by thirty pounds per man, was more experienced, better coached, etc. The lighter, weaker team was being terribly beaten, not only on the scoreboard but also on their bodies. They were bruised and cut and bleeding and several first-stringers already had left the game because of injuries. As they gathered 'round in their huddle late in the final period, the quarterback noticed that they had twelve men on the field, one more than the eleven allowed by the rules. That's all they needed! If the referee discovered the extra man he would assess a penalty, thereby adding to their already deep humiliation. "Look," the quarterback said to his teammates, "we'll try a running play that will take us past the bench. In the confusion, as we pass the bench, I want one of you to drop out. If we can do this fast enough, the referee may not notice and we can avoid the penalty at least." Whereupon, amidst great confusion, they succeeded in running the play right past the bench. When they returned to the huddle to decide on their next play, the quarterback discovered, to his amazement, that six men had dropped out.

EASTER

263   (Celebration; Conversion; Resurrection)

A man named George was accustomed to driving his wife, Rosie, to Church every Sunday. George and Rosie had been married for forty years and they loved each other deeply. They did everything together. They were inseparable in practically every area of their life—except one. When George drove his wife to Church on Sunday, Rosie went in and George remained in the car, reading his newspaper. Rosie died, and for many Sundays thereafter, Church members looked wistfully at the parking lot because George's car was no longer seen there. Several months later, on Easter Sunday, George's car again appeared, and George went into Church. The preacher delivered a stirring Resurrection sermon and then, as was his custom, invited the members of the congregation to respond. Whereupon, George stood up and, with deep emotion said firmly, "Rosie lives!" Then he began to sing: "My wild Irish Rose / the sweetest flower that grows . . ." One person joined in, then another, and another. Finally everyone present was joyfully singing what someone later described as "The most beautiful Easter hymn ever sung in our Church."

264   (Caring; Forgiveness; Good News; Idolatry; Resurrection)

Easter brings us the Good News of Christ's glorious Resurrection. It also brings us a mandate:

> . . . to care about human problems that most people ignore

> . . . to speak up for the downtrodden who are powerless to speak for themselves

Education

> . . . to call for forgiveness when others call for blood

> . . . to give of our resources without asking "What's in it for me?"

> . . . to be loyal to the Rule of God when others have sold out to the idols of money and possessions.

265   (New Life)

Often, to the eyes of man, it is midnight. And midnight means the end! But, to the eyes of Faith, midnight begins with the dawn and ends with Easter morning when life springs forth out of the empty tomb and the dead are more alive than ever before; their eyes open to new light; their spirits gifted with new life.

EDUCATION

266   (Humor; Success)

On the twentieth anniversary of their graduation, members of a college alumni were getting together for a class reunion. As they arrived, they gathered in little groups on the lawn and began reminiscing about their college years. In one group, the conversation turned to a classmate named Harvey. The thing they remembered most about Harvey was that whenever he was asked what he was going to do after graduation, he replied, "I expect to make a million dollars." Harvey fully expected that he would become a very wealthy man. Another thing they remembered about Harvey was that he had been the slowest student in the class, intellectually. He was especially poor in mathematics. Here was a man who expected to make a million dollars, yet couldn't add a simple column of figures. As the members of the group were trading "Harvey" stories, up pulled a brand new, chauffeur-driven Rolls Royce and out stepped Harvey wearing an expensive, tailor-made, three-piece suit and everything that went with it. His classmates quickly gathered around and began throwing questions at him. "Hey Harvey, where did you get that car? Harvey! Wow! What happened? How did you do it?" Harvey said, "Well you see, I came upon an invention that costs me only five dollars to manufacture and I sell it for one hundred dollars. And you'd be surprised how fast that ten percent profit adds up!"

267 (Humor; Reality)

A newspaper ran the story of a memory expert. He had earned a doctor's degree in the study of human memory. He had written books on how to remember. He had fashioned a popular course of study for systematic memory development. And, he had accepted an invitation to deliver the keynote address to a big science meeting in Cleveland. The night of the speaking engagement came and all the scientists were assembled. But, to their great dismay, the keynote speaker failed to appear. Next day, when they asked him for an explanation, he said, simply, "I forgot." There was a man who was unable to connect all the knowledge he had acquired with his everyday life in the real world.

EGOISM

268 (Money; Pride)

James Thurber, the well-known American humorist, wrote a number of "beast" fables. In them he poked fun at our short-

Egoism

comings by having his animal characters act as humans do. One of these fables is entitled "The Mouse and the Money."

It seems a city mouse moved to the country to live in the walls of an old house. From the start, he lorded it over the country mice. He grew handlebar whiskers, wore his hair in the "Dry Look," and talked with an accent. He even told the country mice that they were beneath him, or as he put it, that they came "from the wrong side of the mouse tracks." Every day the newcomer bragged about his forbears, and when he ran out of ancestors he made some up. "My great-great-great-grandfather," he said, "was a theater mouse at the Comedie-Francaise in Paris. My family came to America in the bridal suite of a great French ocean liner. My brother is now a restaurant mouse at the exclusive '21' in New York." One day the city mouse wandered through the forbidden walls of the country house to show his inferiors he knew his way around. By chance he came upon a treasure of money hidden between the plaster and the wood. Despite the warnings of the older country mice, he decided to eat the whole thing. He didn't want any of the other mice to have a cent. "I'm already a mouse of distinction," said the city mouse, "and this money will make me a millionaire. I'll be loaded." He quickly rejected the pleas of some of the young idealistic mice who wanted him to make a contribution to some poor church mice. "Finders are not their brothers keepers," he said. So in a few days the city mouse with the fancy French forbears had eaten all the money. Then he tried to leave the walls of the old country house, but he was so loaded with money, and his head was so swelled, that he got caught between the plaster and the wood. His neighbors tried to help but they could not dislodge him, and so he died in the walls. Only the country mice knew that he had been the richest mouse in the world.

269 (Change; Repentance)

We all know how difficult it is to make profound changes in our lives, though the need may be obvious. We recognize that there are changes for good to be made, but we hesitate. The prospect of change in our lives makes us uneasy. We find it threatening when we realize that substantial change for the better means a repudiation of so much we have stood for all our lives. We find it threatening to be called upon to renounce that which, like nothing else, is of our own special workmanship, namely, our own egos.

EMPATHY

270 (Compassion; Handicapped; Service)

Helen Keller is an outstanding example of a person who lived a rich and fruitful life despite major physical handicaps. At the age of two she was almost totally shut off from the world: she was blind; she was deaf; she could not speak. But she rose above these disabilities to become internationally famous largely for her devotion to the work of helping to enrich the lives of thousands upon thousands of other handicapped persons. Helen Keller was a senior at Radcliffe College when she wrote an article entitled "My Future As I See It," for the November 1903 issue of "Ladies Home Journal" magazine. In it she said:

> Opportunities to be of service to others offer themselves constantly. I am looking forward to Commencement Day . . . Generous friends have assisted me and strewn my path with opportunities. The question now is, what shall I do with this education and these opportunities . . . I often think I shall live in the country and take into my home a blind and deaf child and teach him as someone has taught me . . . I feel that I could

Emptiness

impart to a child afflicted like myself the power
to see with the soul and understand with the heart.
All his needs and difficulties would be intelligible
to me since I know the darkness he sees and the
stillness he hears. The road he must travel, I have
traveled, I know where the rough places are and
how to help him over them.

271 (Children)

Maurice Sendak, author of many award-winning children's
books, was interviewed on a TV "talk show." The master of
ceremonies asked a number of questions designed to uncover
the secret of Mr. Sendak's success at writing children's books.
"Do you have any children of your own?" he asked. "Do you
like children? Do you spend a great deal of time watching children at play?" On-and-on went the questions. It so happened
that P. L. Travers, author of "Mary Poppins," was watching
the program at home. As the questions continued, Travers grew
more-and-more impatient until, finally, he blurted out, "Tell
him you have been a child." Whereupon, as if by magic, Mr.
Sendak said to the TV host, "I have been a child." The two
authors had come to the point simultaneously. Both knew that
the real secret of success in writing for children is to remember
what it was like to have been a child.

EMPTINESS

272 (Despair; Success)

In the film, "La Dolce Vita," the famous Italian Director, Fellini, gave us a devastating commentary on Modern Society. But

of all the mixed-up characters in the movie, a man named Steiner is the one person who seems to have it all together. Steiner has it made. He is a University Professor. He likes good books. He likes good music. He has a fine house. He has a beautiful wife and two lovely children. He is the only character in the film who projects some feeling of hope. On the surface, he seems to know where he is going with his life. Then, suddenly, comes the shocking scene. On a particular afternoon when his wife is out shopping, Steiner murders his own two children in their sleep, then kills himself. He did this because at the center of his being he was malnourished. The sense of emptiness and purposelessness was so overwhelming that he could not stand the thought of his children growing up to experience it nor could he endure it any longer himself. By means of this scenario, Fellini is trying to tell us symbolically something very important about life in contemporary Society: so many of the people who seem to have it made are afflicted with emptiness and decay and degeneration at the center of their being.

END OF THE WORLD

273 (Humor)

A preacher was drawing heavily on his supply of imagery to describe the day of final judgment. "Thunder will boom," he cried out. "Rivers will overflow," he shouted. "Flames will shoot down from the heavens and the earth will quake violently," he warned. "Darkness will fall over the world!" Whereupon a small boy in the congregation nudged his father and asked, "Daddy, do you think they'll let school out early?"

143

ENVY

274

A famous Christian preacher was fond of telling the story of two diamonds. One of the diamonds was out in the bright sunlight, sparkling with life, flashing brilliantly from every one of a thousand facets. The other diamond was in the shadows, very dull and uninteresting. The diamond in the shadows kept saying mournfully, "If only I could sparkle like that." The other diamond said, simply, "Come on out into the sun."

It has been written that "Envy is plain, unadulterated evil. It pursues a hateful end by despicable means and desires not so much its own happiness as another's misery.

EPITAPHS

275 (Death; Humor)

"She lived with her husband fifty years and died in a confident hope of a better life."

"Here lies Jane Smith, wife of Thomas Smith, marble cutter. This monument was erected by her husband as a tribute to her memory and as a specimen of his work. Monument of the same size, $350.00."

"Sacred to the memory of Mr. Gerard Bates, who died August the 6th, 1800. His widow, age 24, who mourns as one who can be comforted, lives at 7 Elm Street, this city and possesses every qualification for a good wife."

"Here lies peas but only the pod/ Peas shelled out and went home to God."

"Now will you believe I did not feel well?"

ESTRANGEMENT

276   (Love)

Alberto Giacometti, the Swiss sculptor, uses thin little stick figures to symbolize our isolation and our inability to love. He arranges these little figures walking all in different directions. As you study it, you realize that their paths are going to cross, but they're never going to meet. Giacometti's art symbolizes our inability to make contact and to love one another. But, when you read about him, you realize that Giacometti understood something of the answer to the problem his work poses. In his whole lifetime, he used only three or four models: his wife, his sister and one or two other people. And when asked why he didn't use more models to enrich his art, he said, "Oh the great joy to me is to look at the same face everyday and see something new there." Many of us have just the opposite reaction: "Oh the same face, day after day! That same old face!" But here is a man with this marvelous insight: to see the face of your wife, the face of your husband, the face of your child, the face of a close friend, everyday, and to see something new there and to delight in what you see and to rejoice in it. What a tragedy it is, in a marriage or a family where, year after year, we live together only to discover that our most intimate loves are strangers. We don't know who they are. We have never broken through. We have missed the fantastic adventure of thinking it couldn't be any better and then, suddenly, crashing through to whole new worlds of love and sharing and understanding—absolutely unlimited possibilities.

ETERNAL LIFE

277   (Education; Humor)

. Recently, some newspapers ran a photograph of a piece of graffito someone had painted on the "Department of Languages" building of a large University. It read, "Where will you spend eternity?" Immediately below, someone else had written, "As far as I can see, it looks like 'German 201'."

278

Toward the end of his life, the great 19th century French poet and dramatist, Victor Marie Hugo, wrote an essay entitled, "The Future Life." It reads, in part:

> I feel within me that future life. I am like a forest that has been razed; the new shoots are stronger and brisker. I shall most certainly rise toward the heavens . . . The nearer my approach to the end, the plainer is the sound of immortal symphonies of worlds which invite me. For half a century I have been translating my thoughts into prose and verse: history, philosophy, drama, romance, tradition, satire, ode, and song; all of these I have tried. But I feel I haven't given utterance to the thousandth part of what lies within me. When I go to the grave I can say, as others have said, "My day's work is done." But I cannot say, "My life is done." My day's work will recommence the next morning. The tomb is not a blind alley; it is a thoroughfare. It closes upon the twilight but opens upon the dawn.

ETERNITY

279 (Devotion)

A Norwegian Cleric on a visit to this country told the story of a devout, old fisherman who lived alone and, when he was physically able, walked 14 miles to Church on Sunday. One Sunday there was a terrible storm and the old man arrived at Church very late. In fact, he was so late that all he heard was the final phrase of the celebrant's Benediction: "Now, and forevermore." His friends tried to console him and tell him how very sorry they were that he had been disappointed after his difficult 14-mile walk. He replied, "Disappointed? Never! It is worth walking 28 miles just to hear those three words: NOW AND FOREVERMORE."

EVANGELISM

280 (American Indians)

At one of the evening sessions of a week-long religious conference in Oklahoma, a local choir of American Indians performed. Led by their American Indian pastor, they sang beautifully, in Indian dialect. Some members of the group used Indian sign language to translate. "Our Father who art in heaven" was portrayed as the "Great Chief" who dwelt in a teepee in the sky—and so on. The audience was deeply moved by the performance and called for the Indian pastor to say a few words when it was over. This is what he said:

> There are many people in our Tribe who are very,
> very bitter toward you White people because you

Evangelism

took our land from us and left us impoverished. I can understand why they are bitter. But I am not bitter because while it is true that you took our land from us, there were those among you who brought us Jesus Christ. And so we rejoice! What would we be if they had not brought us The Christ?

281

There is the story of an angel who asked the Risen Jesus on His arrival in heaven, "Lord, what have you left behind to carry out the work?" "A little band of women and men who love Me," Jesus answered. "But Lord, what if they fail when the trial comes? Will all you have done be defeated?" "Yes," Jesus replied, "if they fail, all I have done will be defeated." The angel persisted: "Is there nothing more?" "No," said Jesus. "What then, Lord?" asked the worried angel, "THEY WILL NOT FAIL," was Jesus' answer.

282   (Disciples; Good News; Joy)

"Crazy Charlie" was an eccentric canary. Unlike other canaries, he sang only when his cage was covered. Moreover, he sang only to the sound of running water. Crazy Charlie lived in the home of a kindly widow named Mabel. Mabel was greatly comforted by Charlie's happy presence and, in return, she did her best to accomodate his strange life style. Consequently, whenever she was going out, she covered the bird cage, moved it near the kitchen sink and turned on the faucet just enough for Charlie to hear the water running. This was a mutually satisfying arrangement! It kept Charlie happy, and Mabel knew that Charlie would be singing his sweet song when she returned.

Evangelism

But the Charlie and Mabel story ended abruptly one summer when Mabel decided to take a two-week vacation. She confidently placed Charlie in the custody of a trusted neighbor who promised to cater to Charlie's special needs. In her desire to please, the neighbor dutifully covered the bird cage, moved it up against the clothes washer and turned the machine on. The big close-up sound of water gushing into the washer was a whole new experience for Charlie: a real challenge! It was the loudest sound of running water he had ever heard, and with all the enthusiasm at his command he began to sing out over the marvelous accompaniment. Charlie joyfully stretched his voice beyond all previous limits. But, unfortunately, the strain on his little body was so great that he fell off his perch and died. Crazy Charlie literally had sung his heart out—for joy.

It would not be irreverent to say that Christ's original band of disciples behaved like a band of "Crazy Charlies." The song of joy in their hearts simply had to spill over, come out, be shared with others. Singing the Lord's song became their way of life. They literally sang their hearts out proclaiming the Good News they had received from Christ.

283

In an ancient story, four men were on a trip through the woods. Suddenly, they came upon a high wall. Intrigued, they built a ladder in order to see what was on the other side. The first man to reach the top cried out with delight at the vision below, and immediately plunged in. The second man did the same. And the third. Finally, the fourth man looked down on the inspiring scene: lush, green gardens as far as the eye could carry; beautiful trees bearing every sort of delectable fruit. Never before had he beheld such a sight. And, like the others, he was tempted to jump right in. But as he paused for a moment to think of his family and friends, he decided to resist the temptation. Then

Evangelism

he rushed down the ladder and set out to preach the glad tidings of the beautiful garden to others.

284 (Discipleship; Religious Education)

A group of high school religion class students were asked to write a scenario for what might have transpired in heaven when Jesus returned after the Resurrection. One student created the following scene:

> Jesus is walking down the golden street, arm-in-arm with the Angel Gabriel. Gabriel speaks first . . . "Master, you died for the whole world down there, did you not?" "Yes!" Jesus answers. "You must have suffered much." "Yes." "And do they all know about it?" "Oh, no! Only a few in Palestine know about it so far." "Well, Master, what is Your Plan? What have You done about telling all the world's people that you died for them? What is Your Plan?" "Well, I asked Peter, and James, and John, and Andrew, and some more of them down there to make the business of telling others about Me the number one priority in their lives. And the others are to tell others, and the others others, and yet others, and still others, until the last men and the last women in the farthest corner of the world have heard the story of how I gave My life for them, because I love them so much."
>
> "Yes, but suppose Peter fails. Or suppose John simply forgets. Or what if their successors, maybe in the twentieth century, fail or forget? What then? Surely You have made other plans!"

In His quiet, wondrous voice, Jesus replies, "Gabriel, I have not made any other plans—I'm counting on them!"

265 (Caring; Compassion)

A beautiful insight into the true nature of Christian Evangelism is contained in the following true-life episode recounted by a man whose life is dedicated to helping the handicapped:

> The other day I was with a friend. We were going into a Church where an old lady was sitting at the door begging. We did not have any money with us. My friend got down on her knees in front of the old lady, looked directly into her eyes and said: "I am sorry but I do not have any money." But she said this with such tenderness that the eyes of the old lady lit up as if for the first time someone had really looked at her, seen her. We went into the Church and prayed with her. On the way out she looked gently and gratefully at my friend, for she had just lived a moment of deep joy. It is good to give a check for the poor whom we do not know. It is even better to touch the wounded person who is close to us, saying by our gestures and facial expressions, "I am concerned about you. I want you to live."

286 (Early Christians; Jesus, presence of; Joy)

A small dog had been struck by a car and was laying wounded by the side of the road. A doctor driving by noticed that the dog was still alive, stopped his car, picked up the dog and took him home with him. There he discovered that the dog had been stunned, had suffered a few minor cuts and abrasions, but was otherwise all right. He revived the dog, cleaned up the wounds and was carrying the animal from the house to the garage when it suddenly jumped from his arms and scampered off. "What an ungrateful little dog," the doctor said to himself. He thought no more about the incident until the next evening when he

Evangelism

heard a scratching at his door. When he opened it, there was the little dog he had treated, with another hurt dog.

That is a story of the "ripple effect." Throw a stone into a lake and the water ripples out, and the circle widens. One of the great characteristics of the first Christians was their ripple effect. Something had happened to them that so filled them with joy they just could not contain it. It was contagious. It spread out among the people in a ripple effect. And the circle grew wider and wider. The reason those early Christians were so filled with joy was that this Jesus who had lived among them, this Jesus who had given them such hope, this Jesus whom they had seen die on a hill outside Jerusalem, this Jesus whom they had seen put into a tomb, this Jesus was alive! It wasn't an hallucination. It wasn't something they dreamed up. It was an event that had happened in their lives. This Jesus had risen and had come back to them.

287   (Humor; Jesus, name of; Marriage)

A man whose wife was sick decided that he would do the cooking. He did quite well at it until one day he became very ambitious. He thought he would bake some bread. As often happens the first time around, he misread the recipe and he put two pounds of yeast into the dough. After faithfully following all the other instructions, he put the dough near the heat and waited. Some time later his wife called down from her upstairs bedroom: "Have you put the dough in the oven yet, dear?" Frantically, he replied, "Put it in the oven? I can't even keep it in the kitchen!" That's the New Testament: the leaven of the Word of God; the Name of Jesus; you "can't even keep it in the kitchen." You can't even keep it in the Church. It just expands into the world.

288   (God, power of; God, presence of)

A pastor received a letter from a young woman with three small children. It is the kind of letter that can sustain a pastor for a long time. She wrote:

I've been searching my own heart to understand all that has happened to me during the past three years. I've wondered who I am, why I am and where I'm going with my life. Of course I don't have all the answers yet, but through persistent prayer to know God's Will for my life I can see the fog begin to lift and even dissappear. As I look back over these last three years I am surprised and bewildered because the events are hazy and I barely recognize myself now as I was then. Through God's Grace I see all in that past as dim, because it was not until three years ago when you introduced me to Jesus Christ that I began to live. I've had many periods of turbulence and depression. I know I will have more, owing to my human nature. But through God's Grace I can never sink too far. I can never turn back because God has made me a new creature through the gift of his son, Jesus Christ.

Beautiful! The overwhelming power of God can change you so completely you won't even know yourself when you look back two or three years. Now that is enough to make us tremble! That is enough to make us alert to what can happen when we enter into the presence of God!

EVIL

289   (Anger; Goodness; Love)

Will Rogers was once asked, "What's wrong with the world?" "I dunno," he drawled, "I guess its people." I guess it is! Individual acts, one-by-one, will be the ultimate determiners of what will happen to this world of ours and its people. The evil in our world is massive, and the goodness is massive too. But when we stop generalizing about them, when we break them down, we discover that it is people—individuals—at the heart of each. The next time an angry word is spoken to you, answer it in anger—and see what happens. One evil piled upon another, a chain reaction is set off. Or, instead, next time an angry word is spoken to you, set off a different kind of chain reaction: answer it with love. God knows where that may lead.

EXISTENTIALISM

290　(Expectation; Paul)

There is a movement in modern philosophy called "Existentialism." It is a rather forbidding word, but what most of the Existentialists are saying is that the past has no reality; the future has no reality, only potential: the only thing that is real is the present moment of existence, so "Live . . . live in it now! Live deeply and fully: taste and smell and feel and hate and love and laugh and cry now!" The Apostle Paul, in the best sense, was an Existentialist. He would say to us, "Live in the present moment of your existence fully." But it didn't end there for Paul. Paul was able to plant both of his feet in the present moment but he was always looking forward to tomorrow. He was always filled with expectation and anticipation and longing and desire. Paul lived in the now with an abiding hope for what lay ahead. Paul lived with his feet on the ground but with both eyes cocked in the direction of his ultimate destiny as a child of God.

EXPECTATION

291 (God, relationship with; New Life)

There seems to be a self-fulfilling quality to expectation. When we are expecting something, actively and vigorously, it seems to make it happen. This theory may not hold up under scientific scrutiny. But on the level of our relationship with God, one can say that when we genuinely expect Him to come bringing us new life, He comes.

292 (Christ, liberator; Serendipity)

The word "serendipity" is derived from an ancient Persian legend about the three Princes of Serendip who went out looking for a certain treasure. Although they did not discover what they were looking for, nevertheless they did keep finding things of even greater value. "Serendipity" is the ability to "hang loose" in anticipation of discovering happy surprises. The serendipitous person is free-spirited enough to expect the unexpected. "Stand fast in the freedom to which you have been called," says St. Paul. "Christ has set us free" to expect the unexpected. Christ has set us free to trust in the Mercy of Divine Providence.

293 (Children; Revelation)

The late Cardinal Cushing often told the story of a little girl who sat on her grandmother's lap to listen to the creation account from the Book of Genesis. As the wondrous story unfolded, the grandmother, noticing that the child was unusually quiet, asked, "Well, what do you think of it, dear?" "Oh, I love it," the child answered, "You never know what God is going to do next." There's the imagination of a Joan of Arc. The conditioning of one's mind and heart to expect the unexpected of God. It is the difference between our preconceived notions of who God is and what He ought to do, and His revelation of who He really is and what He is really doing. It is the difference between being a mere spectator to the revealed Word and the actual addressee of the revealed Word. It is the difference between some vague, general affirmation that God has spoken, and an abiding conviction that God is speaking to me—right now!

EXPLOITATION

294 (Change; Lifestyle)

Thomas Alva Edison, possibly the greatest inventor in history, lived in a large house with a huge fence around it. Visitors had to push open a heavy iron gate in order to enter the compound and then push it back again until it clanked shut. One of Edison's friends complained to him about the tremendous amount of energy it required to open and shut that gate. With a twinkle in his eye, Mr. Edison escorted his friend up onto the roof of the house and showed him an elaborate mechanical device made up of levers and pulleys and pumps. "What you don't know," said Edison, "is that everyone who comes to visit me and opens and closes that gate, automatically pumps a gallon of water into the tank up here on the roof."

People come walking into our lives and we say, "How do you do," meaning, "What can you do for me? How much water can you pump into my tank? Can you amuse me? Can you fatten my wallet? Will you praise me, adore me, exalt me?" But when Jesus Christ becomes real to us, a very subtle but profound change takes place that makes it possible for us to become a

"How do you do, what can I do for you?" person. You begin to feel that you're "O.K." because of the way God loves you and not because of what you've taken from other people.

295 (Insensitivity)

In Edward Albee's play, "Seascape," Deborah Kerr plays the part of a wealthy English woman. Her sister-in-law in the play is going to visit some ex-servants who are destitute in their old age. One of them is ninety-years-old. Deborah Kerr gives the sister-in-law a small coin to buy some little gift for the poor old servants and, as she does, says with a smug smile, "That's why the poor are so useful. One can always help them without being too extravagant."

FAITH

296

A group of clergymen had invited a famous advertising man to lecture them on ways and means of increasing Church attendance and instilling new vitality into their congregations. They hoped that they could profit from this man's knowledge of advertising and the Media. But he shocked them. Without preliminaries, the advertising man began his presentation as follows: "If God has forsaken you, what can a poor advertising man do for you? Do you no longer understand, dear reverends, what actually gave that little group of apostles on the day of Pentecost such tremendous power that it was sufficient to transform the face of the Western World? There was no advertising in the old sense. It was rather the influencing power of faith which accomplished the miracle." And then, later, these few closing sentences which were equally as devastating: "Because you yourselves no longer feel the influencing power of

Faith

faith within you, you try to substitute tactical cleverness for the faith of a strong soul. And when you do that, you sink ever deeper into the realm of no response."

297 (Humor; Trust)

There is a wonderful story about a man who got the idea of walking on a tight-rope over Niagara Falls. Other people had done it, but this man had a new twist. He was going to push a man in a wheelbarrow. He began at once to prepare for the event, even though he hadn't yet found anyone willing to ride in the wheelbarrow. He set up a tight-rope near the Falls and every day he could be seen pushing and balancing the wheelbarrow filled with stones. One day, a young man came up to him to wish him well. "Good luck," he said. "I've watched you practicing and I have confidence in you. I know you can do it." The tight-rope walker answered, "Do you believe I can do this?" And the young man replied, "Yes, of course!" Again, he said, "But do you really believe I can do this?" "Yes, of course," the young man repeated. "Then you're my man. Get in the wheelbarrow!"

298 (Discipleship; Reality)

The world of science has produced authoritative aerotechnical tests which prove that a bumble bee cannot fly due to the shape and weight of its body in relation to total wing area. But the bumble bee doesn't know it, so he keeps right on flying anyway. In this instance, at least, the bumble bee is more at one with reality than the aerodynamics experts. Facing reality through faith in kindliness is like that! In every age, Jesus' true disciples are told that the Christian ideal of life, though interesting, isn't practical. But Jesus' true disciples do not know this, so they keep on loving anyway.

158

299 (God, goodness of; Reality)

The first thing God wants of us, the first thing we must do to be right with reality, is to live in faith. We cannot be right with God merely by keeping the letter of the law; we cannot be right with God simply by disciplining ourselves; we cannot be right with God just by being as good as the next person. We can be right with God only by faith. Which is to say that we must live in the constant conviction that God is good. Genuine faith involves an all-out attitude of reliance on God's goodness. It may be compared to a child's absolute trust in a wise, generous, loving father or mother. There is a world of difference in attitude, not to mention output, between a son who does things for his father out of love and respect, and that of an employee who does things merely for pay, or out of fear that he may lose his job or not get a promotion. They may do the same things, but the difference in motivation inevitably colors their work. There is a world of difference between a doctor who chose his profession because it made him an instrument of vital human service, and one who calculatingly chose the profession because it promised a large income! So it is with Christian faith: what counts is motivation, spirit. Commitment to religious law and formal observance cannot substitute for the conviction that God is good. That is where faith's reality begins.

300 (Children)

A stranger approached a little boy who was flying a kite so high it was out of sight. "What are you doing?" the stranger asked. "I'm flying a kite," the boy replied. "How do you know there is a kite?" "I can feel the pull of it," said the boy.

301 (God, love of; Love; Meaning of Life; Truth)

"Truth, what does that mean?" Pontius Pilate asked. Our answer is born of faith. Without faith there is no answer. But

Faith

with eyes of faith we can see the truth of why we were born, the truth of why we have come into the world. With eyes of faith we can accept the Gospel Truth of a Gracious God who created us out of inestimable love and who promises us eternal fulfillment in the Mystery of His Love. With eyes of faith we can see that the reason we have come into this world is to learn how to love like God, and to testify to God's great love through our love for one another. In order to testify to the Truth, we are called upon to love one another not merely for the love of God, but with the very love God has for us.

302 (Humor)

An elderly woman, who had just traded in her compact car for a larger model, drove her long, shiny, new beauty downtown to go shopping. The only parking space she could find was a parallel one. It appeared to be no longer than the length of the car. The self-assured woman began her attempt to accomplish the seemingly impossible. As she cut the wheel sharply, she noticed two policemen staring at her intently. Unruffled, she shifted into reverse gear and even to her own amazement, parked the car perfectly on the first effort. Contentedly, she got out of the car, walked to the parking meter. Standing next to it was one of the policemen. Much to her surprise, he inserted a coin in it. Then, as he walked away, he responded to her bewilderment with just two words: "I lost." In her best self-satisfied tone, she called after him, "Blest are they who have not seen and have believed."

303 (God, existence of; Preaching)

A young clergyman was asked to preach on "Why I believe in God." He thought it would be an easy sermon to prepare. After all, he could think of a dozen reasons to believe in God. But he soon discovered that they were not his reasons. "My theology books give the arguments for God," he said, "and studying those books has strengthened my faith and confirmed my beliefs. But it would not be honest for me to copy the reasons for belief in God from books and give them as my own. The fact is, I believed in God before I ever studied theology. The more I think about it, the more I realize I believed before I knew the reasons. I know now that it is necessary for me to breathe and that without air I would die. But long before I knew that, I just breathed."

304 (God, silence of; Love; World War II)

One of the worst moments in World War II came when the Nazis occupied Warsaw and proceeded to slaughter the Jewish population. There was a young Jewish girl who managed to escape and hide herself in a cave outside the city. She died there, alone. But before her death, she had scratched on the wall of the cave these words:

> I believe in the sun, even when it is not shining.
> I believe in love, even when feeling it not.
> I believe in God, even when He is silent.

305 (Frustration)

In one of his plays, Tennessee Williams tells about a mentally ill woman who is sitting at a card table set up in her garden, working a jig-saw puzzle. She is extremely tense. Her hands are shaking. She tries to force the pieces together that do not fit. Some of the pieces fall off the table. The woman becomes more and more agitated. Finally, she looks up at her daughter and says poignantly, "The pieces don't fit together! The pieces don't fit together!" That is the way it is for many people today. The pieces just will not fit together for them—and never will until they discover Faith in the Gracious God who is always working in us and around us to give us life.

False Image

306 (Responsibility)

Our Christian Faith offers us no illusion that we are a People chosen for exemption from pain and suffering. It holds no promise of a trouble-free life of easy comfort. It grants us no immunity from evil and its consequences. It makes no exception to the rule of God's judgment. Rather, our Christian Faith provides us with the spiritual equilibrium and the moral stamina we need to face up to the burdens and the fears and the evil days that overtake us—often in the most unexpected ways. With eyes of Christian Faith, we see things as they are in the light of things as they will be. With eyes of Christian Faith we see our own culpability for things as they are and our own responsibility for things as they will be.

FALSE IMAGE

307

Renowned French novelist and Nobel Prize winner, Francois Mauriac, once interviewed the celebrated Swedish-born actress, Greta Garbo. Of Miss Garbo it has been written, "Her profile, honey-colored hair, large blue eyes, and beautiful but mysterious smile, made her an ideal heroine." In 1941, at the peak of her success and still a young woman, she gave up her acting career without explanation, although she had often expressed a dislike for the publicity. Her legendary line, "I want to be alone," is often mimicked by impersonators, using a heavy Scandanavian accent. In the interview with Mauriac, Miss Garbo tried to explain her desire to hide from public view. "Imagine," she said, "how often I have sat way in the back of some theater—whether in New York, Chicago, Vienna, Berlin, or Paris—and in the hazy half-light watched the enormous crowd fascinated by my face. My face! The terrible thing is, all those eyes are desiring a face that isn't mine, is not my real face. Mine is bruised and stained with kisses and tears, it's even a little lined. Pain and grief, you know, leave a mark on any face, no matter how beautiful or cherished it is. But the public doesn't dream that what they see isn't my real face. Even I have forgotten what it's like. I've had to change the face God gave me as a child in order to offer people the ageless miracle they worship on the screen."

FAMILY

308 (Humor)

The children in a prominent family decided to give their father a book of the family's history for a birthday present. They commissioned a professional biographer to do the work, carefully warning him of the family's "black sheep" problem: Uncle George had been executed in the electric chair for murder. "I can handle that situation so that there will be no embarrassment," the biographer assured the children. "I'll merely say that Uncle George occupied a chair of applied electronics at an important government institution. He was attached to his position by the strongest of ties and his death came as a real shock."

309 (Aging)

The highly respected anthropologist, Margaret Meade, stated flatly that our modern "nuclear" families simply are not equipped to take care of the aged as the "extended" families once did. We no longer have aunts and uncles and cousins in our family units into which the old people were absorbed and cared for as a matter of course. Consequently, in many family situations,

Family

putting a parent in a nursing home can be the most loving, caring, rational thing to do. For many others, the nursing home solution is unacceptable. In the recent Broadway Play, "A Texas Trilogy," one of the characters has suffered a stroke, completely paralyzing her. Because of the woman's condition, the total, fulltime attention of her daughter, Lu Anne, is required. A friend asks Lu Anne, "Why don't you put your mother in a nursing home?" Lu Anne replies, "Having mama at home is a burden to my body. But putting her in a nursing home would be a burden to my soul." Said one drama critic, "You could almost see the cloud of guilt arise from the audience when she said that."

310 (Humor)

A man was standing over his baby's crib, staring down at it very intently. His wife entered the room and silently watched him. She saw in his face a wide range of emotion: rapture, wonder, doubt, despair, admiration. Deeply touched, she moved close to him, put her arm around him and, with eyes glistening and voice trembling said, "A penny for your thoughts." Unhesitatingly, he blurted them out: "For the life of me, I can't see how anybody can make a crib like that for $29.95."

311 (Insecurity; Parent and child)

In a family, the children may opt for certain values that differ from those of their parents. Deep rifts occur and the family begins to feel like a collection of strangers trying to make conversation but not succeeding very well. This same alienation is present in classrooms and in Churches where teachers struggle to calm the troubled waters of confusion that accompany social change.

The Norwegian Actress, Liv Ullman, gave a newspaper interview in which she was asked about her relationships with her mother and her daughter. She said, "I grew up in a country which is very traditional and very authoritarian in its teachings. I was always told by my mother that 'Nice girls do this and nice girls don't do that.' She even told me that nice girls don't put milk in their tea. So when I went to England for the first time, and everyone was putting milk in their tea, I thought 'These are not nice people.'" Liv Ullman concludes, "I do not want to be the kind of mother my mother was." She has cast off the burden of programmed insecurity that many parents are capable of imposing on their children. Consequently, she is determined not to impose such a burden on her own daughter.

312 (Humor)

An eight-year-old was being interviewed on TV. The child came from a large family in which mother got up first, got the children off to school, got the father off to work, and then got down to the business of daily household chores. At one point in the interview, the youngster was asked, "What do you think your mother wants most?" Unhesitatingly, he replied, "To go back to bed."

313 (Bad News; Good News; Humor; Marriage)

A father came home from a very rugged day at work and said to his wife, "I've had a bad day. Please! If you have any bad news tonight, keep it to yourself." To which she replied, "O.K. No bad news. Now for the good news. Remember our four children? Well, three of them didn't break an arm today."

314 (Humor; Music)

At a time in his life when his children were still young, the great piano virtuoso Arthur Rubenstein often had to be away from his family for extended concert tours. And always, when he returned, there was a kind of family celebration. Once, after being away for weeks, as he walked through the door his little

165

Family

daughter Eva ran up to him, saying, "Daddy, daddy, you're home! Play for me! Play for me!" Rubenstein was delighted. He had been longing to get back to the family and he sat down at the piano determined to play as he had never played before. But as he began to play, little Eva cried out, "No, daddy, not the piano, the phonograph."

315 (Children; Humor)

There is a wonderful story about a family with one house rule that always was strictly enforced: everyone's plate had to be cleaned at every meal, without question or discussion of any kind. And the rule included vegetables. At first, the children griped a lot, but soon they fell in with the spirit of the rule and eating every morsel on the plate became almost automatic to them. Moreover, the rule began to pay great dividends for the children after a sign was posted in the school lunch-room. It read: "No dessert until you show your empty plate." The children of that family had no problem with that lunch-room edict, and the eleven-year-old even found a way in which to turn it into a fantastic enterprise. This was revealed when his father stumbled onto a cigar box loaded with $38 in small change tucked away in the boy's bedroom closet. The parent had no notion of how his eleven-year-old son had come into such a sum. Fearing the worst, he asked the boy about it. "I earned it at school," the boy explained. "The other kids pay me to eat their vegetables. I charge a nickel for spinach, ten cents for broccoli and fifteen cents for cauliflower."

316 (Humor; Motherhood)

A mother of several small, active children was having a particularly hard day: her husband was out of town; the clothes washer was broken; the car battery was dead; the children were just impossible because it was raining outside. That evening she was talking about this to a neighbor. "It was a dreadful day", she said. "I even got a busy signal when I called 'Dial-a-Prayer'. And when I finally got through, they put me on 'hold'."

317 (Humor; Motherhood)

There is a wonderful story about a home in which there were four active children and an exhausted, harassed young mother. Her husband came home one afternoon with a frisky young puppy as a gift to the family. The children, in their excitement, took the puppy to mother and asked her what they should name it. She said, "You'd better name it 'Mother,' because if that dog stays, I'm going!"

318 ("Mother's Day"; Motherhood; Preaching)

One of America's best-known preachers remembers his first "Mother's Day" sermon as a dismal failure. He says, "First I had all the mothers raise their hand and I spoke about what a great thing it is to be a mother (a subject I personally knew nothing about). But I soon discovered that many in the congregation had been turned off. Apparently my sermon had dredged up a lot of guilt and anger and resentment for many people whose family life had been less than happy. The following year I tried a different approach. I decided to acknowledge the importance of the immediate family relationships and then go down to a deeper level where we could celebrate God's calling us into the Community of Faith: the family for everybody; the family of God.

319 (Idolatry; Parent and child)

Jesus knows that the close-knit family circle can be turned into a substitute for God. Even something so wonderful as family life experience can become destructive if it is turned into idolatry. Honore de Balzac, the 19th century French author, wrote of the suffering, the emotional pathology, and the inevitable catastrophe caused by a father's idolatry of his two daughters. In his memorable novel, "Pere Goriot," Balzac presents a pains-

Family

taking study of how parental love can be twisted by idolatry into a fatal weakness.

Pere Goriot, the father of two daughters, was a well-meaning man. His mistake was not in loving his children, but in going too far. He let his love get hold of him in a way that totally preoccupied him. He worshipped his children in a fanatical, excessive idolatrous way. His children were his God. He learned too late that human wisdom, human values, human understanding are not enough.

Poor Goriot! Sadly, we watch him on his deathbed. He has given all his life to his daughters, but they cannot give him one hour, even then. Goriot cries out to his friend, to himself and to God:

> Oh, my daughters, my daughters! If only I could see them. But, they will not come to bring me relief in the agony, for I am dying now. I will tell God that you have been good children to your father, and plead your cause with God. I tell you they are innocent my friend. I did not behave to them properly; I was stupid enough to resign my rights. I would have humbled myself in the dust for them. They might have asked me for the very eyes out of my head, and I would have bidden them to pluck them out. What could you expect? The most beautiful nature, the noblest soul would have been spoiled by such indulgence. I am a wretch, I am justly punished. I loved them so! I went back to them as a gambler goes to the gaming table. This love was my vice, you see . . . They were everything in the world to me. I, and I only, am to blame for all their sins. When they were little girls, I indulged them in every whim. They have never been crossed. Today they are as eager for pleasure as they used to be for sugar plums . . . I am guilty, not they. But, I sinned through love.

168

FATIGUE

320 (Humor)

An Army unit went on a twenty-five mile hike with full field-pack. When the unit reached the end of the twenty-five miles, there was a message that said, "All men who are physically able to make the return march should do so immediately. The others will camp overnight and return in the morning." The Commanding Officer called a formation, made the announcement, and then said, "All those who do not feel they are physically able to make the return march take three steps forward." Whereupon, the entire unit stepped forward—except one frail, little private who stood drooping under the weight of his pack. The Commander walked over to him and said, "Son, the Army is proud of you." The little private replied, "I don't know why, sir, I can't even walk three more steps."

FEAR

321 (Humor; Travel)

An elderly woman named Maude had a window seat on a big "747" jetliner that had just taken off for Rome. She had been scrimping for years to fulfill her dream of travelling to Europe and visiting the exotic places she'd read about all her life. But it was her first flight and she was terrified! "O Lord, what am I doing up here?" she kept repeating to herself. Even the stately presence of the four bishops seated behind her didn't help. In fear and trembling, she finally opened her eyes and peeped out the window just in time to see one of the plane's four engines break loose from the wing and disappear into the clouds below.

Fear

Maude sounded the alarm: "We're going to die! We're going to die," she cried out. The chief stewardess immediately consulted with the pilot, then announced to the passengers the news that everything was under control. "The captain assures you," she said, "that he can fly the airplane back to New York and land safely on three motors." But poor, panic-stricken Maude continued to cry out, "We're going to die! We're going to die!" The stewardess went to her and said, "Don't worry, my dear, God is with us. We have only three motors but, look, we have four bishops." To which Maude replied, "I'd rather have four motors and three bishops."

322 (Appointed Time; Crisis)

Suppose science developed a super-duper computer, programmed to match every last word in the Bible and every important event in the history of man against all of the available data on the physical aspects of the known Universe. Suppose further that this giant computer then generated the awesome conclusion that all the signs of the end-time would converge before year's end. In other words, suppose mankind believed it had stumbled onto the secret of the "appointed time" and could accurately predict the world's end, say within a week or two. How would people react to the news that it would all come to pass before next Saturday? Is it not conceivable that obsessive fear would cause a substantial portion of the human race to "take to the hills," so to speak? Would it be at all surprising to see every airport in the world in a state of incredible chaos as huge throngs of panic-stricken people madly scramble for flights to the remotest corners of the earth? Would it be difficult to picture a small army of heads-of-state and space scientists collaborating in a frantic effort to launch as many space-flights as possible for the avowed purpose of "saving the human race from extinction"? In other words, can we honestly deny the possibility that, once in on the secret of God's time, mankind would engage in one final, frantic, panic-stricken, all-out attempt to hide from God?

170

323 (God, judgment of; Judgment; Justice)

We must read the signs-of-the-times, knowing that we share in the responsibility for things as they are and that we stand under constant judgment. God's judgment is upon us now for things as they are. We should be fearful of a social order in which some human beings are victims of famine and others are victims of over-eating. We should be fearful of a social order in which the full range of medical resources is available to the affluent and pestilence is reserved for the poor. We should be fearful of a social order permanently afflicted with wars and rumors of wars. Tortures, persecutions, assassinations; hatreds, betrayals and "love growing cold"—we have seen them all; many we have experienced first-hand. And the constant judgment we live under is rendered not merely on the basis of whether or not we are parties to these evils, nor merely on the basis of whether or not we fear them. The definitive judgment we are under is whether or not we fear them enough. Do we fear the evil of social injustice enough to attend to the works of justice—or do we simply cave in? Do we fear the evil of mass killing enough to attend to the works of peace—or do we merely bow and scrape before the false prophets of war and destruction? Do we fear the evil of "love growing cold" enough to tender our own full measure of love—or do we passively submit to the forces of hatred and persecution?

FELLOWSHIP

324 (Celebration; Crisis; Light)

A great darkness came over the land. The lights went out for some 25 million people, in an 80,000 square mile area of Northeastern United States and Southeastern Canada. It was the great blackout of November 9, 1965, caused by a power failure

Fellowship

at New York City's Consolidated Edison. Hundreds of thousands of people were suddenly thrown together in all sorts of unaccustomed situations—some of them weird, some of them absurd, some of them dangerous, most of them highly inconvenient. In New York City, air passengers looked down on the blacked-out city as their planes circled the metropolis in interminable "hold patterns." Thousands of commuters sat in darkened railroad cars, some stalled between suburban "bedroom communities," others standing motionless in underground subway tubes. Above ground, many people were trapped between floors in crowded elevators.

There were the usual grumblings and complaints, to be sure, and scattered incidents of shoddy attempts to exploit the situation. But, in general, the News Media reported a strange overall effect of the technological disaster: it brought an otherwise distant and cold "rush-hour" crowd together in a remarkable spirit of fellowship and good-will. Community song pierced the eerie darkness of skyscraper halls, railroad cars and even stuck elevators. Everywhere people were demonstrating concern for the other's safety, comfort and feelings. "People were wonderful," said a burly subway attendant. "Men were actually letting the ladies out first." (Easily, the ultimate New York City rush-hour miracle.) On the 86th floor of the Empire State Building someone excitedly shouted to his stranded group, "You should see the full moon shimmering in the East River. .. I've never seen anything like it." On a commuter train, a middle-aged couple sitting next to each other asked the conductor if he has the same powers in his car as a captain has on his ship: they wanted to get married. The impersonal, lifeless "crowd" had been converted into a sensitive, vibrant "community." Moreover, the New York City Police reported, in amazement, that although the blackout had enhanced the possibilities for crime, the rate had actually gone down on that eventful day. The lesson of the big blackout in New York City is that the incessant glitter and glare of those neon lights and everything they symbolize had not only shut out the simple beauty of the moon shining on the river, but had closed people off to one another. Suddenly, huddled together in the darkness, they caught a little glimpse of a new and refreshing light. Suddenly, freed from the din of the "rat race," they found themselves speaking and listening to one another with warmth and understanding. Suddenly, they found themselves celebrating the enriching experience in song. Suddenly, "The people that lived in darkness had seen a great light."

325 (Church)

In a little town in Central Europe, "Jacob the Tailor" felt that he had been mistreated in the synagogue. And so he withdrew from the community and isolated himself from his friends and neighbors. Weeks went by until, finally, the Rabbi called on him. After a polite greeting, there was a heavy silence. Then the Rabbi said, "Let's sit in front of the fire." So the two men sat in complete silence. An hour or so later the Rabbi picked up the fireplace tongs, pulled out a coal and placed it on the hearth, away from the fire. Still no word was spoken. The two men just sat and watched the glowing, burning piece of coal become darker and darker until finally it was black and cold and dusty with ashes. A few moments later, Jacob the Tailor spoke. "I understand," he said. "I'll come back to the synagogue."

FIDELITY

326 (Children)

A journalist, through no fault of his own, lost two fine jobs within a single year. He was managing editor of a magazine

Fools for Christ

that failed because of declining advertising revenue. Then he joined the staff of a major newspaper but within months it was sold to an opposition syndicate and he became part of the employee casualty list. When he came home to his wife and three small sons, he told them sadly, "I'm out of a job again." The wife comforted him as best she could. The three boys stared at him round-eyed. Next morning after his sons had left for school, the journalist went into his study. There, in the waste basket, he discovered the remains of three china "piggy banks." On his desk was a pile of pennies, nickels, dimes and a few quarters. Next to the coins was a crudely lettered note which read, "We believe in you, pop." "Be as little children," Jesus says.

FOOLS FOR CHRIST

327   (Compassion; Service)

The late Johnny Parks of the City of Chicago was known to his family and friends as "The Coatless Wonder." He just couldn't seem to keep an overcoat on his back. On cold days he was always giving it to some poor person in the street who had none. He couldn't keep a watch very long for the same reason. On impulse he would give it to the first poor person who walked by. Johnny Parks was a fool. He was always talking about Jesus and he was always giving away valuable things. He was a fool to his family and friends. You don't give your overcoats to people in the street. Only a fool would do that. Or did old Johnny Parks know something.

FORGIVENESS

328 (Death; Hate; Prayer)

A clergyman tells of an episode in his parish ministry that moved him deeply. He says:

> I called on an old man who was dying. The old man wanted to die but he couldn't. When he was a little boy, he had been horribly beaten, almost to the point of death by a man who was supposed to be taking care of him. And he had nurtured an intense hatred for that man for the rest of his life. He confessed to me that because of his bitterness, for all those years he had not been able to pray—not even once. He confessed to me that for all those years he couldn't bring himself to go near a Church. He even compared his anger to the verse in the Psalms that says, "I hated him with a perfect hatred." An incredible case of anger had been festering in that man's soul down through the years. On several subsequent visits, we talked about a man named Jesus who had been beaten to the point of death but who, instead of expressing hatred for those who beat Him, forgave them. And three or four visits later, when I walked into the old man's room, before I could even say "Good morning," he said to me, "I did it last night. Last night I forgave him, and for the first time, I prayed." By the next morning, the old man had died.

329 (Reconciliation)

Some years ago, a pastor in Boston was being harassed by a woman in his congregation. She started false rumors about

Forgiveness

him. She wrote vicious letters about him to his bishop and others. She initiated petitions to have him removed. After several months of this, the woman moved to another city and not long afterward was converted to Christ. Part of the process of her conversion was to realize the terrible wrong she had done and all the pain and suffering she had inflicted on her pastor in Boston. Consequently, she wrote him a long letter explaining what had happened to her and how deeply she regretted what she had done to him. The pastor immediately sent her a telegram with three words on it: "Forgiven, forgotten, forever."

330 (Jesus, mercy of; Repentance; Judas)

There is a very beautiful old legend in which someone has pictured the Last Day: the "Day of the Lord" that the Bible talks about. Up in Paradise on this Last Day everyone is celebrating, dancing and singing and shouting with great jubilation. Everyone except Jesus. Jesus is standing very quietly in the shadows of the gates of Paradise. Someone asks Him what He is doing, in the midst of all this celebration. Standing quietly He says, "I am waiting here for Judas." The story symbolizes the infinte quality of God's forgiving love which He offers even to Judas Iscariot. But the question still remains. Will Judas use his freedom to accept it or will he reject it? And that is the question we must ask about the bit of Judas that is in us all!

331 (Guilt)

A Pastor received a letter from a woman in which she recounted her life experience of the past year. It more or less typifies what life is really like for all of us. She said:

> "What a year! We married my brother George
> last fall. We had our baby, Johnny. Aunt Ida died,

and my father-in-law is dying in a nursing home. With the school referendum and the natural joys and sorrows of four children, I feel as if we're on a perpetual emotional jag. Our next door neighbor has kicked her teenage daughter out of the house and told her not to come back. Another neighbor and mother of four had a nervous breakdown. And the friendly couple down the street have become alcoholics. What we need in this town is for someone to come along to show us what the meaning of this crazy life is and to preach "Forgiveness, forgiveness, forgiveness." Isn't it strange how everything seems to boil down either to being unable on one's own to forgive others, or to feeling guilty and unforgiven oneself.

PROFESSIONAL ADVICE

332 (Humor)

TV personality Hugh Downs tells a story about the problem lawyers and doctors often encounter with people who seek to obtain free professional advice at parties and other social events. It seems that a certain doctor and a certain lawyer were conversing with each other during a cocktail party. While they were talking, a woman approached the doctor and complained about a sore leg. The doctor listened, then told her about applying cold compresses and keeping the leg elevated and taking aspirin, etc. After she had gone, the doctor turned to the lawyer and said, "I think I ought to send her a bill, don't you?" The lawyer said, "Yes, I think you ought to send her a bill." Consequently, the next day, the doctor sent the woman a bill and the lawyer sent the doctor a bill.

FREEDOM

333   (Caring; Healing; Service; Widows)

A young businessman was killed in an automobile accident. His widow was left with several small children to raise and her elderly mother to care for. Over the years, she devoted herself wholeheartedly and lovingly to the task. She had nursed her mother through a long terminal illness. She had supported and guided her children through adolescence and teenage. All five were college graduates and on their own now. And the mother said, "For so long I had wanted to be out from under all these responsibilities and now I am free. But I am worse off than before, because for the life of me, I cannot figure out what I am free for."

334   (Guidance)

In his autobiography, the famous Russian Poet, Yevgeny Yevtushenka recalls a chilling experience of human sheepishness: He was part of an enormous crowd gathered to view Stalin's coffin. The people wedged themselves tighter and tighter into the square, blocked on one end by buildings and on the other by a row of army trucks. People were being trampled and crushed. Some began to scream, "Get those trucks out of the way!" And the policeman's voice sheepishly answered from one of the trucks, "I can't do it. I have no instructions." With that, the crowd panicked. Many heads were smashed against the trucks. "All at once," the poet writes, "I felt a savage hatred for everything that had given birth to those words, 'I have no instructions.' The man we were burying . . . could not be innocent of the disaster."

335 (Grace; Redemption)

Picture yourself for a moment as a slave. You have been brought into the slave market and you are up on the auction block. Someone comes along, bids the highest price, and pays for you. But, to your utter astonishment, instead of taking you into slavery in his household, he says to you, "You are free! I have paid the price for you! You are a free person."

The picture changes. Now you are a criminal. You have committed the crime of which you are accused. You know you are guilty. You stand before the judge, condemned. You are awaiting the death sentence when, to your utter astonishment, the judge pronounces you forgiven and free! Although you had done nothing to deserve it or expect it, nevertheless you are free again! In both instances it was a sheer act of grace—a gift—that made a whole new way of life possible to you.

FRIENDSHIP

336

A London periodical ran a contest for the best definition of "friend." From thousands of entries, two definitions were declared the winners—and they are beautiful. One read,

> A friend is one who multiplies joys and divides sorrows.

And the other,

> A friend is one who comes in when the whole world has gone out.

179

FRUSTRATION

337 (Aging; Humor; Marriage)

A man reached retirement age and decided that he would help his wife more by taking over some of the cooking chores. He began to make notes as he learned things about his newly-acquired kitchen duties. Both husband and wife liked oatmeal for breakfast. Consequently, one of the first lessons he received was on the art of cooking oatmeal. "Be sure to measure the water and the oats, both," his wife instructed. "Use the small saucepan . . . Be sure to stir it carefully when cooling so that it doesn't stick . . . Don't forget to time it . . . When it is fully cooked, turn off the gas, put a lid on the pan and let it stand for a few minutes before serving . . . Before you wash the sauce-pan, soak it in warm water for a while." Later, the wife happened to glance in the husband's notebook and she saw the entry he had made. It read: "Forget about oatmeal."

338 (Gumperson's Law)

Some of you may have heard about the "law" called "Gum-person's Law." "Gumperson's Law" explains why one of the kids always comes down with the mumps the day before you're leaving for vacation. "Gumperson's Law" explains why, when you're in the city and late for an appointment, every parking place is on the other side of the street going the other way. "Gumperson's Law" explains why your last match can never get the campfire lighted, but that same one match can start a forest fire. "Gumperson's Law" explains the forgotten casserole, still in the oven, when the holiday dinner is over. We could go on and on forever. However, there is a sad historical footnote about this. Gumperson, the man who discovered and formulated this law, was killed while walking on a highway. It seems he was walking on the left side, facing traffic (which is what you're supposed to do) when suddenly he was struck by a visiting Englishman who was driving on the wrong side. Now that we've heard about it, we can start blaming "Gumperson's Law" for our ills and the world's ills if we want to.

339   (Meaninglessness)

There are many middle-aged people today who frankly admit they are missing life. They've worked hard on their career; they've put the children through school; they've done many of the things that they were expected to do, but they feel that they have missed so much, and that they have not been experiencing life in a satisfying way. One of the three plays in "Texas Trilogy" is called "The Oldest Living Graduate." In it, old Colonel Kincaid is sitting in his wheelchair going through the experience of remembering his life. He remembers what it was like when he was a young cowboy. He remembers what it was like to spread out his bedroll and sleep at night under a star-filled sky. He remembers what it was like to taste good ranch food after a hard day's work on the range. He remembers his wife whom he had loved very much, but who is now long since dead. He remembers his children. And as he moves through this great panoramic review of his life, finally, with great sadness, he says, "And I let it all slip by. It all slipped by."

340   (Humor)

Someone has come up with a definition of the absolute height of frustration: when a wife discovers a letter she gave her husband to mail three months ago in a coat he gave her three months ago to have a button sewn on.

GAMBLING

341 (Humor)

Harvey Ziegfeld and Charles Dillingham, the famous Broadway producers, were pallbearers at the funeral of the great magician, Houdini. As they carried the famed escape artist's coffin out of Church, Dillingham leaned over and said, "Ziegfeld, I'll bet you $100 he isn't in here."

GOD, AND CREATION

342 (Children; Humor)

In the "Children's Letters to God" book by Eric Marshall and Stuart Hample, a little boy sends the following message to God:

> Dear God, My teacher says the north pole is not really at the top. Did you make any other mistakes?—Herbie

GOD, AND SUFFERING

343 (Faith)

In a scene from "The Big Fisherman" by L. C. Douglas, St. Peter is in prison awaiting his execution. He is visited by his friend, Mencius, an influential Roman Proconsul, who is trying to have Peter's death sentence commuted. "How do you find it possible to live down there in those caverns?" Mencius asks Peter. Peter replies, "It is not so difficult to do what one must do." He goes on to describe how he, a condemned man, ministers day and night to his frightened, beaten, sick and hungry fellow-inmates. "I pray with them . . . I offer words of comfort when they die . . . And I bid them be of good cheer, for the Kingdom is coming!" Mencius then says, "It must take great Faith, Peter, to believe that the Kingdom of Christos is coming when everything they had is lost." To which Peter replies, "That's when our faith is strongest, Mencius, when there is nothing else to lean upon. The spirit of God is very real, and near, to those distressed ones."

GOD, AND VALUES

344   (Coronation; Service)

A certain political leader attended the Coronation of King Edward VII in 1901. The man spent several days in London, amidst all the pomp and ceremony. He attended receptions, the Coronation service itself, the balls and all the rest of it. When he got home, some friends asked him to recall the one thing that impressed him most. And to their great surprise, instead of talking about some glittering moment of glory in the coronation ceremony, he told this story:

> He was returning to his hotel after a reception when he saw two children huddled together in the doorway of a house. Two children with arms around one another, sleeping. It was a very cold night, a bitterly cold night. One of the children was a boy about twelve years old. The little girl, apparently his sister, was about three. He said

this boy had taken off his coat and put it around his sister's shoulders. And he'd taken off his wool cap and put it around his sister's feet. And•there they were, huddled together, sleeping through the cold night. And he said, "It may seem strange to you, but of all the things I saw in London, this picture will always be strongest in my memory."

But was it so strange really when you come to think about it? A simple act of loving concern for another person, even to the point of suffering, is not only impressive and memorable in our sight but in God's sight too. In God's sight, a simple act of loving service is more acceptable than any other human event— even the Coronation of a king. Caring is the Crowning Glory of all human experience.

GOD, FATHER

345 (Children; Humor; Lord's Prayer)

A little girl was having a difficult time learning the Lord's Prayer. Despite her mother's heroic efforts to teach it to her, she kept coming up with her own inspired interpretations, such as, "Our Father, who art in heaven, how-do-you-know-my-name." That is precisely what Jesus is telling us: God, your heavenly Father, knows your name; He knows you—intimately!

346 (Hope; Luck)

Psychologist Erich Fromm has observed that in the "Mickey Mouse" motion pictures there is always the same theme: a little being is threatened and persecuted by an overwhelmingly powerful being. To avoid adversity, the little being runs and runs and runs. Eventually it escapes and, sometimes, even harms the enemy. People are ready to accept this constant theme running through the many variations of "Mickey Mouse" and similar cartoons because they can readily identify with the little being that is always being threatened by a powerful enemy. There is, of course, the "happy ending" always (if Mickey Mouse were to be overcome by the enemy, there could be no more "Mickey Mouse" films). Consequently, the viewer who identifies with the fears and feelings of smallness that "Mickey" endures, in the end is comforted by the feeling that he will survive and the powerful one will be overcome. However, the significant and sad part of this "happy ending" is that his salvation lies mostly in his ability to run fast, and in the sudden mishaps which make it impossible for his pursuer to catch him. In other words, Mickey's luck never runs out. He can depend on it, and the spectator indulges himself with the hope that "Lady Luck" will be his savior too.

Don't be a Mickey Mouse. You don't need to run, run, run away from life. You don't need "Lady Luck" on your side. Your loving Father is with you, always. He will give you strength. He will give you hope. He will give you dignity and integrity and a purposeful goal in life.

347

Out of the depths of our being we all need and want a father. Author Thomas Wolfe looked back over his own life and said that for him it had been a search, for a Father—not merely the father of his flesh, not merely the lost father of his youth, but a Father with whom he could identify in his weakness, a Father who could accept and love him as he is, and give him strength. There are many other writers in our time who have beautifully expressed the need for that kind of Father—literary giants like Eugene O'Neil, William Faulkner, Tennessee Williams, Albert Camus, and countless others.

GOD, CELEBRATION OF

348 (Joy)

In the story of "Zorba the Greek," Zorba's uptight American businessman friend was totally unable to express his feelings about life. Zorba, on the other hand, could go into that joyous Greek dance of his when he saw a donkey! Why? In order to celebrate a God who had sense of humor enough to create a donkey. How many of us have arrived at that level of joy in our proclamation and celebration of the Christ Spirit in the Creative Wonder we call "God"?

GOD, DEPENDENCE ON

349 (Humor; Kingdom of God)

Two middle-aged women were mingling in the after-theatre crowd in a New York City Hotel. A waiter passed by carrying three cups on a tray. One of the ladies asked him what was in the cups. He said, "It's Irish coffee, madam. We make it with a cup of strong coffee, a shot of Irish whiskey and then we put cream on the top." The woman thought for a moment, then replied, "Well, it sounds delicious but do you think you could make it for us with Sanka?"

That should really hit home for many of us because we're always trying to get our spiritual Irish coffee made with Sanka. We're always trying to water it down a bit, dilute it a bit—but Jesus gives it to us straight! He tells us straight that in order to be in union with God, we must acknowledge our total dependence on Him as the Source of our life and as the Source of our life's fulfillment. We want to water down the message because we see that kind of total dependence as a sign of weakness. We want to assert our independence. We decide to come late to the banquet. We've got our own thing to do first. The Kingdom of God is for later. We haven't discovered the secret yet, that the more we depend upon God the stronger we are; the more completely we give ourselves over to God, the more wondrously He gives our life back to us in a whole new dimension.

350 (Incarnation; Magi; King Herod)

A very dignified, austere European theologian always began his lecture series on the "Incarnation" with the same line. He would look out at his audience and say, "I feel like a mosquito in a nudist colony. I can see that it is wonderful to be here but I hardly know where to begin." King Herod demanded of the Magi information about the child Jesus. Two thousand years later people all around us want "detailed information about the Child Jesus," and our Christian duty is to meet that demand. Whether or not we succeed depends largely on knowing where to begin. Unlike the mosquito in the nudist colony, we must know where to begin. Clearly, we must begin with ourselves by acknowledging dependence on God not only for our life but for our way of life.

351 (Children; Homesickness; Humor)

A little girl went to Summer Camp for the first time. She was seated on the edge of her bunk, crying. Her counsellor came in and said to her, "What's the matter, are you homesick?" "No," the little girl replied, "I'm here-sick." We are being told, and perhaps we would agree, that most of us these days are both homesick and here-sick. And some of us are getting sick of hearing how sick we are and how sick the world is. And yet, we seem to just fiddle around on the surface of things and wonder why things aren't getting any better. What Jesus and

God, Estrangement from

the Biblical writers make clear to us is that at the heart of the matter is our unwillingness to acknowledge that God is the God of all of life, that we are not God, that we are dependent on God. And, because the world has been unwilling to do this, it is being drained and diminished and destroyed.

352 (Humor; Psychiatry; Satan)

Said the psychiatrist to the patient, "I'm not aware of your problem, so perhaps you should start at the beginning." Said the patient to the psychiatrist, "All right. In the beginning I created the heavens and the earth . . ." One must say to oneself, "All right, in the beginning I did not create the heavens and the earth. This is God's creation. God is the Source of my life. I need God to tell me who I am and why I am and where I am going. I need God to lead me through the exit from nothingness and into the light of His Grand Design. I need God to tell me where my fulfillment lies. Away with you, Satan. In the beginning God created the heavens and the earth . . . Him alone shall I adore."

GOD, ESTRANGEMENT FROM

353 (God, power of; Heaven; Hell; New Life)

The brilliant writer, C. S. Lewis, wrote a thought-provoking book called "The Great Divorce." It is not about divorce that occurs between husbands and wives. It is about the divorce that occurs between our souls and God. In this book, C. S. Lewis gives us a picture of Hell as a big city, with all its pressures and problems. In this big city, the weather is always cold and wet with a heavy rain. The light is always grey and murky. The people in this City of Hell become more and more aware of the great divorce that has taken place between their souls and God, and they sink deeper and deeper into their dismal surroundings. Except . . . there is a way out! There is a way out of this terrible condition! God has provided a shuttle-bus service from Hell to Heaven: regular bus service. All you need to do is to get on the bus and let the power of God carry you into the light. The incredible thing about the story is that very few people get on board the buses, even though they are coming and going all the time. The people find all kinds of excuses for putting the journey off to some vague future time. Hardly anyone wants to get on the bus now, thereby missing the opportunity to be carried by the power of God from death to new life.

GOD, EXISTENCE OF

354 (Caring)

A little book called "Around A Rusty God" is one of those rare stories: simple and beautiful for children to enjoy, but profound enough for the most thoughtful adult. The action takes place in China, just before the Communists take over. It centers around a little boy named Bengal and his two pet goats. One of the themes that runs constantly through the book is Bengal's deep concern about the way people come into the temple, week after week, to burn their incense and candles and sing their songs and clap their hands and march around a rusty little god. He simply cannot understand how this worship of a rusty god does anybody any good. So he asks a friend about it. And the friend gives him this answer: "The rusty little god is not real because the people do not care about him. He is always covered with spider webs and the temple is dirty. And the things they put in the little dish in front of him are not worth anything." And then Bengal asks, with all the fervency of his young spirit, "If they cared about him would he be the real God?" His older and wiser friend replies, slowly, "Yes. If they cared about him he would be the real God."

355 (Devil)

In a book called "The Cloister and the Hearth," by Charles Reade, two men are shown back-packing their way across Europe during very dangerous times. One of them constantly tries to shore up his companion's courage by repeating the words, "Courage my friend, the devil is dead! Courage my friend, the devil is dead!" What would have been better said, however, is "Courage my friend, God is alive! Courage my friend, God is alive!"

356 (Atheism; Perspective)

"What are you reading?" a passing stranger asked a holy man sitting by the roadside. "I am reading a Sacred Book," he answered. "What is it about?" the stranger asked. "It is about God," the man replied. "Who is God?" asked the stranger. "God," said the holy man, "is the Lord of the World." To which the stranger replied, "I only believe to exist what I can see with my eyes. Where is He? Where does the Lord of the World reside?" Whereupon the holy man arose, held the open book up to the stranger, at a great distance, and told him to read. "How can I read this when you hold the book at such a distance?" the stranger shouted. Then, the holy man held the book so close to the stranger that it touched his nose. "Can you read now?" "But how should I be able to read when the book is so near? Again, I cannot make out anything." "Indeed you cannot see," the holy man said. "You cannot focus your eyes on the print because you are blinded by faulty perspective."

GOD, FEAR OF

357 (God, mystery of)

Do you remember Herman Melville's "Moby Dick"—the story of the great white whale? Most people used to think of it simply as being a great sea story, an adventure story. But the critics in recent years have begun to say that this is one of the greatest theological novels ever written. Whole books have been written to describe and to analyze the religious symbolism on every page of "Moby Dick." Melville portrayed "Moby Dick," we now understand, as the God symbol. The unbelievable whiteness of Moby Dick symbolizes God's omnipotence. And there is always a mystery about him. You remember, his pursuers would sight him and then he would disappear, sight him again, and again he would disappear. And they became obsessed with the elusiveness, the awe and the wonder, of that whale. Captain Ahab, the whale's chief pursuer, symbolizes man, from Adam on: man shaking his fist at God; man trying to subdue God; man striking out at God, trying to "catch up" to God. Through hundreds of pages, Captain Ahab and his crew pursue the whale relentlessly. In the last climactic battle, which lasts for three days, Ahab and his crew are destroyed. On this level, the story of "Moby Dick" symbolizes how man's unwillingness to co-exist with the Mystery of God can lead to his destruction. It is wrong to fear God because we can't capture the full mystery of His Being. If we do, sooner or later we will begin to lash out at Him and to try to destroy Him. But we will destroy only our own humanity.

GOD, GOODNESS OF

358 (Courage)

A Washington, D.C. newspaper announced that Betty Grant was going to retire. Years earlier, she had been stricken with polio. She could talk, see and hear, and had the use of her toes, but the rest of her body was totally paralyzed. She had a daughter to raise. Lying in bed day-after-day, concerned about her life, concerned about her future, concerned about her daughter's future, she thought, "Well, I'll make use of what I have." She contacted the telephone company. They rigged up a switchboard she could work with her toes, and she started a 24-hour-a-day telephone answering service. For 16 years she carried on this business and supported her daughter through college. Interviewed on the occasion of her retirement, Betty Grant's closing words were, "God has been so good to me!"

GOD, LIFE OF

359   (Eyes of Faith)

There is a wonderful story about the father of one of America's great poets, Emily Dickinson. One evening at the dinner hour, the fire-bell started ringing madly. All the people in the little town came running out, clutching their napkins and their silverware, looking for the fire. And there stood Emily Dickinson's father. He had just seen a glorious sunset and didn't want the people to miss it, so he started ringing the fire-bell furiously in order to get them out before it was too late. Most of the people went back to their homes shaking their heads and talking about that "Weird Dickinson man, nuttier than a fruitcake." Now, most of us don't get all that charged up over a glorious sunset. We see it and we get a little inspiration for a moment or two. But when we can look at it through eyes of Faith, it is cause for more than a little inspiration. The whole world around us is throbbing with the life of God, not only a beautiful sunset and the mountains and the storm at sea and the deep-blue sky, but also the wood and the steel and the dirt and the grass and the sweat and grime—all the common things we see everyday.

GOD, LOVE OF

360   (Compassion; Healing)

A man recently visited a home where there were five children. He was supposed to be a kind of "godfather" to them and was trying to get involved with them on their level. He asked one of the little girls about her doll collection: "Which one is your favorite?" "Promise you won't laugh if I tell you?" she answered. "No I won't laugh," he said. She went into the next room and brought back a doll that was the most tattered, dilapidated, worn-out doll he had ever seen—a real refugee from the trash heap. All the hair was missing, and the nose was broken off and an arm was cracked. He didn't laugh, but he couldn't cover his surprise. He said to her, "Why do you love this one the most?" The little girl replied, "Because she needs it most. If I didn't love her, nobody would." Jesus said that God is like that. God is loving us most when we need it most. God is closest to us when we feel broken and abandoned. When we are in need of healing, God is ready to work His miracle, through the Lord Jesus.

361   (Christian Ministry)

At a retreat house called "Dayspring," when a retreat has ended the participants follow a custom of making their own bed and leaving a note for the next occupant of the room. Usually the note contains a little prayer or some word of encouragement.

God, Love of

One retreatant found the following note under his pillow when he arrived:

> Observations of a skeptic. I don't want to be told that God loves me or that Jesus loves me. I want to feel that the people who call themselves "Christian" love me. Then perhaps I can realize the love of God and the love of Christ. I don't want to be told about the love of God and then find eyes averted when I look straight at a Christian. I want to see God's love in eyes that are unafraid to look into mine, eyes that shine from a soul that is sincere. I want to experience God's love through a smile that says, "I love you, I accept you right where you are. I want genuinely to be your friend, now and when we leave this retreat place." Then, maybe, I can begin to believe in that love from God through this strange Christ that Christians talk so much about. And if I believe, then perhaps I too can live in love and give it to others. And, you know, I think I did find ·some of God's love here this weekend. Be ready on your retreat to receive it, and be ready to give it. Peace,—Bob

362 (Cross; Preaching)

It was in the Middle Ages, and a very popular preaching monk had announced that he was going to preach on the "Love of God." On the appointed Sunday, the Cathedral was filled to overflowing with worshippers. Instead of going into the pulpit, the preacher merely sat. The setting sun was shining through the stained glass and flooding the Cathedral with glorious color and warmth. Still the preacher just sat, in silence. Finally, when the Cathedral was dark, he went to the altar and lit a candle. Then he walked over to a statue of Jesus Christ on the Cross. In silence, He held up the candle to the wounded hands for several minutes. Then he moved the candle down to the feet which, like the hands, had felt the sharp nails tearing into the flesh. Then up to the open side and finally after a few minutes, to the crown of thorns. Having done this, the old monk pronounced the Benediction. And everyone left the Cathedral knowing that they had heard an unforgettable sermon on the love of God, even though the preacher had spoken not one word.

GOD, MERCY OF

363   (Love; Service; Trust)

In the opening scene of Paul Claudel's play, "The Satin Slipper," a missionary, the sole survivor of a shipwreck, has lashed himself to the mainmast and is wholly at the mercy of the raging sea. As death approaches he cries out, "Lord, I thank you for sending me down like this. Sometimes I found your commandments painful and my will in opposition to your rule. But now I could not be closer bound to you than I am. However violently my limbs move, they cannot get one inch away from you. So I am really fastened to the cross, but the cross on which I hang is not fastened to anything else. It is floating on the sea." The shipwrecked missionary is approaching the end of his life and he knows it. Already he has nothing left to keep him fastened to the world. Yet, at that perilous, drifting last moment, he discovers his final security. Having expressed his child-like trust in God's mercy, he uses his last breath to utter a prayer of concern, not for himself, but for his unfortunate, wayward brother. "My God, I pray you for my brother Rodrigo," he cries as he sinks into the arms of his heavenly Father. This dramatic enactment of final and total allegiance to God and neighbor, both, beautifully portrays the Gospel truth that authentic trust in God's mercy is necessarily and simultaneously expressed in the performance of brotherly service. Love of God and love of neighbor are inseparable.

GOD, POWER OF

364 (God, trust in)

Some of us have problems, relationships, decisions and duties concerning which we have never once turned to God. We surmise that they are either too hopeless for help of any kind (even Divine help) or they are too small to bother God with. More likely, we see ourselves as being in charge of our lives, and we do not wish to turn these matters over to God. Right now, fix your mind on a problem relationship or a difficult decision you must make. Then say to yourself, "What would happen if I asked God to take charge?" After you have thought about it, you may find yourself ready to trust God's power to become active in this area of your life.

GOD, PRESENCE OF

365 (Atheism)

"Where do you look for God?" "Where do you see God?" These questions were put to a group of elementary school children and adolescents—all Christian. Responses to the survey were reported in a national religious periodical. One eleventh-grader answered poetically: "I find Him in the morning mist/beyond the shining sun/among the wild flowers/in the city lights." Another's answer reflected deep cynicism. "God is a non-existent security blanket," he said. In the same vein, another twelfth-grader found God "in solitude, in friends, in nature, in beauty, in other people, babies, those over sixty-five, in my family," and "even in New York City." Possibly the best of all answers came from a high school lad who asked, simply, "Why, did you lose Him?"

366

Christopher Morley once wrote: "I had a thousand questions to ask God; but when I met Him, they all fled and didn't seem to matter."

367

Pablo Casals, the great cellist of our time, described his experience of God:

> When I awake in the morning I go immediately to the sea, and everywhere I find God in the smallest and in the largest things. I see him in colors and designs and forms. I constantly have the idea of God when I am at the sea. What is God but this world in which we live—alive with His life! What is music but God! Every human being is a miracle. The world is a miracle that only God could make. Think of how no two grains of sand are alike; how there is not one nose, one voice like another; how, among billions and billions of living and non-living things in the Universe no two are exactly alike. Who but God could do that? God must be present all the time! Nothing can take that from us!

368 (Indifference)

A World War II Navy man tells the story of what happened aboard his destroyer when news of the War's end came and

God, Presence of

orders were received to destroy all the big shells on board. "When they started their work," he said, "the men treated those shells with great respect. They cradled them in their arms very carefully, carried them to the side where they eased them overboard. But there were hundreds of shells to be destroyed and, as the day wore on, the men became more and more careless. Toward afternoon's end, I actually saw them tossing the shells to each other and even contemptuously kicking them overboard." The man who tells this story says that he often thinks about the episode to keep himself from taking the big things in life for granted—even God.

369

The famous theologian of the Middle Ages, Thomas Aquinas, went into the chapel to worship and meditate. He came out with his face aglow, and his secretary asked him if he was ready to dictate. "No, my son," Thomas said. "I will dictate no theology today, because what I have just seen makes me feel like all that I have written is so much straw"—the difference between experiencing the reality of God's presence and writing and talking about it as we so often do.

370 (Prayer)

In 1666, a French soldier named Nicholas Herman joined a Carmelite monastery, became known as Brother Lawrence, and wrote a book called "Practice the Presence of God." He was assigned to the monastery kitchen, which became his Cathedral. In his book he explained:

> The time of business does not with me differ from the time of prayer; and in the noise and clatter of my kitchen, while several persons are at the same time calling for different things, I possess God in as great tranquility as if I were upon my knees at the altar . . .

God, Presence of

Our lives can be flat and lifeless or they can be rich and alive with significance. We can live as though unaware of the nearness of God or, like Brother Lawrence, we can be alert to His coming to us, again and again, in every situation.

371 (Bible; Grief; Prayer)

Happy are those who have learned to turn to God in all circumstances of daily living—big and small. One woman learned this secret after years of confident, successful living which included a good marriage, an enjoyable job and an active role in the Church. Then, everything caved in: she became severely arthritic, her husband committed suicide, her father died and her mother had a stroke. Faced with supporting herself and her daughter, and in the midst of her grief and poor health, she turned to God in a way that was different than ever before. She began rising early for prayer and meditation. She began to read the Bible regularly. She began to feel the presence of God at her side, helping her through each day. Leaning on God, one day at a time, she survived years of stress that might have put some of us in a mental hospital. And she did it with grace and dignity, in a life-enhancing way.

372

The great English writer, G. K. Chesterton, was playing a little quiz game with some friends. One question they had to answer was, "If you were cast up alone on a deserted island and had only one choice, what book would you take with you?" One of them immediately said, "The Bible," and gave a very pious reason for his selection. Another said, "A volume of Shakespeare," and gave a very learned reason for wanting Shakespeare. When it came to his turn, Chesterton said, "Well, if I were allowed just one book on that deserted island, I would choose a one-volume manual of instruction for amateur boatbuilders." We can say "Hallelujah" to that because it makes

God, Presence of

us mindful of the New Testament teaching about how God comes to us in Christ at the level of our very practical life. Whatever your hangup—it may be your kids or your spouse or your job or your health or a worry over someone else's problem or some decision you have to make—whatever is bugging you, that is where God will give Himself to you through Jesus Christ, in tangible, concrete ways.

373 (Teaching)

A seminary professor had developed a very close and caring relationship with many of his students. He spent a great deal of time with one student who was experiencing many personal problems. The professor and the student often had after-dinner conversations that extended long into the night. After several of these talks, the student began seeing his problems in a new light. He began to feel good about himself and he asked the professor to join him in a prayer of thanksgiving. Later, in trying to describe the experience to some of his friends, he was hard put to communicate the sense of God's presence he had felt. Finally, he said, "When the professor was praying, I was afraid to put out my hand, lest I touch God." He didn't mean that literally, of course. What he was trying to say was that God's presence was so immediate, so real, that it was almost as though he could reach out and touch Him.

374 (Marriage)

"Emmanuel," Matthew tells us, means "God is with us." Like the selfless lover who commits his entire being to the beloved in the marriage union of two-in-one-flesh, God is with us in the Person of our Lord and Savior, Jesus Christ: in season and out; in sickness and in health; for better or for worse, God is with us.

God, RELATIONSHIP WITH

375

The Danish theologian, Soren Kierkegaard, wrote about a wealthy woman who felt God calling her to the religious life. She felt that she would be able to give up everything, with one exception. She had a garden which was very important to her. It was a place for her to be alone, to be at peace and to renew herself. And she was unable and unwilling to give up the key to her secret garden. What an interesting symbol that is for us! Each of us has a secret garden and we are unwilling to give up the key to God and let Him in. We want God to keep His distance. We haven't yet learned that if we give Him the key to our lives without reservation, He will give life back to us with interest compounded daily.

376

It was said in a novel of many years ago ("Mr. Britting Sees It Through," by H. G. Wells) that "God is the first and the last thing and that until a person finds God and is found by God, he or she begins at no beginning and works to no end."

377 (Jesus, life and ministry of; Jesus, as gift from God)

Imagine for a moment what life would be like if you believed with your whole being that God was against you or, at best, indifferent toward you. Imagine that you believed your life wasn't going anywhere. Imagine that you believed the Creator had cruelly destined you to struggle through life trying to forget that your existence was meaningless. If you can imagine that, then take a full one hundred and eighty-degree turn, and you

201

God, Resurrection Power of

will begin to get the feel of what the Gospel writers are trying to say to us in their stories about Jesus' life and ministry. You will have come full-circle because what they are trying to say is that God is for you, God loves you, God believes in you. What they are trying to say is that Jesus is the supreme gift of a loving God to His beloved human creatures; that Jesus is the gift from God that opens the way to New Life; that Jesus is the gift that keeps on giving—from here to eternity.

378

Francis of Assisi is famous for his great love of nature. He loved birds, for example, whom he called his "sisters." He believed that the birds' singing was their way of praising God. The moon was his "sister," the sun his "brother." He spoke of "brother fox," "brother fire," and so on. But these things are all related to the one thing needful in the life of Francis: his great love for God. Toward the end of his life, he was heard to pray all night long, "My God and my all! My God and my all!"

GOD, RESURRECTION POWER OF

379

It's all there in the lines of the old Spiritual someone has called, "The greatest poem ever written in America":

> Nobody knows the trouble I've seen,
> Nobody knows my sorrow.
> Nobody knows the trouble I've seen,
> Glory, Hallelujah!

Nobody knows the trouble I've seen, but glory hallelujah, God is God. God is a god of Resurrection Power.

380 (Redemption)

Fran Tarkenton, one of football's great quarterbacks, has written a book called "Broken Patterns." The title, of course, alludes to his great skill as a "scrambling" type of quarterback. It happens often that the pattern of an offensive play is broken, either by an offensive player's mistake or by the defensive team's penetration. But a good "scrambling" quarterback can use a broken pattern to gain ground. At one point in the book Fran Tarkenton writes about one of football's great linebackers, Dick Butkus. He said, "Great players make great plays. They change the course of the game. They demoralize the enemy. Butkus has been painted as a dumb football animal, but nothing is further from the truth. He is enormously bright and he never, ever gives up." If you take these two ideas from, of all places, a football book, and put them together, it can help you to see what the Gospel writers are trying to say to us. God has a beautiful pattern laid out for us. We rebel against it, we break it, but God uses the broken patterns. He redeems them. His Resurrection Power is working in and through the broken patterns of our lives. What we need to do is to experience this great thing God is doing and to identify with it. And never, ever, give up! Never give up on the Gospel truth that God will win His victory; God will ultimately fulfill His purpose for mankind—for you and for me.

GOD, RULE OF

381 (Death; World War II)

During World War II, a young Dutchman who was to be executed within a few hours by the Nazis, wrote a farewell letter to his family. The letter was free of any traces of bitterness or hatred. It was clear that in those final hours, God and God alone was at the center of his life. The letter is a powerful

God, Search For

witness to the presence of God in a person's life—so powerful,
that it has been acclaimed as one of the most significant doc-
uments to emerge from the World War II period. It ends with
these words: "God rules everything." To his family whom he
dearly loved, the writer chose those three words to be his last:
God rules everything.

GOD, SEARCH FOR

382 (God, search for)

There was a young Indian boy who came to an old guru and
complained that he could't find God. The old teacher instructed
some of the boy's frineds to take him down to the Ganges River
and hold his head under the water. The boy went along with
it at first because he thought it was a joke. They held his head
under the water so long that he thought they were drowning
him: Those fools! He struggled desperately, frantically, to get
up. And only at the very last moment did they let him up. He
was coughing and choking and sputtering. When he had calmed
down a bit, the old man came up to him and said, "Now what
did you think about when you thought you were drowning?"
And the young man said, "Why I thought about how I had to
breath, I had to have air." And the old man said to him, "When
you want God the way a drowning man wants air—then you
will find Him."

383 (Holocaust; Jewish People; Nazi Concentration Camps)

Elie Wiesel has written many accounts of the pain and suffering
endured by the Jewish people through the ages including, of
course, the horrors of the Nazi concentration camps. Wiesel
tells the story of a certain Jewish official who each day would
visit the synagogue, position himself at the reader'a lectern and
cry out to God, "I have come to inform You, Master of the
Universe, that we are here." Even in the midst of continuing

holocaust, as his people we're being exterminated by the thousands, he would pound the lectern with a determined fist and cry out, "You see, Lord, we are still here." Finally, after the last massacre, he positions himself at the lectern and stares out into the empty synagogue: he is the last living Jew. Then he casts his eyes in the direction of the Ark of the Covenant and gently whispers, "You see, I am still here." Then sadly he asks, "But You, where are You?"

GOD, VOICE OF

384 (Depression; Day of Atonement)

A rabbi was coming to the Day of Atonement in a state of deep depression. (The Day of Atonement, in the tradition of the Hebrew people, is a day of repentance and restoration.) He was depressed; he was lethargic; he was fatigued; he was feeling very down. He was standing in the doorway of his little house and down the road came a shoe cobbler pushing his cart with his tools and his materials on it. And when the cobbler came opposite the rabbi's house and saw him standing in the doorway, he shouted in a very loud voice, "Do you have anything that needs mending?" And the rabbi said it was like the voice of God, because he suddenly saw so clearly what the source of his problem really was. He saw that his life needed mending because God was not at the center.

GOD, WILL OF

385 (Church Attendance; Joy)

A prominent Government official and his several brothers and sisters were raised by their grandmother. He recalls that the grandmother was very strict and insisted that they all go to

Golf

Church every Sunday without exception. If a child rebelled and did not go to Church, the penalty was a triple dose of castor oil. Her theory was that if you didn't have time to go to Church you shouldn't have time to do anything else. "It was years," he says, "before I was able to go to Church without that castor oil feeling." We get that "castor oil feeling" when doing the Will of God means giving up the things we need to give up. It may be a destructive relationship. It may be a passion for money and possessions. It may be a desire to control other people's lives. But, always lurking in the background is the fear of losing the pleasure or the satisfaction we think we are getting from these things. The great breakthrough comes when we realize that genuine joy and satisfaction can come only by seeking the Will of God in these areas of our life.

386   (Aging; Humor)

There was an extremely old man, with a number of health problems, to put it mildly. He suffered from crippling arthritis. He was losing his hearing. He needed surgery for cataracts. He couldn't remember things. He had high blood pressure. Disgustedly, he said to his doctor, "I don't know why God keeps me alive!" The doctor replied, "I'm sure it is because He has something in mind that He wants you to do." The old man thought for a minute, then leaning his full 97 pounds into the doctor and poking his chest with a bony finger, he stamped his foot and snapped, "Well, I'm not going to do it!"

GOLF

387   (Humor)

There is a story about a golfer who set up his ball on the tee, swung mightily and missed. His club hit an ant hill and he killed thousands of ants. He became more and more frustrated as he repeatedly swung and missed. And each time he missed, he slaughtered more ants. Finally, there were just two little ants left. One of them raised his head and hollered over to the other, "It looks like if you want to save your life around here, you'd better get on the ball."

GOOD NEWS

388   (Holy Spirit)

The great Irish poet, William Butler Yeats, said of our confused time: "The center does not hold." The Good News from the Holy Spirit of Truth is that God is the Center and He does hold.

GOOD SAMARITAN

389   (Humor; Religious Education)

A Sunday school teacher told the Good Samaritan story to the class and then asked the children, "What would you do if you were walking along the road and saw a person who was terribly beaten and bruised and covered with blood?" One little girl answered, "I'd probably throw up!" The next question is, "After you have thrown up, what do you do?"

GOSSIP

390 (Clergy; Parish Life)

A certain town had four churches: Lutheran, Roman Catholic, Methodist and Baptist. One Spring day, the four local pastors happened to meet by chance in the village park. They sat on a bench and began to share in confidence some of their parish experiences and personal problems. Said the Lutheran Minister, "Perhaps you can help me with a problem I've been having recently. You see, I've taken to gambling." This evoked a gasp from the other three. The Roman Catholic Priest said, "I must tell you that lately I have been drinking a little too much." There was a second gasp. The Methodist Minister then said, "Lately I find myself preoccupied with an attractive married woman in the parish." This was followed by a third gasp. Finally, the Baptist Minister said, "I hesitate to tell you this, but my problem is I'm an incurable gossip."

GRACE

391 (Parish Life)

A very holy man who had served for many years in a big downtown parish decided to shift gears in his middle-age by settling down as pastor to a small, rural congregation. This is the way he tells the story of his first, big, country meal in a parishioner's home.

> The eating was so good, it was almost sinful: baked
> ham and fried chicken and roast beef; sweet po-
> tatoes and mashed potatoes; vegetable casseroles
> fairly dripping with butter; fresh-baked bread and

rolls; and for dessert, hot blueberry pie topped with huge wedges of home-made vanilla ice cream. But all through that meal something was bothering me. I just couldn't enjoy it. All during the dinner I heard the obvious sound of running water. And it really bugged me. Back in the city that sound was bad news: someone had left a tap open and the sink or tub was about to overflow; or there was a leak in the plumbing and the ceiling was about to cave in. For two hours I listened to little else but that sound of running water. However, since it was my first visit to the parishioner's home I was reluctant to say anything. Finally, I could no longer contain myself. So I asked about it. With a smile, my host explained the situation to me. It seems that forty years before, when the people had built the farmhouse, they discovered a spring of water right in the center of their property. So they built a spring-room around it and then designed the house around the spring-room. And for forty years, the people who lived in the house had been refreshed and nourished by this spring of water that was welling up right at the center of their home. I thought to myself, "That's what Jesus is constantly trying to tell us: that it is possible for us to build the rooms of our lives around the life-giving spring water of God's Grace."

392 (Fulfillment)

An ancient Oriental story tells of a little fish swimming along the edge of the river. Nearby on the river bank a science teacher has assembled his class for an instruction on "water." As the fish swims by it hears the teacher speak: "Water is absolutely necessary to life. Without water we would all perish within a week's time." "Golly," says the fish, "If what that man said is

Grace

true, I'd better find some of that substance called 'water' or I shall die in a few days." It asks every other little fish it sees where water might be found, but none of them knows. Then it puts the question to some older, larger fish, but they are more interested in food for the day. Some think the little fish is crazy: "Go away and let us alone," they say in fish language. From stream to stream the frightened fish carries its quest, but in vain, until finally it comes upon a fish who seems wiser than the rest. "Please, where can I find the substance called water that will give me life?" "Water?" replies the wise old fish. "You are in water this very minute. You were conceived and born in water. Water is your environment. Water supports your very life. Draw on it and you will live."

We too are immersed in a precious substance on which our life's fulfillment depends. Like that little fish, we are born and conceived in it, our lives are sustained by it, we eat, sleep, work and play in it—we are immersed in it. Like that little fish who couldn't see the water for the river, we fail to recognize it and we wait longingly to encounter it . . . and we wait . . . and we wait.

In theology, the word for this precious, life-giving substance is Grace: the Grace of God. In plain language, "Grace" means that God is continually doing for us everything we need to have done for our life's fulfillment—whether we know it or not, whether we appreciate it or not, whether we are worthy of it or not, whether we recognize it or not.

393 (Bible; Good News; Humor)

On one of San Francisco's streets there was a store-front funeral parlor with some beige-colored curtains covering the windows. In front of the curtains there was a sign which read, "Why walk around half dead when we can bury you for ninety-eight dollars." That was a sharp piece of advertising because a lot of people these days are ready to take them up on the offer. But there is a better way to ask the question. And every one of the

Biblical writers, each in his own way, asks the very same question: "Why do you walk around half dead when there is a way of replenishing your strength?" You see, a part of the Good News of the Bible is that the God who created us didn't just create us and then let us be. The God who created us always gives us the Grace to do what must be done. Always and without exception! The biblical writers were aware of this and they rejoiced in it.

394

When John Newton, the composer of "Amazing Grace," received an assignment that took him from a small country Church to a big Church in London, he offered a fervent prayer for "London Grace." When asked what he meant by "London Grace," he replied, with a twinkle in his eye, "London Grace is a Grace of a very high degree; a very intense Grace; a very special Grace; a Grace strong enough to make it possible for me to live a Christian life, even in London."

395 (God, goodness of; God, love of; Hope)

A theologian, about to retire, was reminiscing on his life as a scholar. "The longer I live," he said, "the more value I put on God's sheer Grace, which I take simply to be what by our human standards we would call His 'extravagant goodness.' The utter persistence of His Love: it is our sole hope."

GRATITUDE

396 (Children)

A little boy was looking forward with great anticipation to the annual birthday gift from his favorite aunt. She always had a way of picking out a toy which brought him a great deal of pleasure. Apparently, she had decided her nephew was old enough to start receiving clothing instead of toys, because she sent him a sweater. The little boy sat down and dutifully wrote his "thank you" note: "Dear Aunt Jane: Thank you for the sweater. It is what I've always wanted—but not very much. Love, Johnny."

GRIEF

397 (Healing; Mercy; Service)

A woman lost her husband and went into an extended grief period. She took flowers to the cemetery weekly. She secluded herself, dropped out of organizations and activities. Her doctor became very concerned about her. Symptoms of physical illness began to appear. One day, he told her about two of his patients in a nearby hospital. They did not have families to visit them. They were alone in the world. The doctor said to the grieving woman, "Next Sunday, instead of taking flowers to the cemetery, why don't you take them to those two lonely patients of mine in the hospital? Just say 'Hello' to them, and see if they need anything, see what you can do for them." Somewhat reluctantly, the woman did as her doctor suggested. And by that simple little act, the logjam was broken. It melted the ice around her heart. It washed away the bitterness. More and more often she took the flowers to the hospital instead of the cemetery. She found that the healing power of God, which she had been resisting, had broken through, and she was cured of the kind of destructive grief that had been diminishing her life. And all because of a simple act of mercy.

398   (Death)

A husband and wife whose six-month-old baby had died were grief-stricken. The death occurred in Pakistan where the couple was living at the time. A kind and wise old Punjabi who heard of their grief came to comfort them. "A tragedy like this," he said, "is just like being plunged into boiling water. If you are an egg, your affliction will make you hard-boiled and unresponsive. If you are a potato, you will emerge soft and pliable, resilient, and adaptable. "The mother took these words to her heart and carried them with her over the years. She now says, "It may sound funny to God, but there have been many times when I have prayed, 'O Lord, please let me be a potato'."

GROWTH

399   (Change; God, wisdom of)

> God said, "Build a better world"
>   and I said, "How?
> The world is such a cold dark place
>   and so complicated now!
> And I so tired and useless,
>   there's nothing I can do."
> But God in all His wisdom said:
>   "Just build a better you!"

400   (Human Potential; Humor)

The sexton of a large Church lost his job because he couldn't read or write. It seems that people were leaving written instructions for him which he couldn't read. Consequently, things

213

Growth

weren't getting done and the job just wasn't working out. Finally, he was dismissed. But he was a very enterprising man. He went into business for himself and soon became very successful. So successful was he that when he applied to the bank for a loan to expand his business, the bank official who reviewed his financial statement was impressed. When he discovered that the man was illiterate, he was simply astonished. "Good heavens, man," he said, "you've done all of this and you are illiterate? Just imagine where you would be if you could read and write!" The ex-sexton replied, "Yup, I'd be janitor of the Methodist Church."

401 (Power)

At Amherst College, researchers experimented with a squash seed that had been planted in rich, fertile soil. Eventually the seed produced a squash as big as a soccer ball. Then the researchers placed a steel band around the squash. Attached to the steel band was a device for measuring "lifting power." As the squash continued to grow and to stretch the steel band, it reached a lifting power of 500 pounds. Amazing! Within two months the lifting power went up to 1,500 pounds. A month later it was 2,000 pounds. It was not until the lifting power had reached an incredible 5,000 pounds that the rinds broke. When the squash was opened, the researchers discovered that it had built up a whole network of tough fibers to fight against the pressure that was binding its growth. Moreover, the roots supporting the squash had reached out some eighty thousand feet in every direction searching for more and more nourishment to strengthen the fibers.

402 (Fear)

During one of America's darkest hours Abraham Lincoln bouyed up his aides' spirits with this story from his youth:

Growth

When I was a small boy, I had a terrible fear of the dark. I always tried to get to sleep before nightfall. One night my father taught me this simple lesson. We were fixing harnesses in the barn, and my father asked me to go to the shed for more supplies. I stood at the barn door frozen in fear of the dark night. My father came up to me and said, "Pick up the lantern. What do you see?" "The oak tree," I answered. "Is there anything between you and the oak tree?" "No." "Then walk to the tree and lift the lantern again . . . What do you see?" "The mulberry bush." "Walk to it and lift the lantern again." By the time I'd gotten to the bush, I'd figured out the procedure. And so I made my way, step by step, from tree to bush to coop to shed and finally to the supplies. It was a simple lesson, but it can take you a mighty long way.

403 (God, greatness of)

St. Mark's Cathedral, in Venice, stands in mosaic splendor paying silent tribute to the Byzantine and Lombard artists and others who created it. And yet, as you look at it, you become aware of the problem of trying, over the years, to fit their diverse works together into a unified whole. Although the cathedral gives the impression of an unfinished, rough, uneven, unpolished work, nevertheless it stands as a powerful symbol of the greatness of God. It stands also as a powerful symbol of God's human creatures. Rough, uneven, unfinished and unpolished as it may be, mankind is, nevertheless, God's masterwork. All of us are subject to further shaping and fashioning by the Divine Artist. To become what God intends us to become when He gives us life, we all need our share of "finishing touches."

GUIDANCE

404 (Direction; God, presence of)

The story is told of a man on a journey to a distant city. Being unfamiliar with the route, he became confused and took the wrong road. When he realized his predicament, he stopped his car and asked a passing stranger, "Can you help me, I am lost?" "Where are you headed?" the stranger asked. "I'm going to Duluth," the traveller answered. To which, the stranger replied, "Then you are not lost. You know where you're going. You just need directions."

We, who gather 'round the Table of the Lord, must not imagine ever that we are lost. That's the whole point of the gathering. In Jesus, God, our Father, is present among us. Through Jesus, He assures us that we are never abandoned. From Jesus, we well know where we're going. But, in the Name of Jesus, let us all admit we need directions. "Speak Lord, your servant is listening!"

405 (Star of Bethlehem; Wise Men)

A great artist once painted a picture in which a solitary figure is seen rowing a small boat across the dark waters of a lonely lake. A high wind is churning up the waters causing white-crested billows to rage ominously around the tiny skiff. As he rows on, the boatsman's eyes are fixed on the one lone star shining through the darkness. Under the picture, the artist has inscribed these words: "If I lose that, I am lost." In the manner of that dauntless boatsman, our mission is to keep our eyes fixed on a certain star as we travel along life's way. We join with the Wise Men from the East as the Star of Bethlehem guides us along the way to the place of the Savior's birth.

216

406 (Love)

In the "Jonathan Livingston Seagull" story by Richard Bach,
an old teacher named Chiang greatly influences Jonathan's life.
When Chiang is about to leave Jonathan forever he says it all
in five words: "Jonathan, keep working on love." God's guidance is what makes it possible for us to find our own special
corner of the sky. God's guidance is what makes it possible for
us to "Keep working on love."

407 (Humor)

A traveling clergyman in a strange town asked a young man
the way to the post office. When the obliging boy gave him the
necessary directions, the preacher thanked him, then added,
"You seem to be a bright young man. How would you like to
listen to my sermon tonight so that I may show you the way
to heaven?" "You're going to show me the way to heaven?"
the boy asked, "Why you don't even know the way to the post
office!"

408

It was a very foggy night off the Coast of Maine. Two beautiful
sailing sloops were making their way, hopefully, into Cape Por-
poise Harbor for safety. The first of the boats was manned by
two seasoned sailors. In the second boat, following close behind, was a honeymoon couple who had worked for two years
outfitting their boat for this, its maiden voyage. As the husband
said later, "It was like a doll's house inside." The first boat
took a wrong turn in the fog, the second boat followed and, in
a matter of minutes, they were on the rocks of Folly Island.
Both boats were smashed to bits. Fortunately, none of the four
persons was injured seriously. A few days later, in perfectly
clear weather, an oil tanker steamed into the bay and took on
a harbor pilot—a man who knows his business. The pilot im-

Guidance

mediately misguided the ship up on the rocks. One hundred thousand gallons of crude oil spilled out, killing the wildlife and polluting hundreds of miles of the Maine Coast. Think about this: experienced, competent, well-intentioned people led other people right up on the rocks. How often it is that with the best of intentions we give advice to our children or our friends and lead them right up on the rocks.

409 (Jesus, guidance of)

The film, "Star Wars," became one of the most popular, most profitable movies ever made. Those who have seen it know that the producers may well have had in mind only one purpose: to make a popular movie that would make money. In that sense they succeeded. However, some viewers—including several professional reviewers and critics—have seen in the film a symbolism of deep religious significance. To read meaning into a film that seems to have been produced purely as an entertainment is a risky business and film reviewers, like the reviewers of literature, proceed at their own risk when they try to interpret in this way. There was a highly symbolic moment in "Star Wars" when, in that last, great inter-Gallactic Armageddon, Luke Skywalker (who is fighting for the Force) switches off the computer and relies upon direct guidance from the Force. Let us now look to Jesus for direct guidance, as we fight the good fight. By following His signs we will discover how to win over the Devil. See!: He heals the sick, He feeds the hungry, He gives drink to the thirsty, He forgives His persecutors, He casts out demons.

410 (Humor)

It was on the eve of the great 1938 New England hurricane that a man living in the Stamford, Connecticut suburbs decided to fulfill a long-standing desire. He walked two miles to the Abercrombie and Fitch department store in downtown Stamford and bought a fine barometer. Delighted with his acquisition, he hurried home and proudly hung it on his living room wall. But what he saw made him very angry: the barometer reading indicated "Hurricane!" Convinced that he had been sold a defective instrument, he walked back to Abercrombie and Fitch, handed the barometer to the sales clerk, and snorted, "Fine barometer you sold me. I put it up in my house and what do you suppose it registered? "Hurricane!"" To which the sales clerk replied, "No problem, sir. We'll replace it with a perfect one." Again the man headed for home with his new barometer, but by the time he arrived there, his house had been blown away.

411 (Service)

The late Thomas Merton once wrote that whenever he found himself struggling to identify with God's Will in a given situation, he always resolved the problem by asking himself this simple question: "What is best for the folks around me?" Because we are made in God's image and likeness, because we can allow God to express Himself through us in any given situation, we have the potential to ask the simple question, "What is best for the folks around me?"

GUILT

412 (Christ, cross of; Forgiveness; God, grace of; Healing)

A new product called "Disposable Guilt Bags" appeared in the marketplace. It consisted of a set of ten ordinary brown bags on which were printed the following instructions: "Place the bag securely over your mouth, take a deep breath and blow all your guilt out, then dispose of the bag immediately." The wonder of this is that the Associated Press reported that 2500 kits

Halloween

had been quickly sold at $2.50 per kit. Would that we could dispose of our guilt so easily. There is nothing on this earth powerful enough in itself to dispose of our guilt. We cannot fix ourselves, which is what many of us are trying to do. That which makes it possible to be forgiven, to be cleansed, to be healed, that which makes it possible for us to receive our life back again, fresh and clean and new, is the power of God's Grace in the Cross of Jesus Christ.

413 (Forgiveness; Pardon)

In the time of Andrew Jackson, a Presidential pardon was given to a man who had been imprisoned for a serious crime. The man had a deep sense of guilt. He felt that he should remain to pay for the crime he had committed. And so he refused the pardon. He insisted on staying in prison. The lawyers of the time engaged in a famous debate as they tried to determine whether a pardon that had been refused was really a pardon. They finally decided that until it is accepted it is no pardon at all. But that is the way it is between you and God. In His great love for you He offers you the pardon, the Grace, the wholeness of life. He gives you the fruits of the Cross! But the question is, will you accept it?

HALLOWEEN

414 (Children; Humor)

On Halloween night, a neighborhood "practical joker" wore a costume designed to frighten the young "trick-or-treaters" who rang his doorbell. He wore a floor-length black cape, a black hat fitted with devil's horns, and a hideous mask that seemed to combine the most gruesome features of "Dracula," "Frankenstein," and the "Wolf Man." When his doorbell rang, he turned off all the lights and, shining a flashlight on his mask, he opened the door and pierced the night air with an eerie scream. Then he looked down and saw standing before him a tiny, golden-haired, five-year-old, dressed as a dainty fairy. The little tyke stared wide-eyed for a moment. Then as she raised her eyes up along the massive black cape and looked straight into the hideous mask, she smiled and said, "Is your mommy home?"

HANDICAPPED

415 (Service)

Together, nine physically handicapped persons conquered Mount Ranier. One of the mountain-climbers had an artificial leg. Another was an epileptic. Two were deaf, and five were blind. Despite these handicaps, the nine successfully negotiated the 14,000-foot climb and got back down again. Asked how they managed to perform this amazing feat, one of the blind members of the party said simply, "We had a lot of help from each other on the trip." There is no way, the Gospels tell us, that we can successfully negotiate our life's journey without a lot of help from each other. And the reason is, we are all handicapped. We are all emotionally and spiritually flawed in some way.

HAPPINESS

416

The clue to finding happiness is to stop looking for it, to forget about it. You must lose your life to find it. Self-seeking is doomed

Happiness

to failure. The question that leads to happiness is not "What do I want?" but "What is wanted of me?"

417 (God, peace of)

There was a wealthy man who, in his old age, was asked to recall the happiest experience of his life. He said, "It was when I was in a hospital in a strange town, seriously ill for three weeks with typhoid fever." When his listeners expressed surprise that this was the happiest situation of his life, he continued: "The hospital was understaffed and overcrowded with patients. It was a difficult time for everyone. But there was one nurse who never let it get her down, who treated each one of us patients as if we were royalty. Every time she came into my room, I felt a deep sense of peace. I have never felt anything like it since and I have never forgotten her. It was the happiest period of my life in spite of the physical suffering." This is what Jesus Christ is saying to us. Every time we go into a room we bring the peace of God. He has given us the power to be like that. Not only do we receive the gift from the Risen Christ we receive the power to share it.

418 (Despair; Possessions)

An ancient legend tells of a king who was deeply troubled, weary of life. He withdrew more and more into himself, trying to escape from reality. Finally, members of his family consulted with the official wise man of the Royal Court. "How can we bring joy back into his life?" they asked. After talking with the king and studying his depression, the wise man announced that if the king would wear a happy person's shirt for one week, his spirits would be renewed and he would be happy again. Immediately, the Royal family began to search for a happy person. None could be found at Court, so they went out among the people to look. Again they searched in vain. Then they came upon a beggar lying under a tree. The man's face bore a look of utter serenity. He seemed totally at peace. "Are you a happy man?" they asked. "Oh, yes," the beggar replied, "my soul is filled with joy." They asked him if there was anything he needed or wanted. "Oh no," he replied, "I am quite content." Then they told him of their mission and asked if they might have his shirt for the king. At this the beggar laughed heartily and, as he arose from the dry leaves that covered him, said, "I have no shirt!"

419 (Humor)

Most of us have experienced what happens to motorists when one of those huge graders goes to work on a highway repair job. When the machine is operating on a busy road, traffic is halted and the cars lined up in opposite directions are allowed to proceed alternately. A veteran operator of one of those big machines decided one day to try to relieve the tension that inevitably results from such a traffic backup. Consequently on both the front and rear of his grader a sign now appears, declaring, "The Road To Happiness Is Almost Always Under Construction."

HEALING

420 (Humor)

A good anthology of "American Humor" will likely contain at least one story portraying a New England farmer as a "man of few words." In one such story, two neighboring Maine farmers—"Clem" and "Luke"—engage in the following verbal exchange:

> Luke: Mornin'.
> Clem: What did you give your horse when he had the colic?

Healing

> Luke: Turpentine.
> Clem: Thanks.

End of conversation. A few weeks later, the two meet again:

> Clem: You said you gave your horse turpentine
> for the colic.
> Luke: Yep!
> Clem: I gave mine turpentine and it died.
> Luke: So did mine.

421 (God, presence of; Service)

An inner-city health clinic, sponsored partly by Church funds, was blessed with the volunteer services of a doctor and two nurses from the local parish. These three dedicated Christians had decided to devote one full year of their lives to this mission. It was not only physical medicine they were giving to the people, it was an unusual caring quality they were offering. One night an old man was carried in on a stretcher. He was a skid-row type: alcoholic, dirty, smelly. It takes an experience like this to discover how badly a human being in this condition can smell. The man's leg was a mass of infection. He had suffered an injury and allowed it to go unattended for days. When he was brought in, one of the volunteer nurses immediately knelt beside the stretcher and began to clean the wound and prepare it for the doctor who had been summoned. Next to her stood a newspaper reporter. He had been assigned to do a feature story on the health clinic. Feeling sick from the ugly sight and the unbearable stench, he turned away from the stretcher. With his back turned, he said to the nurse kneeling at the stretcher, "I wouldn't do that for a million dollars." And the nurse replied quietly, "Neither would I." Not for a million dollars, but because we have experienced the living Presence of God loving us; because we have this burning desire, through our servant ministry, to share that Presence with the world!

422 (Humor)

A farmer owned a mule that was very important to him because it was a good plowing animal. The mule got sick one day and the farmer called in a veterinarian. The "vet" looked the mule over, then gave the farmer some extremely large pills. "Give the mule one of these pills three times a day and he'll recover," said the vet. "How do I get those big pills down the mule's throat?" asked the farmer. "Easy," replied the vet. "Find a piece of pipe with a bore large enough to fit the pill into, then put one end of the pipe inside the mule's mouth, put the pill into the pipe, and blow in the other end. Before the mule knows what's happening, he'll swallow the pill." It seemed like a good idea, but in a few hours the farmer presented himself at the veterinarian's office looking terribly sick himself. "You look awful, what happened?" asked the veterinarian. The farmer replied, "The mule blew first."

HEALTH

423 (Humor; Lifestyle)

A cartoon depicts a man saying to a friend, "I worked so hard to make a fortune that I ruined my health. Then I spent the fortune trying to get my health back."

424 (Humor)

A middle-aged man decided to visit a clinic and undergo a complete health checkup. He told the interviewing doctor that he had always taken good care of himself. He said, "I always see to it that I have adequate rest. I exercise regularly. I believe in good nutrition. And I take vitamins C, E and B6 every day." Later, after he had been looked over from head-to-toe by a team of specialists and was waiting for his post-examination interview, he accidently saw the medical history which had been set down in the first interview. In the place labelled, "Deformities," the doctor had written, "Health Nut!"

HEAVEN

425 (Hell; God, relationship with)

There is symbolic truth in the notion of heaven and hell as geographical locations, but it is important for us to recognize that when the question about what happens when our physical bodies die comes before Jesus, he does not speak in these terms. What He talks about is God. He is saying that we must think of heaven and hell in terms of our position in relation to God. The thing in your life that is most important is God—knowing God, being present to God, entering more deeply every day into your love relationship with God, nurturing your relationship with God. Jesus therefore says that when you begin to think about afterlife, just keep on thinking the same way. Heaven is being with God. Hell is being estranged from God and, worst of all, knowing that you are separated from Him. When you think of heaven, think of God. That is all we need to know of heaven. That is all we are given to know of heaven.

426 (Children; Humor)

Will we play games in heaven? Will we have to eat in heaven? Will we need to sleep in heaven? Do you remember those childhood days of earliest exposure to the idea of afterlife and bodily resurrection? In our innocence, it seemed terribly important to get an answer to the question, "As it is on earth, will it be in heaven?" A mother once reported receiving one of those heavenly queries from her five-year-old son who wondered over the following weighty problem: "Mom," the boy asked. "Is God stronger than Superman?"

427   (Travel)

Someone has said that heaven is like this: You land at the airport and there is God waiting to greet you. If you are a travelling person, you are also familiar with the sinking feeling that comes when you try to show people pictures of the places you've been. "Who would like to see my slides?" you ask. And there is silence. All travellers have that problem with their family and friends. Consequently, for the photography nut who travels a lot, the airport imagery describing heaven is uniquely beautiful: not only is God at the airport saying "Welcome! How was your trip?" God also says, "I would like to see your slides."

HELL

428   (Mount Vesuvius; Travel)

A group of American tourists were visiting Mount Vesuvius in Italy at a time when that volcano was in one of its active periods. One woman who was completely awed by the seething mass of lava and steam, cried out, "It is just like hell!" One of the Italian villagers standing nearby turned to a friend and said, "My goodness, these American tourists, they've been everywhere!"

429   (Heaven)

"What does it profit a man"—this frantic pursuit of what we have been conditioned to call "happiness"? A man named John Balderson wrote a play in which a man dies and passes into

Hero

the next world. When he opens his eyes he sees laid out before him more beauty and luxury than he ever dreamed possible, more than he ever dared hope for. He found himself in a state of being in which every wish was granted instantly. At the slightest whim, an attendant would appear to see that it was immediately fulfilled. After a time he grew restless, bored. "If only something different would happen," he said to himself. "If only, just once, there would be a refusal." Finally, the monotony became unbearable and he summoned the attendant saying, "I want something that I can't have unless I earn it." "Sorry," the attendant replied, "that's the one wish we cannot grant here." "Very well," the man said, then let me out of here. I would rather be in hell." Whereupon, the attendant asked, "And where do you think you are, sir?"

HERO

430   (Honesty; Humor; Imagemaking)

A man walked into a fast-food establishment and ordered a ham and cheese sandwich. The girl behind the counter seemed puzzled. "Oh," she said finally, "You mean a 'Yumbo'." "That's right," the man said, "a ham and cheese." "It's called a 'Yumbo'," the girl insisted, "now do you want a Yumbo or not?" Bracing himself, the man said, "Yes, thank you. The ham and cheese." "Look," said the girl, "I've got to have an order here. You're holding up the line. You want a Yumbo, don't you?" Whereupon, the man turned and walked out the door. Symbolically, at least, a modern hero. A slice of ham between two pieces of bread is a ham sandwich. Add a slice of cheese and it's a ham and cheese sandwich. It's straightforward. It's honest. It's what our hero wanted—without the gimmickry. The imagemakers could keep their Yumbo. Our hero would not sell out.

HESITATION

431

A famous aerial acrobat suffered a terrible fall from his high trapeze, narrowly escaping death. In a bedside interview at the hospital, he stated that after his bones mended he would try to resume his career. Asked how he felt about the risk of another accident, he replied, "Oh, I don't fear that happening ever again. I know exactly what happened and why. I got what I deserved, because I hesitated. Once you get into a pattern and set everything in motion, success or failure depends on whether or not you keep up your end of the deal. I took a second or so too long in my leap, you see, and I upset the pattern—so I was late getting to where I was supposed to be. Hesitation is the number one killer in our business."

HISTORY

432 (Truths)

When Sir Walter Raleigh was imprisoned in the Tower of London, he decided to pass the time by writing a history of the world. He had filled about two hundred pages when, one morning, he was interrupted by a loud commotion coming from the prison courtyard. It seems that two prisoners working there had entered into a violent argument. Several blows were struck. Inmates clung to the bars of their cell windows and yelled gibes and words of encouragement until the guards pulled the fighting prisoners apart to avoid mayhem. When the prisoners assembled for mess that noon, they talked of nothing but the fight. Sir Walter Raleigh listened attentively to no less than eight different versions of the encounter. No two stories were the same! As soon as he returned to his quarters in the tower,

Hobbies

Sir Walter took his manuscript of the history of the world, tore it up, and threw it into the fire.

HOBBIES

433 (Ambition; Humor)

It was reported in "Sports Illustrated" magazine that athletes who intended to participate in the National AAU track and field championships were required to fill out a questionnaire. Among the questions were, "What is your hobby?" and "What is your ambition?" One Olympic distance-runner answered, "My hobby is taking apart my Volkswagon . . . My ambition is to be able to put it back together."

HOLY SPIRIT

434 (God, law of; Obedience)

The "Fable of the Birds" is a story about Creation. All the newly-made animals were walking around discovering what it was like to be alive. All except the birds. They were doing nothing but complaining because God had given them a heavy burden that He had given no other animal: those awkward appendages on their shoulders. God must be punishing them somehow. Why did they have to carry these things around, making it hard to walk? "Why?" they asked. "Why us?" Finally, two or three of the more adventurous birds began to move their appendages, to flutter them, and soon they discovered that the very thing they had regarded as a burden actually made it possible for them to fly. And no other animals could fly. The "heavy burden" turned out to be a beautiful gift. Many of us act like those silly birds. We regard God's call to obedience as an awkward appendage to our lives—weighing us down. Thou shalt not! Thou shalt! Heavy burden it is until we discover that God's Law is really the wind of the Holy Spirit, enabling us to fly as no other creature can fly.

435   (Celebration; Pentecost)

There was a man who lived back in the sixteenth century called Lorenzo D'Medici. He was one of the better members of the famous (sometimes infamous) D'Medici family. They called him "Lorenzo the Magnificent" because he was a celebrator of the first magnitude. He would stage huge pageants and public spectacles at religious festival times. And all the people of the City of Florence would become involved in the celebration. On one occasion, he decided to stage the pageant of Pentecost in one of the city's great Churches. He liked realism in his drama and, consequently, he arranged for a system of wires and pulleys coming down from the ceiling so that, at a given time, real fire would come swooshing down. Unfortunately, the entire project backfired. On the day of Pentecost, as the great pageant unfolded, the fire came swooshing down right on cue. But it brushed against some flimsy stage hangings, igniting them. And the Church burned to the ground.

436   (Kingdom of God; New Life; Sermon on the Mount)

A young Hindu student was attending a course on the "Sermon on the Mount," also attended by a young Christian seminary student. The two became friends and they began a long series of discussions concerning whether it was even possible to live according to Christ's teachings. The Hindu student, although he was very impressed with the "Sermon on the Mount," and although he knew that to a large extent Mahatma Ghandi's life had been patterned on it, nevertheless felt that ordinary people simply could not live this way. And he was deeply troubled by

Honesty

this feeling. On the last day of the semester the two students argued the question all through the night. The next morning, the Hindu student came to his young Christian friend and said to him, "I've been thinking about it constantly since last night's talk, and I've decided that if God would give man a new heart, then he could live this way." What the Gospel writers are saying is that by the power of the Holy Spirit we are given a new heart—and New Life.

437 (Future; Happiness)

Many years ago, in the cornerstone for its new office building, a large insurance company placed a number of predictions by community leaders as to what life in the United States would be like fifty years hence. Among the forecasts was one by a leading industrialist. He made some eyebrow-raising predictions concerning population, the economy and living standards. Then he added this wise reminder: "Fifty years from now, and five hundred years from now, men and women will still struggle for happiness—which will continue to lie within themselves." Our happiness lies within ourselves because within ourselves dwells the Holy Spirit of God.

HONESTY

438 (Humor)

Mark Twain once told the following story in a speech he delivered on "honesty." "When I was a boy, I was walking along a street and happened to spy a cart full of watermelons. I was fond of watermelon, so I sneaked quietly up to the cart and snitched one. Then I ran into a nearby alley and sank my teeth into the melon. No sooner had I done so, however, than a strange feeling came over me. Without a moment's hesitation, I made

232

my decision. I walked back to the cart, replaced the melon—
and took a ripe one."

439   (Humor; Sin; Virtue)

A young man filled out an application for admission to a University. In response to a request to "List your personal strengths,"
he wrote, "Sometimes I am trustworthy, loyal, helpful, friendly,
courteous, kind, obedient, cheerful, thrifty, brave, clean and
reverent." Where the form said, "List Your Weaknesses," he
wrote: "Sometimes I am not trustworthy, loyal, helpful, friendly,
courteous, kind, obedient, cheerful, thrifty, brave, clean and
reverent."

440   (Death; New Life)

A man came back from a weekend retreat experience and when
a friend asked him how it was, he said, "I died!" The friend
asked him what he meant. "You see," the man answered, "I
went to this thing not knowing what to expect. But in the
process of that long weekend, I discovered that I had spent my
whole life hiding behind a lot of masks. I realized that I had
never even let my wife see me as I really was. I'd been playing
games with her, and playing games with my children, and
playing games with others—never letting anybody know who
I really am. The worst of it was to discover that even I didn't
know myself. I was not in touch with my own honest feelings
about myself. And, as all of this was being exposed over the
weekend, I died over and over again." It is a painful thing for
a middle-aged man to discover that he is not even in touch
with his own honest feelings about himself. "I am convinced,"
he said, "that I had to go through this death experience in order
to become the new person that I hope to be now." Unless a
grain of wheat falls to earth and dies, it remains alone. But if
it dies, it bears rich fruit.

HOPE

441 (Death; Healing; Rehabilitation)

The late Muriel Lester was an amazing woman. As a teenager she quit the busy round of social life in London and rented a humble room because she wanted to serve the poor. Out of this small beginning came "Kingsley Hall," a rehabilitation center that has restored health and hope to a great many people. Because Muriel Lester especially was concerned about the problem of alcohol, she built Kingsley Hall in the midst of an area containing no less than thirty saloons. She was so effective at bringing rehabilitation and hope to others that people came from all over the world to study with her, and to learn from her. As she moved into advanced years, her concern about our world-situation deepened. A letter she wrote to a friend in the U. S. reflects this. She wrote, in part:

> How can the world recover? Is it moving its last time around the sun? I know God has other worlds and, probably, wonderful beings, managing better than we to preserve their world from the absurd super-sensitivity and pride that start us grumbling and pitying ourselves—and resenting others so much that eventually it leads to the murder and torture of children via war. I will interrupt this letter while I get ready for Church. I must not hurry at all—ever—else the pain comes. What a lot we learn as our bodies grow older and more stubborn! But what a wonderful increase of joy and serenity!

This excerpt reflects a deeply sensitive Christian woman's concern about our world and her feeling about the end of the world (which the Bible talks so much about). But the really poignant thing about the letter is the postcript, added by her nurse. It reads, "Half an hour after writing this letter, Muriel Lester died. She was writing about the end of the world not knowing that while she wrote, she was making her own last turn around the sun."

But these concerns were always against the background of shining hope. Three years before her death, she had experienced a severe heart attack. The doctor gave her an injection, with little hope that she could survive. But with a visible burst of energy, she opened her eyes, looked quizzically around and winked at him—a sign that all was well. In another of her last letters she said:

> How marvelously sufficient are God's ways! He turns the temptation to despair to a sense of harmony and joy. He turns even the palest shadow of that demon, self-pity, into new and delightful experiences. He turns the outworn experiences of silly little personal regrets into total and grateful acceptance of life.

And then she cried out:

> God save this beauteous and precious planet from destruction! GOD IS ABLE!

What a joyous example this is of Our Lord's teaching on the end time. As His followers we are never without hope. Even when we are making our last turn around the sun.

442 (Freedom; Nazi Concentration Camps)

At a University Music Department, there was a piano teacher whom the students simply and affectionately called "Herman". One night at a University concert, a distinguished piano player suddenly became ill while performing an extremely difficult piece. No sooner had the artist retired from the stage when Herman rose from his seat in the audience, walked onstage,

Hope

sat down at the piano and with great mastery completed the performance. Later that evening, at a party, one of the students asked Herman how he was able to perform such a demanding piece so beautifully without notice and with no rehearsal. He replied, "In 1939, when I was a budding young concert pianist, I was arrested and placed in a Nazi concentration camp. Putting it mildly, the future looked bleak. But I knew that in order to keep the flicker of hope alive that I might someday play again, I needed to practice every day. I began by fingering a piece from my repertoire on my bare-board bed late one night. The next night I added a second piece and soon I was running through my entire repertoire, and I did this every night for five years. It so happens that the piece I played tonight at the concert hall was part of that repertoire. That constant practice is what kept my hope alive. Everyday I renewed my hope that I would one day be able to play my music again on a real piano, and in freedom."

443 (God, power of; World War II)

A famous American preacher was invited to England to give a sermon at St. Andrew's Parish, located out on the edge of London. And, for many years thereafter, whenever he recalled the experience, he spoke of a conversation he had had with an elderly member of St. Andrew's congregation: a man in his eighties. The old man told him what it was like on the nights of the great World War II bombing raids, especially on the night that for him was the worst of all. He said that as he stood in St. Andrew's churchyard looking out over the City of London, he could see the whole central part of the city in flame. The sky was filled with black smoke, as far as he could see. With tears in his eyes, the old man said:

> It seemed to me that everything was lost—the War, England, all the values of civilization. I found myself asking, again and again, "Is there any

hope?" I found myself crying like a baby. But then, there was a sudden gust of wind, for just a moment. And it blew the smoke away just long enough for me to see the Cross of Christ atop the dome of St. Paul's. And the instant I saw it, I felt a surge of hope within me. And I stopped weeping, because I knew once again that there is a power that is greater than all the powers of evil, a power that would see us through and that would live on.

444 (Despair; Nazi Concentration Camps; World War II; Worthwhileness)

Dr. Viktor Frankl was one of the several million Jews who experienced the horrors of Nazi concentration camps during World War II. He personally suffered much, and was an eyewitness to the torturing, incinerating, shooting and gassing of his fellow prisoners. But through it all, he also was a keen observer of the conduct of those who survived. In his book entitled "Man's Search for Meaning," Dr. Frankl reports that the majority were overcome by their situation of hopelessness and defeat. Faced with the reality that from the deathcamp there was no escape—no end to suffering, no "light at the end of the tunnel"—many of the prisoners fell apart spiritually even before they were broken physically. Their spiritual transformation was so complete that they literally ceased to function as human beings. They were dehumanized. But Dr. Frankl also observed, and was deeply moved, by others who refused to be destroyed spiritually. Not only did they refuse to give up hope, but also they helped others sustain hope. Although the Nazis were able to strip their bodies bare, take from them every scrap of personal belongings, and subject them to limitless torment and humiliation, nevertheless there was one thing that could not be taken away: the sense of Being or Selfhood; the sense of worthwhileness as human beings.

Hope

445

A remote Polish village had not been visited by a clockmaker for many years. After a while, the clocks in the village were all telling different times. Most villagers gave up on even winding their useless clocks. Finally a wandering clockmaker did show up. The villagers ran to him with their clocks to have them set and repaired. But the clocks had rusted and corroded from long years of disuse—except for one clock, whose owner had wound it each day. Even though he knew it was not telling the right time, he remained hopeful that a clockmaker one day would come to the village. The faithful Christian is often like that one man.

446 (Challenge)

A famous composer was once asked this question: "If you knew you had to spend the rest of your days on a desert island, which of your four hundred compositions would you take with you?" "I'd take some blank paper," he replied. "My favorite composition is always the one I will write tomorrow." That's the "look ahead" spirit of the Gospels: the challenge to live each day hopefully and creatively, whatever the circumstance of life.

447 (Expectation)

It is a matter of the will to "seek first the Kingdom of God" in the spirit of youthful enthusiasm and imagination and wide-eyed expection. Youth, in this Gospel sense, means to approach life in the spirit of adventure and to live in a way which says, "I'm really going someplace." Years may wrinkle the skin, but lack of enthusiasm for life's journey wrinkles the soul.

Whether one is seventy or seventeen, there is in every human heart a great reservoir of child-like awe and wonder, of child-like zest for "What's next?", of child-like hope for the transformation of "things as they are" into "things as they will be." We read in I Corinthians,

> Eye has not seen, ear has not heard, nor has it so
> much as dawned on man what God has prepared
> for those who love Him (1 Cor.2:9).

Only a heart filled with child-like awe and wonder can cherish that prophecy!

448 (Despair, Easter)

There are times when the voices of the prophets of doom begin to get to us, and we begin to wonder if there will be a tomorrow. There are even voices within ourselves that begin telling us to flee to the hills of despair. And then comes Easter, and at the center of our being, both as individuals and as a people, we know that there is a tomorrow and that it is full of hope and full of promise and full of assurance that we are bound for glory.

449 (Expectation; God, presence of)

A pious old man was asked why he remained a man of hope, even in the most difficult days. He replied, "Because I believe that God is new every morning; I believe that God is creating the world today, at this very moment. He did not just create it in the long ago and then forget about it. That means we have to expect the unexpected as the normal way God's Providence is at work."

450 (Future; Lifestyle)

A close friend of Leopold Stokowski, the famous orchestra conductor, has written that Stokowski often said to him, "Don't ask me about what was, but what is to come!" This was typical

Hope

of Stokowski's attitude and approach to life. "Shortly before he died," the friend wrote, "he had signed a contract with Columbia Records to make four records a year until 1982— when he would have been exactly 100."

451   (Devil)

There is a famous painting in which the artist depicts a young man playing chess with the Devil. The Devil has just made a decisive move which checkmates the young man's King. Serious chess players who examine the painting immediately feel sympathy for the young man because they understand that the Devil's move has finished him. He has come to a blind alley from which there is no exit. Paul Murphy, one of the world's great chess players, once studied the painting for a long time. He saw something that no one else had seen. This excited him, and he cried out to the Devil's opponent in the picture, "Don't give up! You still have a move! You still have a move!"

452

Ordinarily, we tend to identify hope with good times. But if we are attentive to the Gospel message, we notice that the great prophets voiced their spirit of hope most eloquently, not in good times, but in bad. That's when hope comes hardest—and when we need it most.

453   (Future; Optimism)

One big theatrical success has been the Broadway Musical "Annie," based on the comic strip, "Little Orphan Annie." The show has emerged as one of the longest-running Musicals in Broadway history. Night-after-night Annie charms the audience with her straightforward, optimistic, always-hopeful attitude and approach to life. Even in the darkest situations, when she seems most vulnerable and helpless, the little orphan waif insists that the sun will come out tomorrow. Again-and-again she sings . . .

> The sun will come out tomorrow, so you've got to hang on 'til tomorrow—come what may!
>
> Tomorrow . . . tomorrow, I love you, tomorrow; you're only a day away!

454 (Mystery)

Dr. Scott Peck is the author of the best-selling book called "The Road Less Travelled." As a psychiatrist, Dr. Peck spends a great deal of time working with patients in a large psychiatric hospital. He says that he has discovered in his practice an almost universal apathy: lack of interest; no desire to ask questions; no desire to seek the new and to grow; "no taste for mystery" as he puts it. He says he has discovered also that if he can cultivate in the patient a willingness to want to search and to grow, then there is some hope. But if not, he sees little hope.

455 (Future)

When news reporter Marguerite Higgins was covering the Korean War she received the Pulitzer Prize for her perceptive, sensitive stories. On one occasion, she wrote about being with the Fifth Company of Marines. It was early evening and the company had stopped the march to have supper. The men were experiencing bone-deep fatigue, anxiety, fear and death. One huge Marine was leaning back against a truck eating his cold meal from a tin can. He had been in the field for many days and his clothes were stiff with dirt and cold. His heavily bearded face, encrusted with mud, was almost expressionless because of the immense fatigue he was feeling. One correspondent in the small group of reporters who were on the scene, obviously trying to get an exciting lead for his next article, asked that

Hope

Marine a strange and perhaps insensitive question: "If I were God and could grant you anything you wished, what would you want most?" The Marine stood motionless for a few moments. Then he looked up at the reporter and said, "Just give me tomorrow!"

456

In A. J. Cronin's novel, "The Keys of the Kingdom," one of the main characters in the book is Father Chisholm, a missionary priest who has worked almost all of his life in China against overwhelming odds. There is a passage in which this good Christian missionary gives a clue to his remarkable courage and hope. He is talking to a distressed friend, a native farmer who was bitterly complaining because his garden has been completely washed out by a seasonal flood. "My plantings are all lost," he cries. "We shall have to begin all over again." And Father Chisholm replies quietly, "But that's life my friend: to begin again when everything is lost."

457   (Christ, and suffering; Persecution)

In the day's of the Roman persecution, one of the worst things that could happen to a Christian was to be sent to the mines of New Midea in Africa. The prisoners were brutally whipped, marched through rocky valleys, burned by the sun, branded on their brow with a hot iron, chained so that they were unable to stand erect, sent into the dark mines to work interminable hours: indescribable suffering. When those mines were opened up to visitors, it was discovered that the Christians had etched little words and slogans on the walls of the caves in which they were working. Of all the many words that appear there, two appear more than any others. One is the word "Christ" (Christos); the other is the word "life."

HUMAN RELATIONS

458

A science professor was delivering a slide lecture. A forest scene flashed onto the screen. In the center of the picture stood an oddly-shaped tree. "I want you to look closely at that tree," said the professor to his class. "You can easily see that its growth was impeded by that big boulder. Because the tree was forced to grow around the boulder, its trunk is bowed. Notice how fire has blackened its bark. Notice that one side is totally devoid of branches. These are all examples of how environment shapes all things in the universe. That monstrous object doesn't look at all like a pine tree!" To which a student responded, "But, professor, it is still a pine tree, isn't it?"

Clearly the student was more concerned with the tree's essence than with its appearance. He looked beyond the twisted base, the blackened bark, the bowed trunk, the dead branches, and he saw a pine tree. Although it was not nearly as robust or as good-looking or as stately as the great majority of pine trees, it was a pine tree, nevertheless. It derived its essential value from its "pine-tree-ness." Similarly, our own essential value is derived, not from appearances, but from our essence, from our condition of "human-ness."

HUMAN PERSPECTIVE

459 (Humor)

In one of the "All in the Family" TV episodes, Edith and Archie are attending Edith's high school class reunion. Edith encounters an old classmate named "Buck" who has allowed himself to become extremely obese. Edith and Buck have a delightful conversation about old times and the things they did together, but remarkably, Edith doesn't seem to even notice how extremely heavy Buck has become. Later, Edith and Archie are talking. She says, "Archie, ain't Buck a beautiful person?" Archie replies, "Edith, I'll never figure you out. You and I can look at the same guy and you see a beautiful person and I see a blimp." And Edith replies, simply, "Yeah, ain't that too bad!"

HUMAN PREDICAMENT

460 (Identity Crisis)

An ancient Greek story says that outside the City of Thebes there was a monster called the Sphinx. To every person who passed by the monster gave this riddle: What creature walks in the morning upon four feet, at noon upon two feet and in the evening upon three? Anyone who failed to answer the riddle was destroyed. It was finally Oedipus who solved the riddle by answering that it is man who crawls on all fours as a baby, walks upright upon two feet at his maturity, and as an old man has to rely on a cane. The interesting thing about this old story is that our generation faces a similar riddle and if we don't answer it we are going to be destroyed. But in our day, "man" is not the answer to the riddle. Man is the riddle! We are finding ourselves involved now in a passionate, almost obsessive search to answer the question, "Who am I and what does it mean to be human?" Unless we are able to solve this problem, this riddle, life on this planet may well cease. "Who am I?" has become the most pressing question of our time.

HUMAN POTENTIAL

461

Several years ago, a book called the "Peter Principle" revealed how, in our complex bureaucracies, the failure to recognize people for who they are often produces chaotic results within the system, and even personal disaster. In a nutshell, the Peter Principle states that in the bureaucratic system a person will most likely rise to a level beyond his or her competence. Happiness and success, we are told, is measured by what the sociologists call one's potential for "upward mobility." Consequently, because moving "up the ladder" is the first priority, people allow themselves to be thrust into areas of responsibility for which they are ill-suited. They soon discover (but hardly ever admit) that they were happier when they functioned at some point down the ladder, performing comfortably a work in keeping with their competence. The author of the Peter Principle contends that this failure to recognize persons as persons, its excessive devotion to "upward mobility" rather than "each according to his own competence," is a prime reason why bureaucracies and corporate hierarchies become such unweildy mazes, why it often seems impossible to "get things done." The person who is thrust into a situation to which he cannot adequately relate, soon discovers that he cannot adequately relate to the people around him as well. Little wonder that the modern high-level executive is usually depicted as harried, harassed, tense, constantly in need of "winding down."The Peter Principle describes the unfortunate effects of the misjudgment of individual potential.

462 (Love)

W. H. Auden, the contemporary poet, has written a long musical work (an oratorio) based on the story of the Three Wise

Human Potential

Men. In it, each man tells why he is following the star. The first one says, "To discover how to be truthful now is the reason I follow the star." The second one says, "To discover how to be living now is the reason I follow the star." The third one says, "To discover how to be loving now is the reason I follow the star." The moving and beautiful climax occurs when the three strong male voices all sing together, "To discover how to be human now is the reason we follow the star."

463 (Compassion; God, children of; Service)

Several critics have called the Japanese motion picture, Ikiru, the greatest film ever made. Ikiru is the story of an old man's struggle to attach meaning to his life after learning that he has cancer and only six months to live. This causes him to reflect on his uneventful life as a minor city hall bureaucrat. The realization that he has made no significant contribution to his fellow man troubles him spiritually. And, despite his weakened condition, he resolves to do something for other people before he dies. With all his remaining energy he gets behind a playground project which has had one obstacle after another thrown in its path by the local bureaucracy. As the result of his efforts, the playground is finally completed and the neighborhood children are presented with their new paradise. The experience transforms the stuffy old ex-bureaucrat into a warm and compassionate human being.

In the movie's touching finale, the old man is seen contentedly seated on one of the new playground swings, slowly moving back and forth and softly humming a tune. There, peacefully, he dies. The symbolism is clear. Only by rendering service to others with a warm and compassionate heart, only by assigning priority in human relations to "What can I give?" over "What can I get?" can we realize our potential as children of God. The childish posture of the old man on the children's swing symbolizes the child-like spirit which enables him to die in peace.

HUMILITY

464 (Mystery)

George Washington Carver, the Black scientist who achieved wonders with the humble peanut, often told this story:

> When I was young, I said to God, "God, tell me the mystery of the Universe." But God answered, "That knowledge is reserved for Me alone." So I said, "God, tell me the mystery of the peanut." Then God said, "Well, George, that's more nearly your size." And he told me.

HUNGER

465 (Poverty)

The American Freedom From Hunger Foundation frequently gave banquets in order to dramatize the world food crisis. At such affairs they waited for the right moment when stomachs were growling and heads aching from hunger. Then one-third of the guests sat down to juicy prime ribs, steaming baked potatoes and all the trimmings. The other guests received a modest portion of rice and tea.

HYPOCRISY

466   (Alcohol; Humor)

In one of comedian Woody Allen's routines, he receives a telephone call from a man who says, "We want you to make a Smirnoff Vodka ad for a magazine." Woody Allen replies, "I'm afraid I can't do that. I don't drink, and if I did it wouldn't be vodka. It would be dishonest for me to do the ad. I can't be hypocritical." The voice on the other end replies, "There's fifty thousand dollars in it." And Woody answers, "Just a minute, I'll call Mr. Allen to the phone." They talk further. Finally Woody Allen says, "I'll think about it. Let me call you back." Then he goes to his rabbi for counsel. "It definitely would be morally wrong for you to do the ad," the rabbi advises. Hearing this, Woody Allen calls the man back and says, "Sorry, I can't do the ad." Three weeks later he sees a Smirnoff Vodka magazine ad in which his rabbi appears, holding up a glass of vodka.

467   (Redemption)

A 19th century pagan philosopher said, "I might believe in the Christian Redeemer if Christians looked more redeemed."

468   (Humor; Marriage)

A middle-aged businessman, returning from a business trip, had just landed at an airport and was met at the gate by his wife. They had walked from the gate together, without too much joy apparently. They were standing waiting for the baggage to be unloaded when an extremely good-looking young stewardess walked by. Suddenly, the businessman came to life. Beaming, he said to the stewardess, "I hope we can fly together again, Miss Fiskle." "How come you know her name?" his wife immediately demanded. Being up to the demands of the moment, the man replied smoothly, "You see, dear, her name was posted right up front in the plane, under the names of the pilot and co-pilot." To which the wife replied, "OK, now give me the names of the pilot and co-pilot." He flunked the course. His hypocrisy was uncovered.

469

A young American and a young man from India were attending an International Conference. During a break in the proceedings, they found themselves talking to each other about religion. The young man from India was very hostile toward Christianity, and the young American was trying to discern the reason for the hostility. "Is it something in Jesus' teaching that turns you off?" he asked. "No," came the reply, "it is not anything like that. The thing I resent most about Christians is that they are not Christian."

470 (Bible; Humor)

There is the story of a man coming down from the Carolina mountains. He was all dressed up and carrying his Bible. A friend saw him and said, "Elias, what's happening? Where are you going?" Elias said, "I've been hearing about New Orleans. I hear that there is a lot of free-runnin' liquor and a lot of gamblin' and a lot of real good naughty shows." The friend looked him over and said, "But Elias, why are you carrying your Bible under your arm?" Elias replied, "Well, if it's as good as they say it is, I might stay over until Sunday."

471

Defense Attorney: I call the defendant to the stand . . . You have been charged, you understand, with a very serious crime.

Hypocrisy

If convicted you could be imprisoned, exiled or worse. In the course of this trial you have openly admitted that you believe in Christ and His authority, and follow His teachings.

Defendant: I have. And I am ready and willing to suffer the consequences.

Defense Attorney: You are certain that you are a Christian? You have no doubt at all that you are a Christian?

Defendant: None whatsoever. And I won't break under pressure.

Defense Attorney: Do you know the following books: The Gospels of Matthew, Mark, Luke and John; the Epistles of Paul, Peter and others, and the Acts of the Apostles?

Defendant: Well, yes, somewhat. Aren't those the books the priest reads excerpts from on Sundays? Naturally, I haven't had time to read them all—I'm a busy man, as you know.

Defense Attorney: Would you say they are the books of the teachings of Christ and the practices of the first Christians?

Defendant: Yes, but due to the complexities of modern living, some of those practices are impractical. In today's world you've got to learn to look out for yourself.

Defense Attorney: Your honor, my client is charged with being a Christian. I am trying to establish the fact that he is not, in fact, a Christian. The books I have referred to are accepted by knowledgeable authorities as containing the central core of faith and practice for the Christian Community. For the purpose of defending my client I would like to enter sections of these books into the record: the Sermon on the Mount, the twenty-fifth chapter of Matthew's Gospel containing the Parable of the Last Judgment, and Luke's report of the conversation between Jesus and the lawyer who asked, "What must I do to inherit everlasting life?"

Defendant: This is outrageous. I am a Christian. I believe in Christ as Lord. I recite the Apostles Creed.

Hypocrisy

Defense Attorney: Your honor, I would also like to enter Matthew 7:21 which reads: "It is not those who say to me 'Lord, Lord,' who will enter the kingdom of heaven, but the person who does the will of my Father." Also a text from the Epistle of the Apostle James (2:17) which reads: "Faith that does nothing in practice is thoroughly lifeless." Moreover, I should like to point out the constant teaching of the Christian Church that being a true Christian involves more than the mere acceptance of, or giving voice to, certain doctrines.

Defendant: You're my lawyer, and I demand that you put forward my evidence. I go to Church. I pay my bills. I shovel my sidewalk. I don't bother anybody. And I am not against helping my neighbor.

Defense Attorney: I am indeed your lawyer. It is my duty to exhibit the truth in your behalf. Please answer this question: Who is your neighbor?

Defendant: You're trying to trick me with that line about loving your enemies. We have enemies in this world that the Christians in Jesus' time knew nothing about. I know what Jesus said, but . . .

Defense Attorney: Your honor, my client is about to refer to the story Jesus told about "The Good Samaritan." Jesus stated it as a basis for Christian conduct. I'm sure we are all acquainted with His proposals: "Love your enemies; do good to those who persecute you." Little has been done about it, but its been told many times. And my client doesn't practice it.

Defendant: I object.

Defense Attorney: To what? The story of the Good Samaritan?

Judge: Objection sustained. Enter in the record that the story of the Good Samaritan is objectionable and has no place in this court or this world.

Defense Attorney: I submit to this court that my client is guilty only of self-delusion. I find no evidence in his life, attitude, or

251

Hypocrisy

in his dealings with people, that he is a follower of Christ in practice. Can anyone seriously charge my client with any remarkable concern for the poor, the oppressed, the imprisoned, the lonely, the homeless—all of whom are the "widows and orphans" of our time.

Defendant: I object. "Charity begins at home."

Defense Attorney: The objection is not well taken. In fact, the precedents against my client's argument are overwhelming. The books of the Gospel clearly show that Christian love admits . . . of no such limitations. Jesus himself stated this over and over again. The Apostle, John, thought it to be the greatest of His teachings. In a short letter written to Christian Communities close to him, he used the word for love or charity no less than 35 times. The gist of the letter is, and I quote, "Let us love in deed and in truth, and not merely talk about it" (1 Jn.3:18).

Defendant: Correct, but with qualifications. As I said before, modern life is complex. You are being too literal. It's not the time for . . .

Defense Attorney: Your honor, may I present another important legal precedent in support of my client's innocence of being a Christian?

Judge: You may.

Defense Attorney: One of the earliest legal defenses of Christians we know about comes down to us from the Roman Courts of the Emperor Hadrian. The following is from the brief of Aristides, who entered it on behalf of those who were regarded as "troublesome Christians": "Christians never fail to help widows; they save orphans from those who would hurt them. If a man has something, he gives freely to the man who has nothing . . . If one of them is poor and there isn't enough food to go around, they fast several days to give him the food he needs . . . This is really a new kind of person. There is really something Divine in them." Your honor, members of the court, citizens

252

of the world, show me the Divinity in this man if he be Christian.

Defendant: Your honor, may I have a brief recess to confer with my attorney?

Judge: You may.

Defense Attorney (after conferring with his client): Your honor, it seems to me that my client is as pragmatic, as secure and as sensible as the rest of us. I'm sure that even he now realizes that Christianity is as much a threat to his own security as it is to ours. Your honor, his crime is merely self-delusion, a little hysteria perhaps, and possibly a little wishful thinking. I ask that the charge be dismissed for lack of evidence.

Judge: Case dismissed.

Do you stand accused of being a Christian? Will the charge hold up?

472

American or Chinese, Russian or British, Moslem, Christian or Jewish, we are all residents of planet earth which has suddenly and dramatically been reduced in size by science and technology. We pilgrims of the "Nuclear Age" are like persons who have sentenced each other to a universal jail that now contains us all, and no one will pardon the other because each can see the other's guilt but not his or her own. It is clear that athiests and believers are equally able to passively accept or actively participate in the proliferation of nuclear arms. Athiests and believers alike are threatening the human race with extinction.

473 (Lifestyle; Prejudice)

There is the story about the head of a law firm who had hired a brilliant young graduate to work in his office. Before starting to work, the young man was sent abroad for further, special

Hypocrisy

studies. When he returned from Europe, he came into the office ready for work, sporting a long, flowing beard. The chief lawyer looked him over and said, "Young man, I have no objection if that beard is how you would like to express yourself. Just don't wear it during office hours!" You see, it's easy for us to claim that we want to let the other fellow be himself, but when it comes down to something that really bugs us, we react in exactly the opposite way.

474 (Compassion; Damnation; Heaven; Judgment)

There is a French play in which all the "good" people are at the gates of heaven on the day of judgment. The gates are about to be opened and they can hardly wait to get in. (We can only imagine what this would mean to a person: to come to the end and realize that heaven is here and I'm here and I'm about to go into my reserved place.) And then a rumor starts. Even at the gates of heaven, it seems, rumors start. "I understand," someone says, "He is going to forgive those others too!" For a moment, the people are absolutely dumbfounded, speechless. Then they look at each other, and start to gasp and sputter in disbelief, all trying to talk at the same time: "After all the trouble I went through!" "If only I had known this, things sure would have been different!" Some are so worked up by the realization that God is going to have compassion on those "others" that they begin to curse Him. And in that instant, they are damned. It all came down to compassion. And the "good" people didn't have it toward those "others."

475 (Education)

Some years ago, there lived a fellow in Los Angeles who went to school all his life. When he finished high school, he went to college. He took degrees in the arts and the sciences, even completing the course of studies for Doctor of Medicine. On and on he went, reenrolling after each graduation. He had a teacher's degree but would not teach. He was an engineer but would build no bridges. He was a doctor but would not heal. He had destined himself for a life of preparation without fulfillment. Why? It seems that a rich relative had left him an allowance of several thousand dollars per year, payable only as long as he remained in school. Consequently, the titles conferred upon this man did not represent a real sense of commitment to a purposeful life—something to be lived and lived up to.

476 (Change; Parish Life; Repentance)

The pastor of a congregation made up of largely upper-middle-class to rich, White people, relates the following example of how God keeps on working to help us break out of our narrowness and exclusiveness. He says:

"We were doing a lot of talking about the social dimensions of our Church ministry and the responsibilities we had toward others outside the narrow bounds of our own little community of believers, especially the inner-city poor. And then God called our bluff by sending us two little boys named Tony and Ricky to test our love, to test whether or not we really were serious about it. Given the makeup of our congregation, they could not have been more different: they were poor, they were Black, they were unwashed and they were undisciplined. We had many a Sunday when they helped themselves as the money basket went by during the offering. They thought this was a great thing: "How long has this been going on?" Some of us responded to this with resentment! "They are disrupting the Sunday School classes; we're not equipped to handle kids like this; this isn't what we had in mind in our discussion." They said all that and more. But others stuck with it and opened themselves up to the situation and to Tony and Ricky. And God taught us so very much about life and so very much about love through those two little boys. God taught us so very much about the kind of change Jesus is talking about when He exhorts us to repent and reform.

IDENTITY CRISIS

477 (Change; Afterlife; Heaven; Service)

A man named "Walter" owned a little variety store and, for years, he extended credit to poor immigrants, helping them get started in their new land. As Walter neared his sixtieth birthday, a group of people whom he had helped in this way decided to give him a party and a gift of money. Walter accepted the money, gratefully, and began to use it for his own revitalization. He had his teeth capped. He bought a new hair piece. He invested in a diet/exercise program and lost a lot of weight. He purchased a whole new wardrobe. Then he boarded a plane and a few hours later the "new" Walter hit the beach at Miami. He met a beautiful young woman, asked her for a date, and she accepted. But before they could go out on the date, a thunderstorm came up. Walter was struck by a lightening bolt and he died instantly. In heaven, he said to God, "After all those years of hard work, I was just trying to enjoy myself a little. Why? Why me?" And God said to him, "Oh, is that you Walter? I'm sorry, I didn't recognize you."

478 (Education; Self Image)

In the movie "The Graduate," a son comes home to his parents after four years in college. He's been a "big wheel" on Campus. He's won honors in athletics. He's won a grant for graduate study because of his scholastic ability. He comes home and he begins to drift. Finally his father can't take any more of it and demands to know the purpose of those four years of work and all the money that was spent on it. The boy acknowledges, quite frankly, that he hasn't the slightest idea what the purpose was. A Vassar College graduate, daughter of a wealthy New York family, was widely quoted as saying, with considerable bitterness in her voice, "My parents gave me everything I could have wanted, except one thing. They forgot to tell me who I am. What's the use of having money, an education and friends if you don't know who it is who has them?" This is the cry of today's young people. And we hear it more and more these days from older people as well. More and more, it seems, older folks are beginning to realize that financial security and the "respectable" image in the community are not the ultimate goals—important as they may be.

479 (Humor)

Sam Levinson, the humorist, once said, "I go pay my psychiatrist sixty dollars an hour and all he does is ask me the same question my father used to ask me all the time: 'Who do you think you are anyway?' " Whether it's a sixty-dollar-an-hour psychiatrist or a wise father or just that small voice within us, it's the same question: "Who do you think you are anyway?"

480 (Caring; Healing)

A man we shall call John was having an "identity crisis". He joined a "Growth Group" in his Church. In that Growth Group he was learning to deal with his feelings—a whole new thing for him and it was very uncomfortable for him. His wife had insisted that she didn't know who he was because even he didn't know where he was coming from. John had been meeting with the Growth Group for some time when he learned that a colleague of his at the office had been hospitalized with a heart

Identity Crisis

attack. In the hospital, the routine blood tests revealed that the patient also had leukemia. John called on his colleague in the hospital and he later described the visit in these words:

> Up until a few months before, in a situation like that, I would have just chit-chatted. We would have talked about the weather; about the football season; about recent TV shows. Just friendly passing the time and "hope you get to feeling better." But, I couldn't do that. I found myself telling him, first of all, that down at the office we really needed him, we really missed him, and we were saving some matters that we felt that only he could handle properly. Then I said something that was hard for me to say—very hard. I had worked with this man for 20 years and I had never said anything like this to him. What I said was, "I want you to know that I really care about you." Then I remember blinking twice before I said, "I love you." Then, I left. Another co-worker who had visited the patient shortly after I had gone later told me that the patient, with tears in his eyes, had said to him, "You know, John just told me the two things that I needed to hear more than anything else. I needed to know that I am needed, and he told me that. And I needed to know that I am loved, and he told me that."

481 (Psalm 139)

Francis Thompson was a man who lived through a severe identity crisis. Although he had not the slightest intention of becoming a doctor, nevertheless he spent six years of his life preparing for a career in medicine. Why? Because his father wanted him to be a doctor. He did it to please his father. When, after six years, he couldn't stand it anymore, he dropped out of school. He sold encyclopedias. He worked as a clerk in a retail store. Finally, he joined the Army but was soon discharged because he was physically unable to be a soldier. Then he started wandering around, as a kind of vagrant. He became a heavy cocaine user. He contracted tuberculosis and died at age 48. But just a few years before he died he had discovered his identity: it was to be a writer. There was a gift within him that he slowly became aware of and then began to share with others. And he wrote a poem which has been acclaimed as the greatest ode, or lyric poem, in the English language. It is called, "The Hound of Heaven."

The poem is a direct commentary on the 139th Psalm and it is the story of Francis Thompson's relationship with God. It is the story of how God had been chasing after him through all those years of knocking around. He was always running away from God, but God was always in hot pursuit—the "Hound of Heaven" padding after him, relentlessly, lovingly! At one point in the poem, Francis Thompson hauntingly refers to the God who constantly pursued him as "This Tremendous Lover." Only when he turned and allowed himself to be caught by "This Tremendous Lover" was he able to live in a fulfilling way.

IDOLATRY

482   (Frustration; Possessions)

One of John Steinbeck's best-known characters is a World War II soldier named "Bugs." The story of "Bugs" is a satire on the souvenir-hunting American GI. Bugs discovers a big, beautiful mirror in the ruins of Sicily. It is six-feet high and two or three feet wide, with a heavy gold-leaf frame on which there are delicately carved cupids and flowers and scrolls. When Bugs sees it his eyes light up. This is the souvenir to end all souvenirs. He decides that he must get this thing back home. At first he plans to bury it—hide it and come back and get it later. But

Immortality

he decides that burying it would be too risky; he doesn't want to take a chance on losing it. So he devises a sling which makes it possible for him to carry this heavy mirror on his back, in addition to all his other gear. Wherever the outfit goes, there is Bugs with his big mirror. His buddies call him the "moving billboard." He has to be very careful to guard it against theft and see that it doesn't crack or break. Every time the outfit settles down for the night he has the problem of what to do with the mirror. He is enslaved by this thing, obsessed by it. Finally the outfit is billeted on the second floor of a house in Palermo. The stairs are narrow so Bugs devises a rope-hoist and pulls his mirror up outside of the house and into a second-floor window. He puts a nail in the wall, hangs the mirror on it, and steps back to look at it. The nail comes loose from the wall, and crash! The mirror hits the floor, breaking into a million shattered fragments. End of story.

IMMORTALITY

483 (Afterlife)

Several years back a tough-minded realist made an interesting observation. "Millions," she claimed, "long for immortality who don't know what to do with themselves on a rainy Sunday afternoon." Her statement holds some truth but she might also have noted that those millions who do "long for immortality" are as likely to do so on a Sunday afternoon as at any other time. Man's hunger for immortality has never been restricted to this or that time of the week or month or year, or to this or that period of human history. From time immemorial, immortality has been in the forefront of man's imagination. Whether out of fear or hope or longing or some other emotion, man's imagination has worked overtime conjuring visions of life in the hereafter.

INCARNATION

484 (Children; Christ, divinity of)

A famous artist was commissioned by a great Church to do a sculpture for the building's vestibule. The assignment came at a time in the artist's life when he felt the need to summarize in a work of art everything he was feeling as a human person. He worked very hard on the statue and, when it was nearly finished, he called in some children to look at it. One of the children said, "It is a statue of a great man," and the others agreed: "a great man." The artist shook his head and went back to work for several more weeks. Then he called the children back. This time the consensus was that it was a likeness of a "good man." Again the artist shook his head and went back to work. Weeks later, the children came a third time and, immediately, one of them said, "It is Christ." Then the artist was satisfied because what he was trying to say in the statue is what the Gospel Writers are trying to tell us in every line: "It is Christ!—not merely a good man, not merely a great man, but the God Man."

485 (Christmas; God, love of)

Once upon a Christmas Eve, a man sat in reflective silence before the fireplace, pondering the meaning of Christmas. "There is no point to a God who becomes man," he mused. "Why would an all-powerful God want to share even one of His precious moments with the likes of man? And even if He did, why would He choose to be born in an animal stall? No way! The whole thing is absurd! I'm sure that if God really wanted to come down to earth, He would have chosen some other way." Suddenly, the man was roused from his reverie by a strange sound outside. He went to the window and saw a small gaggle of blue geese frantically honking and aimlessly flopping about in the

Incarnation

snow. They seemed dazed and confused. Apparently, they had dropped out in exhaustion from the flight formations of a larger flock on its way from the Arctic Islands to the warmer climes of the Gulf of Mexico. Moved to compassion, the man tried to shoo the poor geese into his warm garage, but the more he "shooed" the more they panicked. "If they only realized I'm only trying to do what's best for them," he thought to himself. "How can I make them understand my concern for their well-being?" Then, this thought came to him: "If for just a minute, I could become one of them, an ordinary goose, and communicate with them in their own language, they would know what I am trying to do." And suddenly . . . suddenly, he remembered Christmas and a smile came over his face. Suddenly, the Christmas story no longer seemed absurd. Suddenly, he pictured that ordinary-looking Infant, lying in that stable in Bethlehem, and he knew the answer to his Christmas problem: God had become one of us to tell us that He loves us.

486 (Children; Christ, presence of; Humor)

A little girl came home with an "F" in spelling on her report card. When her mother demanded an explanation, the little girl said, "Mommy, words fail me." That's exactly where we are in trying to explain the Incarnation: mere words fail us. But the experience of the Christ Presence in our life will not fail us.

487 (God, presence of)

The Incarnational presence of God is the very heart of our Christian Faith, and if we are not experiencing it, either individually, or as a Church, we are malfunctioning as Christian people. The story is told of a huge atomic energy plant that was malfunctioning. None of the plant's engineers and scientists could figure out the cause of the trouble. Finally, an eminent professor in the field was summoned from his University for consultation. The professor surveyed the situation, then asked for a hammer. He took the hammer in hand, walked over to a pipe and struck it a heavy blow. Immediately, the plant began functioning again: everything was back in working order. Later, he submitted an itemized bill for his services in the amount of $5,005. It read as follows:

For striking the blow—$5.00

For knowing where to strike the blow—$5,000.00

If your life is bogged down, if you feel as though you are malfunctioning as a human person, I have Good News for you. God is hammering away at the very center of your being to get you started again. He is striking blow after blow after blow on the window of your soul to get you to open up to His Incarnational Presence in Jesus the Christ. Again and again the Gospel writers strike a heavy blow for the Incarnation. Again and again they tell us why Christians love the Lord Jesus, why we say He is the center of our life, why we say He is Our Lord and Savior, why the Wise Men of Old "fell down and worshipped Him" at Bethlehem (Mt.2:10). Jesus is not just a great teacher. Jesus is not just a great man. He is the Christ. He is the One in whom God became one of us to tell us that He loves us and is present to us always. This is why we love Him and why we give our lives to Him and for Him.

488 (Trust)

Two men were walking through a dark passage with the aid of a flashlight. The man holding the light turned the beam upward. He said to the other man, "Wouldn't it be something if you could walk up that beam of light! Why don't you try it?" "You can't trick me," the other replied. "I know that when I get to the top of the beam, you'll turn the light off." The Incarnational Presence of God is the light that leads us through even the darkest passages of life. It never malfunctions and God never tricks us. He never turns it off. We can stake our life on it.

489   (God, presence of; Paul)

"The unsearchable riches of Christ" is a phrase Paul uses to try to help us understand that when the Incarnation becomes real to us, we can experience the wholeness of life we all need and want. In Paul's time and in our own time, there are those who say that the way to become a whole person is to reject your humanity, to withdraw from the rest of the human race, to wash your hands of the human drama. Paul says an emphatic "No!" to this sort of religious elitism because God's coming to you in human form is the confirmation of your humanity. God is saying to you, "The way for you to become a whole person is not to reject the humanity I have identified with, but to plunge deeper into it." The Incarnation means that your life now is good because God is in it. It means that God is working in every area of your humanity: in your joys and in your sorrows; in your laughter and in your tears; in your hopes and in your fears.

INCENTIVE

490   (Humor; Motivation)

An industrial organization once sponsored courses in human relations for its employees. During one session on employer-employee relations, the instructor experienced difficulty in getting feed-back from the class, after he had carefully drawn the fine distinction between "motivation" and "incentive." Finally, a factory worker arose to give the following illustration: "When the boss tells me that if I increase my production to a certain number of units a day I'll get a raise, that's incentive. When he tells me that unless I increase my production to a certain number of units per day I'll be fired, that's motivation."

INDIFFERENCE

491   (Crucifixion; Good Friday; Resurrection)

A young boy was taken to church to hear his uncle preach on Good Friday. The uncle preached eloquently on the Crucifixion and the boy was so moved that he began to cry. He looked around, suddenly aware that the people around him were unmoved and were looking at him as if he were some kind of oddball. Later he said, "They all walked away as if nothing had happened." And he could not understand that. We do that Sunday after Sunday. We celebrate the Crucifixion and Resurrection of Our Lord and walk away as if nothing had happened.

INDIVIDUALITY

492   (Self-identity)

The uniqueness of living things is one of life's most awesome wonders. No two blades of grass, no two roses, no two insects, or birds or dogs or cats are precisely alike. Each human creature of God is different from all the rest—each a unique creation of God. Geneticists tell us that prior to birth, each person has an array of genes unlike that of any other person, living or dead. Each set of fingerprints, footprints, and voiceprints is unique, individual, unmatched. Heart specialists tell us that no two cardiograms are alike. Neurologists tell us that no two brain-wave tests produce the same results. Over seventy-seven billion persons have lived on the planet earth, which means

Inflation

that each of us is a seventy-seven billionth wonder of the world—
each a unique marvel. It is also true that modern computer
technology has the capacity to record a variety of the distin-
guishing marks of every living person, as well as all those yet
to come. We have reached the point where it is relatively easy
to establish one's identity and virtually impossible to conceal
it. Yet, fingerprints, footprints, cardiograms, voiceprints, and
brainwaves notwithstanding, we never cease to ask ourselves
and each other, "Who am I?" "Who do you say I am?"

INFLATION

493 (Change; Humor; Lifestyle; Work)

For many complex socioeconomic reasons, many of us are being
forced these days to adjust our lifestyle and live more simply
than before. One of the problems we all face is the ever-rising
"cost of living": inflation. Consider, for example, the lawyer
who called a plumber to his house to fix a leaky pipe under the
kitchen sink. The plumber repaired the leak in exactly one hour,
whereupon he presented the lawyer with a very large bill. The
lawyer protested. "I am a lawyer," he said, "and I don't get
that much money for an hour's work." To which the plumber
replied, "Come to think of it, when I was a lawyer, I didn't
make that much either." Whether we're lawyers or plumbers,
or whoever, we are being forced, in these changing times, to
change our ways.

INSECURITY

494 (Loneliness; Parent and Child)

The famous cartoonist, Jules Pfeiffer, was discussing a cartoon
strip he did for the newspapers. In it, a little boy didn't want

to go to school because he feared his parents would move away while he was gone. He didn't want to go to bed at night because he feared that his parents would die while he slept. Coping with these fears is a terrific battle for a child. "It's like being on 24-hour guard duty," Pfeiffer said. He also said he had received many letters about that cartoon from adults who told him, "That's the way it is, all right. But you don't have to be a child to feel it."

INSENSITIVITY

495 (Fools)

Someone has likened people who remain insensitive to the needs of others—unloving people—to two foolish shipwrecked men sitting together at one end of a lifeboat, doing nothing. They watch intently as the people at the other end bail furiously, trying to keep the boat afloat. One man then says to the other, "Thank God, that hole isn't in our end of the boat!"

INSINCERITY

496 (Romantic Love)

An impetuous young man spied a beautiful young woman walking through the park. Immediately, he began to follow her. After a time, the young woman turned and confronted him: "Why are you following me?" she demanded. "Because you are so beautiful," he answered fervently. "I am madly in love with you and wish you to be mine." To which the young woman replied, "But why don't you take a look behind you to see my younger sister. She is far more beautiful than I." The young man quickly wheeled about but saw no one. "You're putting me on," he said. "You have lied to me." To which she replied, "If you were so madly in love with me, then why did you turn around?"

INSPIRATION

497

"I wish I could write with both hands at the same time," Teresa of Avila once said. Sometimes the ideas about God and about Jesus were coming to her so fast that she was unable to write them down fast enough.

INVOCATION

498 (Humor; Politics)

William Allen White, famed Editor of the Emporia Gazette, was a staunch member of the Democratic Party. On one occasion, however, he found himself attending a Republican Party convention as a political reporter. At the opening session, the presiding officer saw Mr. White in the audience and asked him if he would give an invocation. William Allen White replied, "No. I will not pray in this place for two reasons. First of all, I am not trained in the fine art of public prayer. Secondly, I don't want the Lord to know that I am here."

JESUS

499

Francois Mauriac, the famous philosopher of religion, once said: "Once you get to know Him, you cannot be cured of Him."

Thomas Carlyle once said: "If Jesus Christ were to come today, people would not even crucify Him. They would ask Him to dinner, and hear what He had to say, and make fun of it."

JESUS AND CHILDREN

500 (Fulfillment)

Good parents do everything they can to help their son become a man and their daughter become a woman. But there are times when the weight of this responsibility gets very heavy and for just a moment the wish comes that their sons and daughters remain children, chasing butterflies and flying kites for a while longer. The wispy, wistful nostalgia of childhood! But then you read the New Testament and you're in all kinds of trouble. This wispy, wistful nostalgia suddenly becomes a life or death matter because Jesus said that unless you become like a child you will never enter the Kingdom of Heaven; you will never become the beautifully fulfilled, complete, whole person you were made to become. Never! And He said that not just once, but several times. You can pay your taxes, you can be Chairman of the Board, you can go to Church every Sunday without fail, but unless you recapture this, Jesus said, you will never become who you ought to become.

JESUS, AS SERVANT

501 (Bible; Service)

Before the Communist Revolution in China, a group of Chinese clergymen invited a U.S. seminary professor to their country to conduct a seminar on modern Biblical scholarship. The professor began the exercise by proposing a series of questions on the Bible. His purpose was to discover the present level of the Chinese clergymen's Bible learning. Among the questions he asked was the following: "What is the most impressive incident in all the Gospels?" After retiring for a time to talk this over, the Chinese clergymen reported back that they had arrived at an answer unanimously. It wasn't the Crucifixion; it wasn't the Resurrection; it wasn't the Sermon on the Mount that impressed them most. It was Jesus kneeling to wash the feet of His disciples.

502 (Service)

A highly placed executive of a major airline company was talking about how very difficult it is to recruit persons and then to train them for that industry. He said, "Service is the only thing, really, that we have to sell, but it is the toughest to teach. Nowadays, no one wants to be thought of as a servant." He is right: nowadays, no one wants to be thought of as a servant. This presents us with a serious problem, because the Gospels make it perfectly clear that Jesus intended for each one of His followers to be precisely that: a servant. Moreover, one of the most striking things about the Gospels is that Jesus Christ, our Lord, applied this image to Himself.

JESUS, BREAD OF LIFE

503

A poor Mediteranean family had decided to emigrate to the United States. At a "going away party" given by village friends, the family received the very practical gifts of several loaves of hard bread and several heads of cheese. The day after the party, the family boarded the large ship on which they had booked passage. Never before having been away from the village, the family was rather intimidated by the hubbub and excitement that obtains on a large ocean-going ship prior to sailing. Consequently, they immediately went to their third-class cabin where they lived on the gifts of bread and cheese for several days of the journey. On the next-to-last day of the voyage, one of the boys in the family said to his father, "Dad, I have had it with bread and cheese. May I leave the cabin and explore the ship?" The father said "Yes" and the boy left, but he didn't return. The father went looking for him and found him down in the fifth dining room. He was sitting at a table that was overflowing with food: soup and salad and meat and vegetables and wine and desserts. The father was aghast. He had visions of spending his first days in the United States behind bars because he could not pay for all the food his son had ordered. The boy said to him, "Dad, we have been living on bread and cheese all these days. I came down here to the dining room and I discovered that we could have been eating like this all the way. I discovered that the meals are included in the price of our tickets."

Many of us journey through life as though we were unaware of the incredibly enriching banquet God is constantly offering us: Jesus, our Bread of Life!

JESUS, GOOD SHEPHERD

504

An American travelling in the Middle East happened upon several shepherds whose flocks had intermingled while drinking water from the same brook. After an exchange of greetings, one of the shepherds turned toward the sheep and called out, "Manah . . . manah . . . manah." (Manah means "follow me" in Arabic.) Whereupon, his particular sheep separated themselves from the rest and one of the two remaining shepherds called out, "Manah . . . manah . . . manah," and his sheep left the common flock to follow him. The traveller then said to the third shepherd, "I would like to try that. Let me put on your cloak and turban and see if I can get the rest of the sheep to follow me." The third shepherd smiled knowingly as the traveller wrapped himself in the cloak, put the turban on his head and called out, "Manah . . . manah." But the sheep did not respond to the stranger's voice. Not one of them moved toward him. "Will that flock ever follow someone other than you?" the traveller asked. "Oh yes," the shepherd replied. "Sometimes a sheep gets sick, and then it will follow anyone."

Sick or well, we are called to follow the Lord Jesus, our one, true Good Shepherd.

JESUS, GOSPEL OF

505 (Humor; Parent and Child)

The principal of an elementary school decided to honor the three best students by presenting each of them with a special award at the end of the school year. One prize—for excellence

272

in science and mathematics—was called "The Right-Thinking Award." When the prize-winning students were selected, the parents were notified by letter. The mother of the "Right-Thinking" award-winner wrote back and said, "This is quite an honor for a boy who just tried to make two quarts of lemonade in a one-quart pitcher."

The problem for many of us is that even when we know certain things, even when we are thinking right about certain things that are absolutely essential to life, when we begin working with them, it's like making two quarts of lemonade in a one-quart pitcher. Somehow, they don't work out.

God knows how we right-thinkers can go wrong sometimes. That is why He gives us Jesus to show us the way. The Gospel of Jesus Christ is the ultimate "how-to-do-it" Book. Not only does it tell us to love God with our whole mind and heart, but also it tells us how to do it. Not only does it tell us what is God's, it tells us how to give God what is His.

JESUS, HUMANITY OF

506

The Gospel reveals Jesus as a man of intense feelings, intensely human feelings. We see Him moving about in the real world, manifesting real human responses and real human emotions. We even see Him as an adroit practicioner of the art of reading motives. But above all, we see in Jesus' humanity, the complete man, the super self-analyst, who not only knows what He is doing but why He is doing it.

JESUS, IN GETHSEMANE

507   (Anxiety; Christian Ministry)

An anonymous author has given us a wonderful little story
called, "The Talking Picture." It is about a young lad, large for
his age, going away from home to work in a distant city. His
mother could hardly bear to see him go. He seemed so young
and vulnerable. She worried inwardly: Would he consciously
be taking along the faith in God she had tried to instill in him?
A few days before his journey was to begin, she said to the boy,
"John, before you leave, I would like you to visit the art gallery
and see a certain picture that hangs there." The boy protested:
He "didn't care very much about art"; he was "too busy" getting ready for his big journey. But the mother insisted, "Son,
in a little while you will be a long way from home where I will
not be asking you to do things. Please do this one last thing for
me?" Hearing this, the boy agreed to go the next morning.
When he arrived at the art gallery, he went to the room to
which his mother had directed him and opened the door. But,
on the threshold, he paused. At the far end of the room a man
was kneeling in prayer on a platform. The boy closed the door,
waited a few minutes, then opened it again. Seeing the man
still at prayer, he again waited. When he opened the door the
third time, he entered the room to investigate. As he approached the platform, he realized that he had been mistaken.
The man at prayer was the picture his mother wanted him to
see: a life-size painting of Jesus in Gethsemane, beautifully
lighted and framed in black velvet. He moved closer, eager now
to study the picture that had misled him. "What a wonderful
face," he thought. "And yet, it bears a look of deep worry and
care." His mother had taught him that Jesus was not afraid to
die. Why then, that look of worry on his brow? At home that
evening, he put the question to his mother: "Mother, you have

always taught me that Jesus had done no wrong and did not fear death. Then why the look of anxiety on his face, and why do His hands seem to be pleading so?" His mother answered, "Son, He had only been a teacher for three years and there was so much more that He wanted to teach and do. Now, He was about to die, and I think he feared that those whom He loved and trusted would forget his teaching and leave the work undone. Even now, the three that He had asked to watch with Him for one hour were lying asleep. I think He feared that down through the centuries it would be the same: His followers would be sleeping when they should be performing the work of His ministry. I think that might have caused the worried look on His brow." The boy then returned to the gallery, stood for a long time before the picture, his head sinking lower and lower as he gazed steadily into the face of Jesus at prayer. Then he raised his head, straightened his shoulders and said, "Oh, Man of Galilee, if there is anything that you have left undone, anywhere, anything that I can do, you can count on me." Then he went out, and away to the distant city to work, and to live a life of loving service according to the Gospel of Jesus Christ.

JESUS, "MAN FOR OTHERS"

508 (Service)

In a phrase that has become well-known in contemporary Christianity, Pastor Dietrich Bonhoefer, who died for the Christian Faith in Nazi Germany, called Jesus "The Man For Others." Jesus said, "I have come not to be served, but to serve."

JESUS, MINISTRY OF

509

Sean Connery and Michael Caine are the stars in an adventure film entitled "The Man Who Would Be King," based on a story by Rudyard Kipling. Each plays the part of an ex-sergeant— Danny Dravot and Peachey Carnehan—from Her Majesty's Royal Army in India. Their love of adventure takes them on an arduous journey to the faraway mountain Kingdom of Kafiristan. There, Danny Dravot is able to fulfill his lifelong ambition. He always has wanted to be a king. All his life he has longed for the power and prestige and pleasures that come with kingship. Consequently, through a combination of trickery and superior Western "know-how," Danny Dravot becomes king and, for a short time, thoroughly enjoys it. But the same drive which led him to want to be king soon proves his undoing, and Danny loses not only his kingdom, but also his life. The film is not likely to win any awards, but the title reminds us that, from the beginning of His public ministry, "the Man who would not be king" becomes a dominant theme in the life of Jesus.

JESUS, NAME OF

510 (Names)

In Matthew's Gospel, we read, "You must name Him Jesus (meaning, 'God saves') because He is the One who is to save His people" (Mt. 1:21). Thus, our understanding of the Messiah (Immanuel), faintly traced by the Prophets, is now brought to full light in the Name of Jesus. The One named Jesus is the fulfillment of God's Plan for our salvation. Often, the names of historical figures are remembered for something merely incidental to their lives, rather than for who they were and what they did. Although Duns Scotus was a brilliant philosopher and writer of the Middle Ages, his name is memorialized in our word, "dunce." It seems that he was caught in a Church-State argument over taxation. Government officials regarded his position in the matter as evidence of gross stupidity. Thus, a "dunce" came to mean one who has no capacity for real learning or intelligence. General Ambrose E. Burnside is remembered, not for his Civil War exploits, but for his bushy whiskers: sideburns. The Earl of Sandwich, an able politician and administrator of Eighteenth Century England, has been memorialized for inventing the universal lunch: the sandwich. In such cases, the invocation of the person's name does little or nothing to recall who he was and what he did. It is not a person or a life we describe, but only an anecdote, an incidental happening.

JESUS, PRESENCE OF

511

An old man had a beautiful dream in which he and Jesus were walking together along a sandy beach. He was able to look back and see two lines of footprints in the sand, one made by him, the other by Jesus. And, as he walked along with Jesus, the man began to mentally look back on the major events of his past life. It was after his reflections had taken him to the time of his conversion to Christ that he noticed a curious thing happening: one set of footprints disappeared whenever he thought about a particularly painful event in his life. He protested to Jesus, saying, "You promised that if I would be your disciple you would never leave me. Why is it that when I was hurting the most, when I needed You the most, there is only one set of footprints: my own." Jesus replied, "You know that I love you,

277

and you know that I will never leave you. When you were hurting the most, when you needed Me the most, there is only one set of footprints because it is then that I carried you."

512

When we look at Jesus in the Gospels, we see that He was totally present to His life's situation. All the way through, we can see Jesus as a man living His life situation to the hilt. This is a very helpful thing for many of us to see. We have been so cautious and so afraid, holding back in our relationships, never getting very close, always ready to look down on and to back away. And opportunity after opportunity to live, to relate, to forgive, to show compassion, to generate warmth, to understand, to give, to put another's interest before our own, to exalt another, is lost!

JESUS, SAVIOR

513 (Salvation)

In Eugene O'Neil's play, "Days Without End," John Loving, a Roman Catholic boy, prays that his parents, both of whom had been injured, might not die. But their lives were not saved by the kind of miracle he had expected and he loses his Faith. Outwardly, at least, he becomes a skeptic and a cynic. Inwardly, however, John Loving keeps searching deeply for some answer. He tries Oriental religions, he tries philosophical cults, he joins secular meditation groups, he even becomes a member of an atheist club for a while. A friend of his—a priest—stands by him through it all. One evening, when John Loving and his priest friend are discussing the situation, John says "A new savior must be born who will reveal to us how we can be safe from ourselves." The priest replies, quietly, "You are forgetting that men have such a Savior, Jack. All they need is to remember

Him." But John Loving is not to remember Him until much later. The setting was a small chapel silhouetted against the sky at dawn. John has been out walking, God is much on his mind and yet he is still in a state of rebellion. And so, it is partly against his will that John reluctantly opens the door of the Chapel and walks in. Then, almost before he knows what he is doing, he kneels before a cross and, for the first time since his parents' death, he feels peace within himself, and he offers this simple prayer: "Thou has conquered, Lord. Forgive the tortured soul of John Loving." A beautiful example of someone who comes to that once-and-for-all moment of being able to say "Yes!" to God.

JESUS, SUFFERING SERVANT

514 (Fulfillment; Sacrifice; Suffering)

Jesus is the supreme example of how God shows Himself to us in unexpected ways. Jesus was an outcast. Therefore we should not be surprised to discover His presence among the outcasts of our time. Jesus was a servant. Therefore, we should not be surprised to see signs of His presence among those who serve. Jesus was a member of an oppressed minority. Therefore, we should not be surprised to hear His voice echoed in the concerns of today's oppressed minorities. If we follow in Jesus' path we are following after God. Often the way will seem strange, especially when the signposts declare that the road to fulfillment is laced with detours marked "suffering" and "self-sacrifice."

JOURNEY

515 (Humour)

A highly-placed corporate manager recently announced, tongue-in-cheek, the establishment of an annual "Better Management Award." The first person to be so honored, he said, would be Christopher Columbus — posthumously. "We are honoring old Chris as the 'Greatest Manager of All Time'," the announcement read. "He started out not knowing where he was going; upon arriving, he didn't know where he was; and upon returning, he didn't know where he had been."

JOY

516 (Paul; Persecution; Praise; Thanksgiving)

The closing scene of Sholem Asch's great novel, "The Apostle," takes place in a dungeon in Rome. Hundreds of Christians have been lowered into the dungeon through a little trap door and they know that they will never come out except to die in the arena. Many of them die in the dungeon. The scene as described by Sholem Asch is one of darkness and horror. Suddenly the trap door opens and there is a shaft of light for a brief moment and a man is lowered. And as the man is lowered into this place of indescribable darkness and death and despair, he is singing songs of praise and thanksgiving to God. The word spreads like wildfire among the people in the dungeon: "It's Paul! It's Paul! Paul has come!" And Paul's joy is so contagious that before long he has all the people in the dungeon singing songs of praise and thanksgiving. A whole new spirit has taken hold of them.

In this, Sholem Asch has given us an accurate description of the New Testament spirit. Even in the darkest dungeons of life God gives His people joy and, through His people, He gives joy to the world.

517 (Crucifixion; Resurrection)

In the original stage version of "Godspell," the Gospel spirit of joy is beautifully conveyed. It brings to the stage the same movement that carries you along as you read the Gospels: joy in the announcement of what God has done through Jesus Christ; joy in the liveliness of the parables that elaborate on this Good News; joy in the father whose lost son came home; joy in the woman who found the lost coin; joy in the shepherd who found the lost sheep, and on and on. In the first act of "Godspell" you are swept along by this mood. The second act begins the same way, but soon it gets heavier as the opposition unites against Jesus and death draws near: the scene in the "upper room" when Jesus says farewell to His disciples, one-by-one; the Crucifixion; the death. But "Godspell" doesn't end there as "Jesus Christ Superstar" did. In "Superstar" there is no hint of Resurrection. "Godspell" ends with the disciples carrying Jesus' body on their shoulders right down the center aisle of the theater. And as they go out they are singing the victory song, "Long Live God...Long Live God." God, not death has the last word. LONG LIVE GOD who "so loved the world that He gave His only Son."

518 (Resurrection)

A gifted public speaker was asked to recall his most difficult speech assignment. "That's easy," he answered. "It was an address I gave to the National Conference of Undertakers. The topic they gave me was, 'How to Look Sad at a Ten Thousand

Dollar Funeral.'" Now, that's a difficult assignment. But I can think of an assignment that would have been even more difficult: "How to Teach the Early Christians to be Sad." The early Christians' absolutely irrepressible joy is one of the dominant characteristics of the New Testament writings. Something so tremendous has happened to these people that it permeates their lives and their beings. And if you try to put a lid on it, it just comes bubbling up again. There's no way to hold it back. It's contagious. It's healing. It's beautiful. They were filled with joy because this Jesus who had lived among them, who had brought them hope and life, whom they had seen die, seen put in a tomb, this Jesus is alive! And it isn't an hallucination. It isn't something they had dreamed up. They report it as fact, incontrovertible fact. He was alive! They had experienced it!

JOYLESSNESS

519 (Parent and Child; Parish Life)

A small child was turning around smiling at everyone in church. He wasn't making noise or doing anything destructive. He was just smiling. Suddenly his mother tugged at him, and in a stern whisper said, "Stop smiling. Don't you know you're in Church!" Then she slapped his bottom and when the tears began rolling down the boy's cheeks, the mother said, "That's better." Then she returned to her prayers.

520 (Parent and Child; Parish Life)

Consider this real-life scenario: It was Sunday morning, "after Church." Several members of the congregation went to a nearby restaurant for breakfast. As one of the church-goers settled into a booth, she noticed that the adjoining booth was occupied by a young lad of about eleven and his father, both of whom she had seen earlier that morning in Church. At first she tried her best to avoid eavesdropping. But, as the father's voice rose, she found herself listening very intently. The boy, it seemed, had slept in Church, much to his father's embarrassment. "You disgraced us both," the man said. "You'll be punished for this. You should have been sitting up and paying attention. Everyone was looking at you. I was ashamed of you. What's wrong with you? Can't you even behave yourself in Church? What will people think?" On and on the diatribe continued, for fully ten minutes. Finally, when the boy had taken all he could endure and his eyes filled with tears, the father issued the one-word command: "EAT!" By this time the boy had absolutely no stomach for eating, which resulted in a second cruel discourse aimed at the boy's disobedience. "What will the waitress think?" the father asked. Finally, the punishment was prescribed. "Next Sunday," the father said, "I'm going to take you to Church twice—for punishment." The woman in the next booth could stand it no longer. She too had lost all appetite for food. Leaving her breakfast behind, she approached the man, saying gently, "What a fine looking son you have! By the way, did you notice how stuffy the air was in our crowded Church this morning? It made me so sleepy I couldn't keep my eyes open!"

521 (God, love of; Jesus, Good News of)

"The Stranger," by Albert Camus, is a powerful novel which deals with those fundamental life-and-death questions that concern us all because we are human: What does God mean to us right now? What does our ability to reason mean to us right now? How are we to act as human beings right now? Is life meaningful or absurd? Albert Camus' "stranger" can find no answer to give him hope, no answer to give him reason for being, no answer to give meaning to his life. He lives an empty, joyless existence. He is a stranger to his own life. He attends his mother's funeral but has no grief, worrying only that people might notice that he has none. He has a love affair which is empty because he has no genuine feeling for the girl. Finally, he commits a senseless murder and when the death sentence is pronounced, he is scornful. He couldn't care less. So many people who have read this book have said, "That's me sometimes. There are times when life seems more an absurdity than a priceless gift of God." Jesus did not come to take the joy out of life. Jesus came with Good News: life is the gift of a God who loves and cares, right now! And we really have not understood Jesus' promise of eternal life until we realize that it has already begun. It comes down to this: it makes little sense to worry about afterlife if you are not serious about learning how to live now.

522 (Motherhood)

One September morning, a doting mother was preparing her two small children for the first day of school. She was still in her housecoat. Her hair was disheveled. She was barking commands: comb your hair, brush your teeth, put on the new blouse I bought you, wipe the jam off your face; hurry up! It was a real battle, and by the time the children were ready to go they were a wreck. As they went out the front door, the mother said, "Wait! I want to take your picture." The children dutifully posed and as the mother looked through her camera's viewfinder, she barked "Smile!" But the children simply would not smile. The hassle of getting ready had been too much for them. Finally, in a voice that could be heard throughout the neighborhood, the mother screamed, "Smile, darn you. If you don't smile I'm going to punish you."

JUDGMENT

523 (Parish Life)

There was a clergyman who found a great deal of judgment going on among the people in his Church and he found a wonderful way of dealing with it. Everytime someone in the congregation started to make a judgmental statement about someone else he took out a notebook and a pen and he said, "Now will you please repeat this? I want to be sure I get it down exactly as you said it." It's simply amazing how the people would disappear into the night.

524

A Princeton University alumnus remembers the day when, as a "cocky freshman," he was rushing toward the campus library between classes. He saw a crew of maintenance men who were diligently raking and hauling the autumn leaves. All except one man who was wearing a wrinkled pea jacket and a small knit hat. This person seemed to be just standing around soaking up the sun, content to let the others do all the work. The "cocky freshman" was outraged. "Look at that old loafer," he said to himself. He wanted to call out, "Old man, you had better shape up if you want to keep your job." He recalls that he had walked about ten paces when, suddenly, "A bell rang in my head. I did a quick U-turn and sauntered back as casually as I could, trying not to stare too obviously at Albert Einstein."

JUSTICE

525 (Humor)

"I Want What I Want When I Want It"—so goes an old song title. But the wise person knows that justice is not always served as the result of getting what we want. Take the case of the farmer who ordered a dozen chickens from his livestock dealer. "I'll be away all day," he advised the merchant, "so just leave them on my front porch." When he returned home that evening, the farmer found only an empty crate on his porch. It seems

285

Justice

the crate had a faulty latch and the chickens had escaped. Immediately, the man set out on a frantic search of the countryside. Next morning, he called the dealer to complain. "Look here," he said, "because of your negligence I spent half the night going over my farm and my neighbors' farms looking for those lost chickens. It took me four hours to find all twelve." After a brief silence, the dealer replied, "Twelve? You have done well, my friend. I thought you ordered half a dozen. There were only six chickens in that crate."

526 (Heaven; Humor; Prayer; Preaching)

The story is told of a clergyman and an ordinary working man: a bus-driver. They arrived together at the gates of heaven. An angel gave the clergyman a plain cotton gown, a wooden halo and modest living quarters containing only the bare necessities of eternal life. To the bus-driver, the angel presented a complete wardrobe of the finest materials, a golden halo and lavish living-quarters containing every imaginable luxury and convenience. When he saw this, the clergyman protested: "Why does he get so much and I so little?" The angel checked the records and said, "It seems that when you were preaching, your congregation slept; when he was driving, his passengers prayed."

527 (Humor; Prison; Vacation)

Once a year, in a modern day "Rite of Spring," thousands of college students from all parts of the U.S. converge on the Florida beaches for "Easter vacation." Most of the students seem to have fun, and they come and go without incident. But so large has the army of young vacationers become that, not surprisingly, there are always a few who find trouble and get themselves arrested. Such was the case one April when six students were taken to the police station on the complaint of a local resident. They were charged with "disturbing the peace." As the arresting officer herded them into a cell, he told them they would be held there until morning when their case would be heard by the toughminded local Magistrate—a man who seldom tempered justice with mercy. Whereupon one of the students demanded his right to make one phone call. After he had made the call, the student joined his companions behind bars. Twenty minutes later, a delivery boy entered the police station carrying a square, flat, white box. He said to the desk sergeant, "Who ordered the pizza?" Obviously, the student who made the phone call had a radically wrong idea of the situation he and his companions were in.

528 (Children; Humor)

The reknowned British novelist, Daniel DeFoe, once said that "Justice is always violent to the party offending, for every man is innocent in his own eyes." This observation comes alive in the story of the little boy who was being particularly mischievous in a Sunday School class. After enduring as much as she could bear, the teacher called him to her desk and rebuked him saying, "Christopher, I'm very much afraid I'll not meet you in heaven!" To which the little rascal replied, "Why, teacher? What have you been doing now?"

KINDNESS

529 (Humor)

A travelling man went into a diner for his evening meal. The stress of the day's business had made him physically tired and emotionally drained. Consequently, when he placed his order for dinner, he said to the waitress, "I want only two things: an order of pot roast and a few kind words." The waitress scribbled down his order and began to walk away. The man called after her, "Hey, how about the kind words?" The waitress replied,

"Sir, the kindest words I can think of right now, " 'Don't order the pot roast!' "

KINGDOM OF GOD

530 (Children; Humor; Marriage)

In the average week how many times do we think about the Kingdom of God? How many times does it enter our conversation? How many times does it become a part of our decision-making? For most of us who claim to be His people, the Kingdom of God, which meant everything to Jesus, is not an important part of our lives at all. It doesn't tie into the way we're feeling, loving, laughing, and crying. We know very little about it, or we misunderstand it. We're like the little boy in religion class who was asked, "What did Jesus say about people getting married?" He answered immediately, "Forgive them, for they know not what they do."

531 (Change)

A college student was working in her first political campaign, After two tedious days of door-to-door canvassing she sighed, "There must be some better way to change the world." Perhaps so, but the other ways are equally tedious, equally unsatisfactory, equally slow in yielding their results. History itself is an unsatisfactory business. That's the whole point. If history were quite satisfactory, there would be no need of yearning for the Kingdom of God. Christians are those who see the unsatisfactory present in the light of the promised future.

532 (Adolescence; Christmas)

There is in every life an adolescent period in which we want to break away from the familiar bonds of family and childhood

288

friends, in which we want to strike out on our own to discover a larger and more exciting world. This is a perfectly healthy impulse and we would indeed worry about any young person who never felt the siren call to venture into the unknown. Sad to say, however, many of us remain adolescents all our lives long. In a very deep sense, we should be discontented and restless for the new. This is because we were made for the Kingdom of God and we must remain unsatisfied with anything short of the Kingdom. But at Christmas God lets us know that the signs of that Kingdom's coming are to be discovered not in adolescent fantasizing but in grown-up commitment to the concrete and particular.

533   (God, will of; Will)

"Purity of heart is to will one thing," wrote Soren Kierkegaard, the 19th century Christian philosopher. "Blessed are the pure in heart," said Jesus, "for they shall see God." But to will one thing! How very difficult that is! Christians are to will one thing—to desire one thing "with all your heart, with all your soul, and with all your mind." Christians are to will that God's will be done, that His Kingdom come. "Seek first the Kingdom of God," said Jesus, and you shall lack for nothing else. Divide your loyalty between the Kingdom of God and some other goals—even one other goal!—and, no matter how successful you may seem, your life is incomplete.

LAST DAYS

534   (Humor; Preaching)

A fire-and-brimstone preacher was delivering his usual doomsday sermon about the end of the world. "Reform!" he boomed. "Reform your lives because sooner or later the signs of the end time will appear in the sun, the moon and the stars. On the earth nations will be in anguish, distraught at the roaring of the sea and waves. Men will die of fright in anticipation of what is coming upon the earth. The powers in the heavens will be shaken" (Lk. 21:25-26). Then, lowering his voice, the preacher said, "God hasn't told us when He would bring the world to an end. That's not for us to know. It could be a billion years from now." Whereupon a worried voice from the back of the Church rang out, "How long did you say?" "It could be a billion years," the preacher repeated. To which the much relieved voice replied, "Thank God! I thought you said a million years."

LAW

535 (Golden Rule)

Legend has it that back in the time of Jesus, a young Divinity student went to the second most famous Rabbi in Jerusalem with a problem. He said that the 667 Old Testament laws were too confusing for him. "Can't you give me a summary of the law in the time that I can stand on one foot?" he asked. The Rabbi picked up a big stick, started beating the young man with it and finally chased him out his study. The Rabbi considered the young man's question as an act of impertinence. He had spent his whole life studying and interpreting these hundreds of laws and it was an insult to be asked to summarize them so briefly. The young man then visited the most famous Rabbi in Jerusalem and asked him the same question. The Rabbi said, "Stand on one foot." The young man obeyed, and as he stood on one foot the Rabbi said, "Do not do to anyone else what you would not have done to yourself. This is a summary of the law." The Rabbi had summed the law up into a negative "golden rule."